Couples Counseling

A Step By Step Guide For Therapists

Marina Williams, LMHC

Text Copyright ©2012
Marina Williams
All Rights Reserved

Contents

ii

Preface

We are living in a society with increasingly negative views towards marriage. People typically don't marry intending to one day divorce, and yet half of all couples eventually will. Sadly, the average marriage only lasts for three years (Elliot & Simmons, 2011). And although divorce has become common, it is far from easy. Going through a divorce has been compared to experiencing a death in the family. Even in the most amicable divorces, couples endure intense feelings of hurt, sadness, and anger (Amato, 2000). And if there are children involved, the process of going through a divorce can last for years.

It is no wonder that so many couples are simply "opting out" of marriage all together. In the mid 1960's, 80% of adults were married. Current research shows that only 52% of adults are married (Pew Research Center, 2010). Effective and confident couples counselors are sorely needed in our society. Unfortunately, few graduate programs cover this very important form of counseling, leaving therapists to either "sink or swim" when faced with real clients.

When I started my private practice I initially only provided individual counseling. However, I soon started receiving requests from my individual clients to provide couples counseling as well. Initially intending to refer them to local couples counselors, I became aware that this was an area lacking in the community. Many professional counselors do not receive formal training in treating couples issues during their graduate training. Few internship or practicum programs exist that offer couples counseling as well. Although so few of us receive proper training in this therapy format, most counselors in private practice offer couples counseling as one of their services anyway. It is probably due to this reason that so many clients find themselves feeling unsatisfied with their couples counseling experience and that couples counseling as a whole has such a dismal reputation.

I have also found few couples counseling methodologies to be based on science and proven treatments. It seemed that many of the treatment methods being advocated were based on the author's own spiritual beliefs or personal background, factors which rarely translate for the overall population of those seeking treatment for their relationship issues. In the end, what I had really hoped for was for a book like this to have existed. A book that would walk you through the process step by step, as well as to provide room for personal growth as you became a more skilled therapist.

I'm going to use the term "therapist" to refer to all psychologists, professional counselors, coaches, social workers, pastoral counselors, and other healing professionals with an interest in providing couples counseling. Although it is common for therapists to offer couples counseling in the list of services they provide, there are few training opportunities that provide the step-by-step guidance necessary to deliver effective couples counseling. We therapists are simply encouraged to take what we've being taught in providing individual counseling and translate it into a couple format. Unfortunately, this approach rarely works. When I was first starting out with couples counseling, I found myself taking turns focusing on each partner individually rather than addressing them as a team. This lead to increased arguing during sessions and the perception that I was "taking sides." In other words, it lead to nowhere. Progress cannot be made in this fashion.

Through my own trial-and-error and experiences providing couples counseling, I have developed a system for delivering effective couples interventions and I lead you through this every step of the way. Together we'll go through each session, starting with the initial phone call all the way through termination, so that you can better help couples heal their relationship. Although I lay it out for you step by step, it is still up to you as the therapist to use your skills and education to bring this method to life. As you practice and gain more experience, feel free to modify any of my suggestions to better suit your needs or personal style. As you become more confident in your abilities, you'll find you have less of a need to refer to the session outlines and will eventually develop your own method.

The method I created for treating couples is based heavily on the research by American Psychologists Albert Ellis (founder of Rational Emotive Behavior Therapy), John Gottman (founder of the Gottman Relationship Institute), and Harville Hendrix (founder of Imago Couples Therapy). In my journey of strengthening my skills as a couples counselor, I have found the work of these three psychologists to be the most effective and helpful for treating couples. However, if you have your own favorite theorist or treatment method, I invite you to experiment with using it in a couples format. Ultimately, it is the techniques and methods that feel the most comfortable to you that give you the most success.

You will find that this book works best if you read it all the way from beginning to end before attempting to help any couples. You want to have a general feel for the flow of couples counseling and know where you will be heading in future sessions. If a client asks "what will we be working on next session?", you don't want to answer "I haven't read that chapter yet." In general, the more knowledgeable you are and the more prepared you are, the less anxious you will feel when performing couples counseling. The more confident you appear in session, the more confident your clients are going to feel that you can help them in their relationship difficulties, and that goes a long way towards progress.

Chapter 1

Getting Started

The most important thing you can do to be successful at couples counseling is to understand that it is not the same thing as individual counseling, only with two clients in the room instead of one. If you go into it with that mindset, you are in for a shock. While individual therapy can be quite passive at times, couples counseling is much more active and structured. And unlike individual counseling where you might see the same client for years, couples counseling typically only lasts for ten to twelve sessions.

Your relationship with your clients will also be different. When seeing your client individually, you are always on your client's side. However in couples counseling you must never take sides, no matter how much the couple may try to force you to. You will probably not feel as close of a connection with your couples as you do with your individual clients, and your couples will probably feel the same way. It's rare to hear someone say "I love my couples counselor."

This is not to say that you will dislike the couples that you work with or that your couples will dislike you as well. If you do good work with the couples that come to you for help, they will most likely feel a deep respect for you and your expertise, a feeling of fondness for the way that you have helped them, but they will not miss seeing you once counseling has ended. Because your attention must be divided between two people, there is not that opportunity to have a deep connection like there is in individual counseling. Because you are dealing with two people that are in conflict, sessions can also have more of a hostile tone than we are used to seeing in individual counseling. As a therapist, it can take time to adjust to the initial negativity you experience in couples counseling sessions.

Something that is important to understand, is that many of the people who come to couples counseling have poor relationship skills, and social skills in general. Often they have a history of being in dysfunctional relationships. Not just with romantic partners but also with family and coworkers, and yes, even therapists. It is not uncommon for those in couples counseling to also have anger management issues and to take an adversarial stance with the therapist. It makes it especially difficult to provide therapy to individuals who seem to take issue with everything you say, interrupt you, and talk over you when you are trying to provide a therapeutic intervention. Many therapists charge more for couples counseling since they find it to be more challenging and emotionally draining. You may want to consider doing the same.

It is because of all these factors that couples counseling has taken on a reputation among therapists as being a challenging form of therapy to administer. However, I feel that this is mostly due to the therapist's lack of experience. I feel that once couples counseling has been mastered by the therapist, it feels no more challenging than administering individual counseling. Of course, like any new skill, it takes guidance and time to master it.

Practice what you preach

Does your own relationship lack something to be desired? If you find yourself facing some of the same problems in your relationship that your clients are, you will not be an effective counselor. Have you ever heard the expression "you have to get your own house in order before trying to tell other people what to do"? Whoever invented that saying may have had therapists with emotional baggage in mind.

No matter how hard you try to prevent it from showing through in sessions, if you are experiencing your own relationship difficulties, your clients will be able to tell. However, there is no more an effective therapist than one who has overcome their own struggles. If you have ever considered doing your own couples counseling, I recommend doing so now. Not only will you improve your relationship, but it will also educate you about what it is like to see a couples counselor. Make notes during the process of what you liked or didn't like about the experience, and use it in order to become a better therapist yourself.

Even if you do not have serious enough problems to warrant seeing a couples counselor, you can benefit by trying out some of the recommendations in this book in your own life. Make your own list of relationship goals, practice the communication skills from chapter five and six, and make notes of your own successes and challenges in implementing these new skills. Make a special note of any emotional blockages that got in the way of changing your behavior. It can be helpful to better understanding your clients when they experience their own emotional blocks. Having an intimate understanding of the process can be useful in helping your own clients avoid the common pitfalls that prevent change.

Although it is helpful to have your own experience in improving a relationship, avoid comparing your client's relationship with your relationship. This can sometimes be interpreted by the client as being condescending or judgemental. I choose not to talk about my marriage to my clients because it is not helpful to them in their relationship. Even if you come across a couple that seems to be in almost the exact same situation you were in once, every relationship is simply too unique for you to be able to prescribe to them the same solution that worked for you.

Talking about your own problems or life story in therapy is generally considered to be unethical and should be avoided. If you ever find yourself unsure about if you are revealing too much in counseling, ask yourself "where is the focus?" If the focus is still on the couple, then you are doing an excellent job. If the focus is on your personal life or how amazing you are as a therapist, put the focus back on the client.

10 most common reasons people are in couples counseling

Although my session outlines are the same no matter what reason people give for seeking out your services, It is helpful to have an understanding of the most common reasons people are in couples counseling, and making "tweaks" or adjustments when necessary.

1. Poor Communication: As a therapist, I am a big fan of communication. I feel that if people could just talk to one another properly, any problem could be solved. Most couples counselors agree with me on this point, and so improving communication is a major focus in most couples counseling methods. You will notice that the biggest changes in counseling happen after the couple has learned some good communication skills and start implementing them. Since there are literally hundreds of communications skills and styles, we are going to focus on just the basics and the ones with the most scientific evidence backing them up. You don't want to risk "overloading" your client to the point that they can't remember any of them when it comes time to use them.

Yes, it all comes down to communicating better. You may wonder why something so simple is at the core of so many broken relationships. We pick up our communications styles at an early age, usually from watching our parents interact. If we grow up witnessing a lot of conflict, a conflictual or adversarial way of communicating becomes what feels most natural to us. You will encounter more resistance in changing the way a couple communicates more than in any other endeavor in counseling. Changing the way you talk just feels "weird." Acknowledging this to the clients is very important. They should also be educated that although it will inevitably feel weird at first, it will become natural over time and eventually they won't even notice it.

You may come across a couple that claims to already have great communication skills, but I want you to teach them the skills outlined in this book anyways. Respond with, "I'm really glad to hear that" or "that's great." Don't argue with the client even if you've witnessed them using poor communication in the session. You might want to present these as "advanced communication skills" if they already consider themselves an expert.

In my experience I have seen couples that really did have good communication skills, but for whatever reason, they chose not to use them with their partner. They seemed to think that you shouldn't have to use communication skills when talking with a loved one and that the loved one should naturally "get them" or "know them by now." Even though they claimed to already know the skills, I still reviewed them and made them practice them in session, but I also dealt with the dysfunctional belief that one shouldn't have to use good communication skills with their partner. Some people feel "we've been together for years, she should know what I mean by now." Challenging the expectation that your partner can read your mind is an important, although difficult, part in changing dysfunctional communication.

2. Infidelity: Infidelity can take on many levels in couples counseling, from having sex outside of marriage to posting an ad on a dating site but never acting on the ad. So if a client says "my partner cheated on me", it's important to find out what that means. People have different definitions of "cheating"; some very strict and others quite lenient. There are so-called "emotional affairs" that never end in sex or intimate touching. What's important is how serious the people in the relationship view the betrayal. Is the cheated partner still angry or ready to move on? Is infidelity still occurring in the relationship. Be clear that any affairs outside of the relationship must end before couples counseling can begin. Infidelity is a common reason people seek couples counseling, and it is useful to know the facts about infidelity.

It is hard to come up with an estimate of how many people have affairs. Surveys are completely dependent upon responders being honest and some people might have difficulty admitting to having had an affair even in an anonymous survey. It is also important to note that the definition of "cheating" has expanded recently to include emotional affairs and affairs done over the internet. Current estimates are that between 30% and 60% of married individuals in America will commit infidelity at some point during their marriage. Men are more likely to cheat, but women are quickly catching up with them (Drigotas & Barta, 2001). After all, these cheating men must be sleeping with somebody, right?

It used to be that people accused the unfaithful of being sex addicts, or just being selfish. Although this may be true with a small percentage of cheaters, the research reveals that most people cheat when their emotional needs are not being met in the relationship (Treas & Giesen, 2000). It has more to do with filling an emotional void of feeling unappreciated, lonely, and unloved, than just needing to have sex with someone.

In the case of infidelity, it may seem obvious who's right and who's wrong in the conflict. However, I have heard plenty of cheating spouses defend themselves quite strongly and argue that the other person is 100% to blame. This is another reason why the therapist should always avoid taking sides; each person believes they are innocent no matter how bad the transgression in the relationship. Attempting to prove the client otherwise will most likely result in them never coming back. Having spent so much time with clients that have cheated on their spouses (both in couples counseling and in individual counseling), I can tell you that most of them are shocked by their own behavior. They never imagined that they would ever be unfaithful, but that after a series of events, they felt pushed to commit the inevitable. For them, it is like they never had a choice.

You have probably heard the saying "once a cheater, always a cheater." Although I think it is true that once you do something for the first time it makes it easier to do it again, I do not think that cheating is a compulsion that can't be stopped. The first step is to help the client identify the triggers, situations, and places that lead to cheating. Next, educate the client on how preventing those triggers will prevent the "inevitable."

You will find the partner that cheated to be sensitive to being perceived as the "bad guy." This can hinder progress because the client will close themselves off to your suggestions in order to defend themselves from further scolding or humiliation. I usually let the clients know early on that I don't pick sides or consider anyone in this situation to be the "bad guy." The way I see it, people cope to the best of their ability depending on their own unique situation. Learning better coping can prevent this type of thing from happening again, both partners have done things that have contributed to the problems in the relationship, and both partners can do things to make it better.

Ask yourself, how angry is the partner that was cheated on? Is that anger going to be a problem in couples counseling? I have found that the anger of having been cheated on is not something that can be let go of easily. If that anger is preventing the couple from making progress in counseling, it is vital that that person seek out their own individual counseling. Yelling at your partner and expressing hurt and anger in every session is not the purpose of couples counseling. Individual hurts are best dealt with in individual counseling. The purpose of couples counseling is to make productive changes and learn new skills of communicating and relating to one another. Bashing your partner does not fit into that equation.

3. Abuse: Domestic violence is a serious problem in our society. Current statistics show that 1 in 4 women will be abused by a partner at some point in their lives (Tjaden & Thoennes, 2000). In fact, women are more likely to be assaulted by a partner than by any other assailant (U.S. Department of Justice, 2006)! Some seek out couples counseling to help in these relationships (and the abuser may play along as part of their manipulation), but couples counseling is never appropriate in situations of domestic violence.

This is because counseling depends on complete honesty, and abusers lie and manipulate. Couples counseling doesn't take sides, but abuse is always wrong. Couples counseling involving abusers creates an unsafe situation for everyone involved, including the therapist. Always screen the client over the phone for signs of domestic violence. The client should then be referred to a domestic violence hotline 1-800-799-SAFE (7233).

4. Meddling in-laws: Conflicts with in laws is a common element in couples counseling. In an age of helicopter-parenting, parents are having a harder time letting go of their children once they reach adulthood. And depending on how controlling the parents are, it can cause a lot of strain, if not outright destroy a relationship. It becomes increasingly complicated considering the number of young adults that are still financially dependant on their parents. Parents may feel that they should continue to have a say in their adult child's life since they're still paying some of the bills or providing day care for grandchildren. Adding fuel to the fire is that the client may complain regularly to their parents about their partner.

In general, clients should be taught to be self-sufficient, independent adults. Some people were never taught to make sacrifices or taught how to make a budget. It then becomes the therapist's role to teach the client these virtues in around the fourth session. It should also be stressed to clients that they should never complain about their partner in front of their friends or family members since they're friends and family are not as forgiving as they are and will develop a skewed perception about the partner. The conflicts you face in your relationship should be considered private or personal information. It is also not fair to your partner because they are unable to defend themselves and there are always two sides to every story.

Conflicts with in-laws puts people in a difficult place. Even if you know your mother is meddling, your mother is still your mother. So what is one to do? I believe that one should always side with their partner. Part of growing up means forming one's own family. That family consists of you and your partner, and any children you have if you choose to have them. Parents and in-laws should not be allowed to criticize or otherwise demean your partner. Clients should be encouraged to set up firm boundaries between them and parents if necessary. Partners should also not be forced to go to family gatherings if it is likely they will be treated in a disrespectful manner while there.

5. Parenting: Multiple studies have shown that marital satisfaction drops drastically after the birth of a child and doesn't return back to normal levels until after the child grows up and moves out (Twenge, Campbell, & Foster, 2003). There are multiple reasons for why this is the case. Being a parent generally means less sleep, and being sleep deprived increases the likelihood of a person being cranky and snapping at their partner. Parenting also takes a lot of time. Time that was once spent doing enjoyable activities with your partner is now being spent changing diapers, calming temper tantrums, disciplining, and cleaning. We are also raised with the expectation that being a parent is supposed to be endless joy. When reality doesn't live up to the expectation, we may put the blame on our spouse.

The role of the therapist in this situation is to help the couple transition to their role of parents. This may mean making the division of labour more equal, making sure they schedule time to be a couple and time for just being alone, and dispelling the myths about parenting. There may be other issues as well, such as one partner feeling like the birth of the child means their youth is over or they can no longer have their own identity. Ask the couple what being a parent means to them. Brainstorm solutions that can make the transition to parenthood easier. Work through any guilt the couple may have about taking time for themselves.

6. Jealousy: Jealousy can take many forms in relationship conflicts. One partner may feel jealous of the other partner's relationship with their family. They may feel jealous that the other person makes more money than they do. Or they may falsely accuse the other person of cheating simply because they have opposite-sex friendships. The jealous partner may also display angry outbursts at perceived slights and have a fear of being alone. Often these individuals don't have a lot of their own friends, have a lot of anxiety, and are very insecure. If the jealousy is severe and you suspect the individual may also be paranoid, you may want to suggest that the individual see their own individual therapist in addition to couples counseling.

The focus of therapy should be on eliminating the controlling and jealous behaviors and also restoring feelings of trust. The jealous individual should be encouraged to make their own friends in the process and be reminded that you cannot count on your partner to fulfill all your needs. You may have to devote a session early on to educating the couple that it is okay for the other person to have their own friends (so long as they are also making equal time for their partner) and also teaching the other partner the social skills necessary to make their own friends.

There is also the possibility that one partner is doing certain behaviors to make the other partner jealous. These behaviors should be identified and then discouraged. Unfortunately, no one knows how to push our buttons better than the people we love, and the other partner may have their own motivations for wanting to make the other person feel jealous (i.e. it makes them feel cared for or important to the other person). Encourage the other partner to employ behaviors that have been successful in the past at quelling the other person's anxiety instead.

7. Financial Problems: There are two types of people in this world: spenders and savers. Spenders feel "I've worked hard for this money. I deserve nice things. I should spend it now while I'm still young and healthy enough to enjoy it." Savers feel "We shouldn't spend our money on things we don't need. Money is a valuable commodity. It should be saved so that if we ever experienced a financial crisis we wouldn't have to worry about becoming homeless. I want to retire comfortably someday." As fate would have it, we often find in the couples who inevitably wind up in couples counseling, that one is a spender and one is a saver.

I don't think having a different philosophy about money dooms people to a lifetime of relationship conflicts, but for a lot of people, money is not something they like to talk about. Increasing communication about finances with their partner is key. The solutions to money problems are usually pretty simple: prioritize your spending through making a budget; or either make more money or spend less. But because the thought of making a budget can fill people with so much anxiety, it is simply never brought up until there's a serious problem. It may also be revealed in session that one or both partners grew up poor or had a bad role model on how to handle money. Although this is no excuse, it helps to understand where the other person is coming from. If the couple is unwilling to see a financial planner or debt counselor, ask each couple to write down three unnecessary expenses they would each be willing to give up. Then add up the monthly or yearly savings they would achieve from this and remember to provide plenty of positive reinforcement.

If a couple is experiencing serious financial difficulties, I advise them to see a financial planner since teaching the couple how to manage money or get out of debt is generally outside of the scope of couples counseling. This does not mean that you should then ignore the issue in your counseling with the couple. I have found that breaking the silence about money and dealing with the anxiety it brings is meant to help clients change their spending and saving habits. In general, people intrinsically know how to budget, it's getting them to do it and follow through that's key.

8. Job Stress: Work and careers are a major part of most adults' lives. We actually spend more time at our jobs then we do with our partners. Sometimes when people feel an overall dissatisfaction with their lives, it often makes sense that the probable cause is the job, since that is where they spend the majority of their time. However, since the nature of anxiety is to avoid, people may place that anxiety on a safe target. Often that safe target is the person we love the most and the person that least deserves it. It's too painful to be consciously aware of the real source of the anxiety, so we avoid thinking about it. According to the 2011 Deloitte's Shift Index survey, 80% of Americans are dissatisfied with their jobs. Some of these Americans are faced with the reality that they spent four or more years in college, have huge student loans, and are not in the right career. This can be a tough truth to swallow. When it feels like your life is a mess, it's easier to blame things on your partner than to accept the reality of changing careers.

As a therapist, you can begin to identify that this is the case if the person is unable to give clear or legitimate reasons for feeling dissatisfied in the relationship, devotes a lot of time to their career, and complains about their job. Complaints may take the form of complaining about their employer, rather than the career in general. This is a tricky one because the client will not readily admit (both to themselves or to anyone else) that the job is the real problem. I would delay confronting the client about this issue until at least the fifth session. The client will be more receptive to your ideas in later sessions after they've developed some trust in you. A gentle confrontation, such as "I've noticed you've mentioned not liking your job a lot. I wonder if the job is more responsible for your discontent than the few problems you've mentioned in this relationship. It would make sense, we do spend more time at work than we do with our partners. What do you think about the possibility that your job is the source of your anxiety, rather than this relationship?

Not everyone with job stress hates their job. Some people may love their career and be fully devoted to it, but have it cause strife in the relationship. Jobs with long hours, traveling, high stakes, and risks can cause stress for the other person in the couple. Specifically, if the long hours cause the other person to become responsible for the majority of childcare and housework, that person can grow resentful. There needs to be a balance in all things, and the therapist will need to help the couple find a work/life balance. This can involve making chores and responsibilities more fair, and scheduling time to work on their relationship.

9. Substance Abuse: Dealing with a partner's substance abuse is very hard on couples. However, if there is current or ongoing substance use, the couple should be advised to seek out their own individual counseling until the addict is in a stable recovery. A person who is currently abusing drugs needs to be able to focus all of their strength on overcoming the addiction. Couples counseling will not be helpful or productive during this time. If the person is in a state of fragile recovery, it is possible that the process of couples counseling could be stress-inducing enough to cause the individual to relapse. Also be aware that many health insurances and licensing boards require you to have a special license if working with addicts.

Even if an individual has been clean and sober for years, there may still be couples work to be done. Their partner may hold lingering resentment from the days when they were actively using. The behaviors that go along with drug addiction can be very damaging to a relationship and unless dealt with, the resentment can last a lifetime. The time a person has spent in a relationship with an addict is often filled with lies, false hopes, financial hardships, and very real danger. For many couples, the memories don't go away once the person is sober again. Often the other partner holds on to anger, mistrust, and any dysfunctional behavior they learned to utilize while the other person was on drugs. The therapist should focus on themes of forgiveness and restoring the relationship back to it's original state prior to any drug use.

10. Disillusionment with the relationship: There are considered to be five stages to relationships (Schultz , 2007). The first stage is Infatuation (also known as the honeymoon stage). During this stage, the oxytocin is flowing in your brain and you feel crazy in love with the other person (Diamond, 2004). You experience ecstasy when the other person is near, and agony when they are away. The relationship feels easy during this stage, and each partner does things to "court" or please the other person. There is disagreement as to how long this stage lasts, but in general it lasts from one to two years.

The second stage is Reality (sometimes called the "power struggle stage"). During this stage you realize that you and your partner are not as similar or perfect for each other as it once seemed. You realize that your partner is their own person with their own flaws. This is where disillusionment usually sets in.

The third stage is the Adjustment stage. This is where most divorces happen. The couple must be willing to adjust to each other and make changes necessary to improve the relationship in order for the relationship to survive. If these adjustments do not occur, the result is often divorce. The Challenge stage (also known as the commitment stage) is where both individuals actively work on the relationship. In the process, not only does the relationship improve, but they each grow as individuals as well. The final stage is Mature Love. Both individuals are able to continually grow and change in the relationship without their being a crisis. They satisfy their own needs and their needs as a couple.

Some people confuse the infatuation stage of the relationship with love itself. When infatuation ends, they assume that there must be something wrong with the relationship and start over with someone new. You may know people like this from your own life. I can think of one person in particular who has had a series of intense relationships only lasting about two years. During this time, she is just as happy as can be, will discuss getting married and having kids with the other person, but inevitably ends the relationship once things settle down. I think it is entirely possible to get addicted to the infatuation stages of love, going from one "high" to the next. Sometimes these people end up in couples counseling. Deep inside they know something is wrong, but can't quite pinpoint what it is.

It is helpful to educate the clients on the stages of love and the fact that everybody goes through a period of disillusionment but that few people admit to it since it's such a scary feeling to suddenly wonder if you're with the wrong person. In this case, the therapist acts like a guide to help move the couple into the mature love stage. This is done through teaching communication skills, the art of compromise, helping the couple identify and change unhelpful behaviors, and bringing romance back into the relationship.

When clients have a hidden agenda

Sometimes clients come into couples therapy with a "hidden agenda." They've already given up on the relationship and are just doing couples counseling as the final step before ending the relationship so they don't have to feel guilty. Secretly, they may even hope that the therapist will recommend divorce so they don't have to. Obviously this can create problems for the therapist as these clients are far less likely to follow through on suggestions or homework assignments and are unlikely to put any effort into saving the relationship. They may even sabotage the therapist's attempts during sessions through being belligerent, interrupting, lying, and talking over the therapist.

The way I have handled clients with a hidden agenda is to try to show the client that it is still worth their while to cooperate in therapy even if the relationship inevitably cannot be saved. I let the clients know that learning communication skills is something that can also help them get ahead at work and just makes life easier overall. If you can convince the client to "play along" for now, you will often see an attitude shift in later sessions once they start to see some improvements.

I once had a client whom I suspected was planning on leaving his long term girlfriend from the very beginning of couples counseling. I was able to convince him that even if the relationship didn't work out in the end, that these were skills he would be able to use in future relationships. This was motivation enough for him to participate in the process. At the fifth session he walked into my office with a big smile on his face and proclaimed excitedly "this communication stuff really works!" Although reluctant at first, after seeing that progress was possible, he had been converted into a believer that the relationship could be saved.

Sometimes people view couples counseling as an opportunity to punish their partner. They may see it as an opportunity to humiliate their partner in front of a professional, or hire someone to professionally gang-up on their partner. This happens more often than you might think. This behavior needs to be ceased as quickly as possible as it can only be more damaging to the relationship. Such individuals should be encouraged to seek an individual counselor where they will be allowed to vent their feelings of frustration about the relationship without hurting their partner.

One way to prevent this is by educating clients, either in your initial phone call or at the first session, what couples counseling is and isn't. Couples counseling isn't about discovering who's right and who's wrong. Couples counseling is about finding solutions and learning new skills in order to heal the relationship.

Dealing with difficult clients

In my experience, client hostility during couples counseling tends to decrease over time. Typically, the first three sessions are the hardest, but you should notice increasing cooperation and decreasing angry outbursts starting around the fourth session. Think an adult has too much dignity to have a full-blown temper tantrum in front of a therapist? Think again. I have seen the most sophisticated and educated people reduced to the level of screaming children in my office during couples counseling. Nothing brings out the worst in us like a dysfunctional relationship, and typically in couples counseling you are seeing worst-case scenarios. Thankfully, there are some things you can do to decrease these negative behaviors.

For some of our clients, their relationship with the therapist will be the first time they have experienced an interpersonal relationship that is mutually respectful and not dysfunctional. Simply by having appropriate interactions with the clients, you are providing a powerful role model. It is important to be aware of your body language during the sessions. We are trained to have accepting body language during therapy sessions, but this can backfire during couples counseling. If a client is acting inappropriately during a session and you are sitting there nodding your head, you may be sending a signal that inappropriate behavior is acceptable.

Practice body language that shows that although you are not condemning the client, inappropriate behavior is not acceptable. While arguing, you will notice that each partner will occasionally turn to you to judge your reaction. By not giving them the satisfaction of a sympathetic nod, you will be surprised how quickly the argument dies down on it's own without you even having to say anything. In my experience, actively trying to break-up an argument rarely works. The couple will typically just ignore your attempts or direct their anger towards the therapist. It is not your job to be a referee.

In addition to being a good role model, do not argue with the clients. Couples may be resistant to your input and suggestions especially in the early sessions. However, just because they are resistant, doesn't mean they didn't receive the message. When I was just starting out as a therapist, my supervisor taught me the concept of "planting seeds."

The job of the therapist is not to tell people what to do, but to plant seeds. When we give an idea or suggestion, even if the client outwardly rejects it, a seed is still planted. The client will continue to think about the ideas we've presented to them outside of the session and this will cause the seed to be nourished and eventually grow. Of course, we can continue to nourish these ideas slowly in later sessions and help these seeds grow little by little. It's important to realize that the client may have motivations for outwardly rejecting your suggestions, such as not wanting to look weak in front of their partner or misconceived notions that therapy is a test of wills, even if inwardly they agree with you.

Starting from the very first session, the best way to handle disagreements between therapist and client is for the therapist to practice validating the client. This is important to model to the client because in later sessions you will be teaching the couple this very same method. It is helpful to the clients if they have already become familiar with it from working with you.

The first step is to reflect (also sometimes referred to as "mirroring" or "editing") or paraphrase what you heard the client say. You then validate what the client said, such as saying something like "I could see how you could feel that way." The third step is to express empathy, and finally you ask the other person if they have a solution. In the situation of a client disagreeing with a suggestion from the therapist, it works this way:

> Client: That might work very well in theory, or sound nice on a bumper sticker, but that's not going to work with us.
>
> Therapist: (reflecting) It sounds like you're saying you've tried similar solutions in the past and they haven't worked. (validating) After all, you two are really the only experts on your relationship and what will work best for you. (empathy) It sounds very frustrating. (solution) Could you tell me about some things you've tried in the past that have worked?
>
> Client: Nothing we've tried has really worked. I guess that's why we're here.
>
> Therapist: Would you be willing to at least try some of the techniques I am suggesting?
>
> Client: I suppose we could try it.

The beauty of this technique is that it shows the client that there are effective ways of responding to a disagreement without someone having to be right and the other person wrong.

As mentioned earlier, it is very important to avoid taking sides in couples counseling. Don't even allow yourself to mentally take sides. No one is completely innocent in relationship problems and no one is ever 100% to blame. Even in a situation involving infidelity, the unfaithful partner will try to the best of their ability to convince the therapist that they are the victim.

Playing the "who's right and who's wrong game" is unhelpful and will get you nowhere, even if it seems at times that that is what the client wants from you. Some clients have the misconception that couples counseling is just "fighting it out" until the therapist declares one of them a winner. Due to this, it is useful to explain to clients periodically that you do not take sides. Also be careful in therapy not to focus on one partner more than the other, as this can be perceived as taking sides even though you do not mean to. You may also be perceived as taking sides simply due to your gender. For instance, if you are a female therapist, the husband may assume you are on the wife's side since you are both women. It is important to be aware of this at all times.

You are doing worthwhile work

You may wonder at times if it's better for the couple to just end the relationship rather than continue hurting one another, and for some couples that may be true. However, the research has been very clear that simply ending the relationship is not a solution. People in dysfunctional relationships tend to have a history of dysfunction. The odds are against them that after this relationship they'll "learn their lesson" and have a functioning relationship next time.

According to the Enrichment Journal on the divorce rate in America, the divorce rate for second marriages is 60%, and 73% for third marriages (Franck, 2000). They have to break the cycle at some point. It might as well be this relationship. And if the couple does decide to end their relationship, at least you will have provided them with the skills and insight to better serve them in their next relationship.

Although couples counseling may sound more difficult than individual counseling, because it involves two people holding each other accountable, progress happens much more quickly in couples counseling than in individual counseling. I find that the length of ten to twelve sessions is the perfect amount of time for instituting real changes in a relationship. Most insurances also only allow twelve sessions before requesting further paperwork, so it works from a technical standpoint as well. I find it to be very rewarding to be able to witness a couple laughing and smiling with their arms around each other at the tenth session, knowing that when I first met them they were at the brink of ending the relationship. For me, it makes the three sessions of crying and yelling back and forth completely worth it.

A word of warning: although you will find this couples counseling method to be effective with the majority of your clients, it is not appropriate for dealing with cases of substance abuse and domestic violence. Those are really instances where you should refer the client to a specialist. Couples counseling is not appropriate when one or both partners are violent or currently addicted to substances. Ideally, the couple should seek individual counseling until either of those issues have been resolved. This is why it is so important to screen all potential clients before they make it to their first appointment.

Many therapists don't like to give initial phone consultations because they see it as free labour or a waste of their time. I feel that thirty minutes on the phone with a client is definitely worth the time.

Not only does it help you screen clients that would not be appropriate, but also given the amount of clients that no-show their first appointment, forming that initial connection with a client is crucial in getting them in the door. I found that advertising on my website and promotional materials that I offer a free initial phone consultation was not only a good marketing device, but it also increased the percentage of clients following through with their appointments. Definitely invest the time for that initial phone call. It is worth it.

First contact

For most of your clients, your first contact with them will be over the phone. Some clients will be calling for more information while others will be ready to make their appointment right then and there; either way, it is worth your while to spend some time (about 30 minutes) talking with the client. I have found that investing time over the phone has led to an increase in clients showing up to their first appointments, as well as less conflicts during the sessions.

Ideally, in your phone calls you're going to want to focus on educating your clients about couples counseling, allowing the client to give you a brief description of the reason for coming to couples counseling, forming an initial connection with the client, and expressing confidence that you are able to help the client with this problem. This also allows you the opportunity to screen for any red flags that would prevent successful couples counseling, such as domestic violence and substance abuse.

Throughout this book I'm going to be using fictional dialog between a therapist and a couple to help illustrate the concepts I am using. The name of our fictional couple is Sarah and Mark. Although it is highly unlikely that any couple you work with is going to follow the exact same script as Sarah and Mark, I've designed Sarah and Mark to be typical of most couples you will encounter. And like most couples in counseling, Sarah will be the partner to make the initial call. I have noticed that about 80% of the time, the female partner is the primary contact. This may be because women tend to have a more positive view towards couples counseling than men do (Bringle & Byers, 1997).

Therapist: This is (therapist's name) speaking. How may I help you?

Sarah: Hello, I'm calling to make an appointment for couples counseling?

Therapist: Sure, I'd be happy to help you with that. Were there any specific appointment times you were interested in?

Sarah: Would it be possible to do a Wednesday at 6pm?

Therapist: Wednesday at 6pm works fine for me. I'll schedule you in... So, what brings you to couples counseling?

Sarah: Me and my boyfriend, Mark, have been having some problems. It seems like we argue nonstop.

Therapist: Is there anything in particular you two argue about?

Sarah: It's just stupid stuff mostly. But we do argue a lot about trust. I feel like I can't trust him anymore. He cheated on me two years ago and sometimes I wonder if he's still cheating on me. He swears he isn't, but I feel like I can't believe a word he says.

Therapist: Have your arguments ever gotten physical?

Sarah: Oh no, Mark would never lay a hand on me.

Therapist: Do you suspect any drug use?

Sarah: No, not at all. To be honest with you, Mark is overall a good person. We've been together for six years now and I feel like it's time to get married soon, but I don't want to marry him while we are still having these problems.

Therapist: I understand. You are making the right decision to try to resolve these problems before you get married. Is Mark in agreement about doing couples counseling?

Sarah: Yes, Mark said he was willing to give it a try.

Therapist: Good. I am glad to hear that. I've helped lots of couples in similar situations and feel confident that I can help you and Mark as well. If it's okay with you, I like to email my clients a copy of my office policies and a consent form prior to the first session. I also like to send reminder emails the night prior to appointments. Is it okay if I have your email address?

Sarah: Sure. That's no problem.

Therapist: Thank you so much for contacting me. I look forward to seeing you Wednesday.

I like to email the intake forms to the client ahead of time. I find that this frees up more time for actual counseling and gives the client plenty of time to read through my office policies and HIPPA beforehand. This information is also posted on my website, jpcounseling.com, making it available to clients, or prospective clients, at any time. In addition to this, I also email the client an article I wrote called "How to make the most out of counseling."

I've found that many clients go into counseling with misconceptions and these misconceptions can hinder progress. When clients don't do "their part" to be productive partners in counseling, I've found that it not only makes my job harder as the therapist but it also makes things harder for the client who went into counseling expecting to make progress just by showing up to appointments every once in awhile. Rather than devote sessions to discussing how to be an active partner in counseling and the importance of taking responsibility for your own mental health, I decided to just write an article explaining all of the points I wanted to make. I titled it "How to make the most out of counseling" because I thought that would be a title people would feel more motivated to read rather than "How to not frustrate your therapist."

Since no one wants to waste their time, clients generally appreciate getting this article. And since the article teaches the client how to be productive in therapy, it makes the therapist's job easier too. Although I've included the article in this book, I recommend rewriting it in your own words. You may also find there are things you want to add and things I've written that you find unnecessary or don't agree with. Feel free to modify this article to better suit your needs:

How to get the most out of counseling

No one wants to waste their time, and let's face it, those copays add up, so I decided to write this article to help you get the most out of your counseling. As a therapist, I love seeing clients get better. Some of the turn-arounds I've witnessed have been simply amazing and I consider myself to be fortunate to have played a part in a person completely changing their lives for the better. Because I want all of my clients to be able to experience this type of change, I started keeping notes on the characteristics of my successful clients. I asked myself, why is it that some clients improve so quickly and dramatically while others linger in therapy for years without making any real improvements? Was it something innate and unchangeable about the clients themselves?

As it turns out, the characteristics that make someone an "ideal" client are quite simple and anyone can implement them. I've found that just sharing this information with my clients has caused all my clients overall to improve. Please continue reading if you too would also like to get faster and better results in counseling:

1. You make your appointments a priority. *If you've ever tried to learn a new skill or get in shape at the gym, you know that consistency is key. Frequently cancelling and rescheduling appointments are going to hinder or prevent progress in therapy. It is the reason why I terminate counseling if missed appointments become excessive. The clients that get better the fastest come to every appointment without exception. I had a client in the past whose car broke down, so he actually rode his bike through the snow for two hours to make it to the appointment! This client in particular also eventually became one of my greatest success stories. When you make appointments a priority, wonderful things start to happen.*

2. You are willing to take risks and try new things. *Anytime you learn new skills, it feels strange and unnatural. If you hired a coach to help you improve your tennis game, the way he teaches you to hold the racket would probably feel "wrong" at first but with practice it would become second nature and improve your game. I'm going to teach you skills and techniques that are going to sound weird at first, but trust me, with practice it will eventually become second nature and you won't even think about it. But what I need from you is a willingness to at least try the skills I teach you. My ideal clients show a curiosity and an eagerness to try new things and follow through with recommendations outside of the office.*

3. You take responsibility for your mental health. *If you went to a doctor's office and when the doctor asked*

"So what brings you here today?" and you just shrugged your shoulders, naturally you would leave the office without having received any care. The same is true for when you visit the therapy office. Ideal clients come prepared to each session with an agenda of issues they would like to have addressed by the therapist in that session. Ideal clients make notes (either mental notes or in writing) of the improving or worsening of symptoms between sessions. Ideal clients have clear goals of what they would like to achieve in therapy, and actively work on those goals.

4. You give direct and honest feedback. The more feedback I get from you about what is working and what isn't working, the more I can tailor my services to be more effective. I never want you to be afraid of hurting my feelings. I value honest feedback from my clients. It allows me to do my job better and it allows services to be made more effective to you so that you get better faster.

I find it best that as soon as you are done talking to the client on the phone that you immediately send the client a follow up email. The email should thank them again for calling, include the date and time of the appointment, directions to your office, and of course an attachment of the documents discussed earlier. Sending the email immediately communicates to the client that you are organized, prompt, considerate, and sets a tone for them to be the same way in their communication with you. It also tells the client that they are important to you. A sample email would look like this:

Good Afternoon, Sarah!

Thank you so much for scheduling an appointment with me!

I've attached some important information to this email. Some of this information I am required by law to give you. I've also included a copy of my office policies and a consent form to sign. Please print and bring the filled-out consent form with you on Wednesday. Copays are due at the beginning of the therapy session. I do not take credit card or check. You can pay me in cash or use the paypal button on my website before the session.

I am located at (your address). (Describe your location

*and what the building looks like in order to minimize con-
fusion).*

I look forward to seeing you!

(your name and credentials)

(your phone number)

(website if applicable)

If you are not in private practice, depending on the policies of the agency you work for, you may not be able to send email to your clients. In that case it is appropriate to spend a portion of that first session explaining to clients how they can get the most out of counseling.

When clients contact you via email

Some busy individuals prefer communication via email and may contact you first that way. Although I consider phone to be the best option aside from face to face contact, people are increasingly turning to email as a primary mode of relaying information. One nice thing about email is that it eliminates phone-tag. Something to be aware of however is that some people may choose to contact you via email because they are less committed to the idea of counseling. They may be "kicking the tires" so to speak. Keep in mind that the sender may have also sent this very same email to a dozen other therapists in the area. This is especially obvious when the person doesn't provide any contact information other than a nondescript email address. Here is an example:

> *Hello, my wife and I have been together for 4 years of mar-
> riage now. It has been tough but we survived so far. Our
> married is falling and falling fast. There are a lot of issues
> that need addressing in order to save this marriage which
> we both want. How do your services work and payment
> work? We really need help... please. ty for listening. Hope
> to hear from you real soon.*

This person did not provide so much as their first name. I can also tell they did not spend much time looking at my website since all of the information they have asked for is easily available. Because I give out my email address on my website, I receive several emails like this each week. Even though this person has probably emailed several other therapists, it is still worth it to give a thoughtful response. The thoughtfulness and timeliness of your response may be what sets you apart from the other therapists they have contacted. An appropriate response could look like this:

Thank you for contacting me!

To answer your questions: Payment works by charging either you or your wife's insurance. I only need one person's insurance and one copay. I am a contracted provider for (name the plans you are contracted with). I can also bill any other insurance so long as you have something called "out of network benefits." The good news is that most people have these benefits. If you could give me your insurance information I could find out if you are eligible. For those without eligible insurance, I charge (be upfront about your costs) per session.

As far as couples counseling goes. . . there are typically ten to twelve sessions, about 50 minutes in length, meeting once a week. The purpose of the sessions is not to determine who's right and who's wrong or to assign blame. I will not be choosing sides. But in the course of these 10-12 sessions we will be creating solutions and learning new skills based on what your own unique needs are as a couple. I can't say what those solutions and skills will be at the moment because I will need to know more about the problem. I have found my methods of delivering couples counseling to quite effective and that those that stick with the sessions tend to see a decrease in problems.

What times are you and your wife available for appointments?

(your name)

(your phone number)

(your website)

This is an appropriate email because it addressed all of the sender's questions, thanked them for their email, educated the client on what counseling is or isn't, and provided the client with the next course of action (providing their insurance information and scheduling an appointment). Although you probably won't hear back from this client right away, I have had similar clients contact me again (sometimes months later) and turn into regular clients.

Final thoughts

I wanted to end this chapter with one final thought about the work you will be doing. At times you will feel unappreciated and maybe even downright despised during couples counseling. It's important to realize that your clients also feel unappreciated and despised in their own relationships and that these feelings and negative attitudes are brought out during the sessions. Sometimes they become projected onto the therapist. This is part of the process, but it will get better in successive sessions. Keep in mind that your clients are hurting, and when people are hurting they sometimes lash out. Of course, you should never take outright abuse, and being a model of respectful interactions goes a long way towards preventing inappropriate behaviors in session. If clients are inappropriate, let the client know that counseling will not be successful until behaviors become appropriate.

Not every couple is difficult to work with. You will find couples that are motivated and easy to work with. However, you should try not to categorize these couples as being "good" just because they are easier to work with. Couples that are really hurting also deserve your very best and often have the most to gain from your services. It is by working with "difficult" couples that you will really hone your skills as a therapist and grow as a practitioner.

For my fictional couple that I'm going to be using in my examples, Sarah and Mark, I've chosen to depict Mark as being resistant to therapy. Although he is not abusive to the therapist, he can at times be condescending and argumentative. I am characterizing Mark in this manner not because I am implying that most clients will act in this manner, but because I want you to feel prepared for when you do encounter difficult clients.

Chapter 2

First Session: Intake

If you work for an agency or other employer, they may have very specific guidelines to follow for the first session, and you probably have a lot more paperwork to fill out than someone in private practice. If that is the case, then by all means follow agency protocol and make modifications as necessary to the guidelines I have provided for this session. If, however, you are in private practice and were able to email the client paperwork ahead of time, make sure you print out that paperwork and have it ready anyway.

I have found that a third of the time the client will say something along the lines of "I read the documents but I wasn't able to print and sign the consent form because my printer is broken." The client may also have questions about HIPPA or your office policies, so it's good to have a print-out to refer to during these discussions. I have found though that most of the time the clients sign the forms without needing further explanation.

Step 1: Build rapport

Building rapport or forming a connection with the client is essential work in therapy. If you have been practicing as a therapist for a while, then you should have lots of experience with this. It starts with greeting the client with a big warm smile. Although it's common for clients in individual counseling to have seen a therapist before, most clients have never seen a couples counselor before and don't know what to expect. They may be dreading the experience and have an expectation that couples counseling is a cold and dour affair. A warm smile and a couple of minutes of small talk from you can help your clients relax significantly. Mentioning "the big game" last night or talking about the weather ("Unbelievable weather we've been having lately, am I right?") are popular topics for small talk that your client will have an easy time engaging in.

Part of the process of building rapport is making the client feel that you are similar to them. This does involve changing your personality and mannerisms to better match the client's, but it is easier than it sounds. One way of doing this is by mimicking the client's body language. Few people are aware of their own body language, so there is a slim chance that the client will pick up on this consciously, but their unconscious brain will pick up on it and send signals to their conscious brain that "this person is like me." You will also want to mimic the way the client talks. If the client uses specific words or gestures when talking, incorporate those same words. If a client tends to talk plainly, tone down the vocabulary. Give longer explanations to client that talk in long explanations, and talk in short bites to clients that only give a sentence or two at a time. Pretty soon they'll feel a connection with you but not be quite sure why. People usually dismiss it as charisma, but it is really much simpler than that.

After having been a therapist for so many years, building rapport comes naturally to me and I don't even realize I'm doing it half the time. It is a great skill to know if you are at a party or meeting new people. It also helps to watch popular television and keep up on the news so that you can more easily talk with your clients about what interests them. Don't forget to pay your clients compliments! Everyone likes a good compliment, and I give them often. If I like a client's outfit, I say so. If the client raised a good suggestion or utilized a communication skill, I let them know. In general, you want to try to give four positive statements for every one criticism. This is a ratio most people are comfortable with (Gottman & Silver, 2000). If you give too much criticism, clients are more likely to not listen to you and may even drop out of therapy.

The only exception to building rapport by mimicking your client is if your client acts in an inappropriate manner. You do not want to mimic disrespectful or negative behaviors and ways of speaking. You also do not want to mimic "defensive body language." Use an open, non-defensive posture in therapy. Above all else, the therapist should be a model of what the client can become. Showing people that there are alternate, more mutually respectful ways of responding to inappropriate behavior is a valuable lesson to clients.

Step 2: Gather information

After introducing yourself to the client, it is time to get down to business. You may want to have a notepad and pen handy so you can take notes because you are going to be receiving a lot of information. I make it a point to let clients know that I am only going to be taking notes during this one session since I have a lot of questions to ask them. This sets the expectation that there will be a lot of questions, and also that they don't have to worry about the stereotype of the therapist constantly scribbling down notes during sessions. I've noticed that taking notes during sessions can be distracting for the clients and that the clients are often curious to know what exactly you are writing. Sometimes that curiosity can take on a paranoid tone; "are you writing something negative about me?." Taking notes also takes away from maintaining eye contact and an open posture with your client. Because of this, I only take notes on the first session.

Even though you have already talked with one of the couples over the phone prior to the first session and got the gist of the problems in the relationship, you are going to ask for this same information again. You may notice that the person seems calmer this time around since they've already had a chance to tell you their story. It is important to hear the other person's side of the story as well. They may disagree with their partner's reasoning, and frequently do. There is also some other information you are going to need to ask for. The information you are going to want to gather for the intake includes both of their occupations, who they live with, any medications or medical conditions, psychiatric history, trauma history, and presenting problems or concerns.

When doing an intake, I ask for a brief history of relationship difficulties. Some clients can go on for hours about the difficulties in their relationship, especially if these difficulties have been going on for years. Some people also want to provide you with every detail of their partner's transgressions, as if they are presenting evidence in court. Any attempts by the client to shift the blame onto the other partner or try to convince you of who's right and who's wrong, should be discouraged. Although clients may feel it is important for you to know all the details "in order to make an informed decision", you really only need to know the gist of it. You are not writing the great American novel. A basic history of the relationship difficulties, a list of symptoms, and then a list of goals, is all that is needed.

When clients describe the problems in their relationship, you want to hear about specific behaviors or feelings they are experiencing in the relationship. Some clients are very good at doing this while others will tend to give a vague response like "the relationship is just dysfunctional." Unfortunately, we need more details than that and must provide enough description in our diagnostic in order to measure progress later. Some people have a hard time describing relationship problems in terms of symptoms or behaviors, so I've provided a list of behavioral symptoms to help get you started:

- Arguments

- Yelling at partner

- Hostility towards partner

- Angry outbursts

- Critical remarks or demeaning statements made towards partner

- Throwing or breaking objects during arguments

- Anxiety

- Putting all the blame on the other partner without recognizing one's own contribution to the problems

- Feelings of low self esteem within the relationship

- Depressed mood

- Avoiding spending time with partner

- Withdrawal from partner

- Resentment toward partner

- Jealousy

- Infidelity

- Excessive use of pornography that is upsetting to other partner

- Financial worries

- Lack of sexual interactions

- Disagreements over parenting

For your intake, you want to define the relationship problems behaviorally using terms similar to the ones listed above. You also need to establish the frequency of these behaviors. Doing so will allow you to more easily track progress over time. If a couple tells you they are still yelling everyday after eight sessions, it can sound discouraging. But if at the beginning of therapy they were yelling five times a day, and now it is down to just one time a day, that is actually a huge improvement! This is why you want to establish a frequency. Most of your clients have never thought of their problems in terms of behaviors or frequencies before and might have some trouble with this. Let them know that their best guess for a daily or weekly average is all you're looking for if they become frustrated by the process.

Now that you've defined the problem, it's time to set goals. Goals can also be done behaviorally. For example, a goal might be "decrease arguing from two times a day to two times a month." A goal of "to never argue again" is probably not attainable. An easy way to help your couple think in terms of goals is to ask them "How would you know if couples counseling was successful? What would be different from the way things are now?" Having a vague response like "I would just feel happier" is probably not going to be helpful. You are looking for answers like "We would have a working budget and stick with it. We would discipline our daughter as a team. We would have sex at least once a week" etc. Setting clear specific goals is important because it gives your clients something to work towards. Just knowing what is expected of them is sometimes enough to get them moving in the right direction.

Step 3: Educate clients about the process of couples counseling

By this point, you have already spoke with the client over the phone, sent an email or two, and gave them an article you wrote about how to get the most out of counseling. However, you most likely only spoke with one member of the couple, and you cannot assume that that information was passed along to the other partner or that they had a deep meaningful discussion about couples counseling before today's session. Given all of the misconceptions about couples counseling, I almost feel that you cannot educate clients about the process enough. I have found proper education to be the most important element to making couples counseling successful.

For clients that have been in individual counseling before, it is important for them to understand that couples counseling is much more structured and we will be actively working towards the goals we just set for couples counseling through problem solving and weekly homework assignments. Couples counseling is far more active and directive than most individual counseling. Also let the couple know that you will not be taking sides and will intervene during arguments if necessary. Many couples feel that the point of couples counseling is to argue in front of a professional until the professional chooses a winner. This couldn't be further from the truth. Both individuals have to be willing to make changes and move past a mentality that couples counseling is about winning at the other person's expense. Let's take a look at what couples counseling is and isn't.

Couples counseling is:

- Neutral

- Structured

- Educational

- A way to grow as a couple

- Making changes to improve the relationship

- Owning up to your own mistakes

- Forgiveness

Couples counseling isn't:

- About proving who's right and who's wrong

- Professionally ganging up on your partner

- "Fighting it out"

- Making yourself happy at the other's expense

- Forcing the other person to change

- Proving the other person wrong

- Blame

Educating the couple also includes educating them about the process of couples counseling. Most people I meet have no idea how long couples counseling lasts or what is expected of them during these sessions. I inform clients early on that couples counseling typically lasts ten to twelve sessions, happening once a week for about fifty minutes each. I also inform my clients that I don't expect any overnight miracles and most couples don't notice any improvement until about the fourth session.

I try to give my clients a realistic idea of what they can expect from counseling and ask for their patience during the process. Because we are going to be dealing with some challenging topics, it's important that the couple give a firm commitment for ten sessions. They have to promise that they will hold off on coming to a decision about ending the relationship and not ending couples counseling until after the tenth session.

Step 4: Express confidence that the relationship can be saved

Many of the couples coming to counseling are so used to conflict and failure that they hold little hope for the relationship or whatever you have to offer as a therapist. One of the best things that you can do as a counselor is to express a feeling of confidence to the couple that you can help them and that the relationship can be saved. This is not the same as giving a "guarantee", which should be avoided in counseling. Most of the conflicts couples bring to counseling are actually pretty easily solved so long as both partners are onboard with making some minor changes. You are not asking them to change their whole personality, just utilize a few new skills. Of course, you do not want to trivialize their suffering either. It's easy as the therapist to see how simple the solution is, but when you are emotionally attached to a person, it can be hard to see past the conflict.

Overall, you want your couple to leave that first session feeling like things are going to improve. Does wrapping up the first session with saying "Well, we'll see how it goes" inspire much hope for change in your clients? The research shows that if people feel hopeful about their situation that they are much more likely to take action to fix the problem (Willis, 2007). They are also much more likely to follow through with recommendations made in therapy and attend all of the sessions. So, what can you as the therapist do to inspire hope?

1. Normalize their experience. Because people don't like to talk openly about problems in their marriage or relationship, people don't realize how "normal" or common it is to have these problems. Letting a couple know that they are "not alone" in their difficulties can be helpful. Let's look at some statistics about relationship problems. A Gallup Poll found that 40% of married individuals in the United States had considered leaving their partners, and 20% said they were dissatisfied with their marriage about half the time.

For many couples, difficulties in their marriage start early. A study of newlywed couples found that 63% had serious financial problems, 51% had serious doubts about their marriage lasting, 49% had significant marital problems, 45% were not satisfied with their sexual relationship, 41% found marriage harder than they had expected, and 35% stated their partner was often critical of them (Olson & Defrain, 1994). Simply saying "A lot of couples are struggling with similar issues" can help normalize their experience.

2. Let them know that you can help. If you've had success working with similar couples, say so! Let them know that based off of what they've told you today that you are going to create a treatment plan that can really help them, but it's going to take some cooperation from them. Inform the couple that upcoming sessions are going to address the specific concerns that they have raised today and that you know of some solutions to these specific problems that the science has proven works. All of the treatments that I suggest herein this book are evidence-based. You can feel confident that these treatments really do work. Try to help your couple feel this same confidence.

3. Highlight the good points of the relationship. Sometimes people get so used to focusing on what's wrong with the relationship, that they don't see what's already good about it. There's good and bad in every person and every relationship. Just the fact that they are even considering couples counseling shows the level of love and commitment for each other. Has the couple overcome many challenges together? Do they have love and respect for one another? Is their communication basically good? Do they have the same goals and a similar outlook on life? Really highlight all of the positives that you see in the current relationship. Just hearing from a professional that the relationship is not as bad as they thought can give the couple hope that change is possible.

First session vignette

At the end of each session chapter I'm going to include a vignette involving our fictional couple, Sarah and Mark. This vignette is demonstrating Sarah and Mark's first session with the therapist. I will then provide a brief analysis about the session. The session vignette will include all the steps mentioned earlier in this chapter and will show you how they might flow in a real therapy session. So, let's get started:

Therapist: Thank you so much for coming! It's so good to see you two. Beautiful weather we've been having lately.

Mark: Yes, the weather has been amazing the past few days.

Therapist: Well, come on in and make yourselves comfortable on the couch. Did you remember to print out and sign the consent form I emailed you?

Sarah: Yes, it's right here.

Therapist: Great. Thank you. I appreciate you taking the time to do that before today's session. Did you have any questions about my office policies or your rights?

Sarah: No. I found it to be pretty straight forward.

Mark: I think we understood everything.

Therapist: Good. Now, because this is our first session, I'm going to be asking a lot of questions. These questions are going to be used to help me create a treatment plan later. I usually don't write during sessions, but because I will be gathering so much information I'm going to have to take some notes today. Is that ok?

Sarah: That's fine.

Mark: Sure. That's not a problem.

Therapist: Great. So, what do you two do for a living?

Mark: I'm a civil engineer and Sarah's a real estate agent.

Therapist: Do you feel happy in your careers?

Sarah: I think we both are pretty devoted to our careers, and we're okay with that.

Therapist: Would you agree with that Mark?

Mark: I'd say that sounds accurate.

Therapist: Good. Do you two live alone?

Mark: Yes, it's just the two of us unless you also count the dog.

Therapist: Have either one of you ever seen a therapist before?

Mark: Never.

Sarah: I saw a therapist briefly while I was in college. I was having some problems with panic attacks, but I feel I've gotten past all of that.

Therapist: Do you still get panic attacks sometimes?

Sarah: Only rarely. I don't feel it is a problem anymore.

Therapist: That's great to hear. It sounds like you've had some success with therapy in the past.

Sarah: I feel like I got better because I wanted to get better, not because of the therapist.

Therapist: That's so true, Sarah. It sounds like if you put your mind to something you tend to accomplish it.

Sarah: I'd say so.

Therapist: Any medications or medical conditions?

Mark: I'd say we're both pretty healthy. Neither one of us are on any medications and we go to the gym regularly.

Therapist: Any history of traumas or childhood abuse?

Mark: My parents never abused me or anything, but they fought a lot. It was not always a happy childhood.

Therapist: Do you think that those childhood experiences still have an effect on you?

Mark: Of course. Everyone's affected by their childhood, good or bad.

Therapist: Do you think it has had an on effect on this relationship?

Mark: Of course.

Therapist: Mark, I want to thank you for your honesty. I know that childhood stuff is not always easy to talk about. Sarah, have you ever experienced any traumas?

Sarah: I think me and Mark have had very different upbringings. I would describe my childhood as having been normal.

Therapist: Good. I had already talked to Sarah over the phone and she gave me a brief description of some of the things you would like to work on in counseling, but now I would like to hear from both of you what are the problems or concerns that you are bringing to couples counseling today?

Sarah: Well, like I said over the phone, me and Mark argue a lot.

Therapist: How often do you and Mark argue?

Sarah: Every day.

Mark: Oh come on, Sarah. We don't argue every day.

Sarah: Mark, be honest. We find something to argue about every day. Sometimes more than once.

Mark: So now you're saying I'm lying?

Sarah: I didn't say that!

Mark: You're always accusing me of lying about something.

Therapist: Mark, how often would you say you and Sarah get into arguments?

Mark: No, I'm not going to play that game. What ever I say is just going to be used against me.

Therapist: Mark, this information is important so that I can establish a baseline to use to measure progress. I am not going to use it against you. And the for the record, I don't think you are a bad person or that everything is your fault.

Mark: But she does!

Therapist: That's not what I hear Sarah saying, but let's move on... What other difficulties are you experiencing?

Sarah: I feel like I can't trust anything Mark says anymore since the affair.

Therapist: So I'm hearing there's a lack of trust-

Mark: That was two years ago! It's time to get over it, Sarah. I am not going to allow myself to be accused and under suspicion for the rest of my life. I will not stand for this!

Sarah: ::bursts into tears::

Therapist: There's a box of tissues on the table next to you if you feel you need them.

Sarah: Thank you...

Therapist: Mark, is there anything you can do to comfort Sarah right now?

Mark: ::crosses arms defensively and leans away from Sarah::

Therapist: Do you think it would help if you put your arm around her?

Mark: This is a game she plays. I speak the truth and then she bursts into tears in order to shut me up.

Therapist: It sounds like you're saying you feel like you can't defend yourself without Sarah getting upset. I could see how her crying could make you feel like she's trying to manipulate you or silence your voice. That must be frustrating.

Mark: It is!

Therapist: I wonder if it would have went differently though if you had spoken less harshly.

Mark: That's your perception.

Therapist: Sarah, tell me what thoughts are going through your mind right now.

Sarah: That he doesn't care.

Mark: That's not true!

Therapist: But could you see how she could feel that way?

Mark: No.

Therapist: You don't have to agree with someone in order to see how they could feel a certain way.

Sarah: Exactly!

Mark: But it's not true. I'm not going to acknowledge something that isn't true. We each have our own perception about it and that's that.

Therapist: That's true, but Sarah's feeling hurt right now. You can argue with someone about facts, but you can't argue with someone about the way they feel. You may feel that her reaction was overblown but the reality of the situation is that someone you love is hurting right now and I can tell that it makes you feel hurt too when you see her like this.

Mark: Of course it does. It makes me feel really guilty and I don't like to see her like this.

Therapist: What if I told you that I could teach you both how to handle disagreements in a way that doesn't end in anger or tears?

Mark: Your pearls of wisdom or whatever else you have to offer may sound good on a bumper sticker, but me and Sarah are pretty set in our ways.

Therapist: Any time you try to learn something new it feels weird at first, but I've worked with lots of couples just as skeptical as you are and I can tell you that with practice it becomes second nature and eventually you get to a point where you don't even realize you are doing it anymore.

Sarah: I want to try. Mark, we have to at least give it a chance. We've tried everything else.

Therapist: Are you willing to give this a try, Mark?

Mark: I'll follow through with all your advice, but I'm warning you ahead of time that we are not your typical couple. That's why we're here.

Therapist: Good... Now, let me tell you a little bit about how couples counseling works. Sessions are about fifty minutes each and we will be meeting once a week for ten to twelve weeks. I'm not going to sugar coat it, people find the first three sessions to be very difficult and usually don't start to see any improvements until around the fourth session. I'm not expecting any overnight miracles and neither should you. Because of that, I need you to commit to ten sessions and promise not to break-up during those ten sessions. After the tenth session, you can decide what you want to do; end the relationship, continue couples counseling if necessary, or find yourself happy with the improvements you've made during those ten sessions and terminate counseling. Can you make that commitment?

Sarah: Yes.

Therapist: What about you, Mark?

Mark: Yes, I'm willing to do whatever it takes.

Therapist: I want to let you know that I have a lot of confidence that this relationship can be saved. I've worked with a lot of couples with similar problems and have seen the change people are capable of. It just takes an open mind and a willingness to try something new. Overall, I think the foundations of your relationship are very good. It's obvious you have a lot of love and respect for one another. We just need to change maybe 10%. Sound good?

Sarah: Yes.

Mark: Sure.

Therapist: Well, I hate to do this to you, but we've run out of time. Will I see you again the same time next week?

Mark: Yes.

Therapist: Thanks again for seeing me today. I look forward to our next session.

Like many first sessions, the session started out civil but then the couple quickly reverted back to their normal mode of communicating with one another. Clues were also given early on that the couple went into the session already feeling tense. When the therapist asked Sarah if she still experienced problems with anxiety, she was quick to minimize it, not wanting there to be any implication that her anxiety or tendency to become overwhelmed easily could have any contribution to the problems in the relationship. Sarah then went on the defense, taking a jab at therapists in general. Rather than also becoming defensive, the therapist chose to disarm the client by agreeing with her, and then managed to put a positive spin on the exchange by emphasizing "yes, the responsibility for change always falls on the client."

Mark also revealed how tense he was by becoming defensive when the therapist asked about childhood traumas. Although Mark was quick to admit he had a dysfunctional childhood and poor role models for how to behave in a relationship, he became angered when the therapist asked if those experiences could be influencing his current behavior. His quick temper confirmed for the therapist that yes, it does influence how he behaves with Sarah. The therapist is going to refrain from mentioning Mark's childhood and Sarah's possible anxiety disorder until more trust is established during the sessions. I mentioned "planting seeds" in the previous chapter, and that is exactly what this therapist is doing now.

Mark's hostile reaction during counseling can be upsetting, especially when he turns that hostility onto the therapist. There could be many reasons for Mark's negative reaction during the session. The first could be a simple misconception about what couples counseling is all about. He may have heard about a friend's experience with couples counseling where the therapist sided with the wife and then recommended they get a divorce (sadly, not unheard of). The therapist took steps towards rectifying this when Mark was told that the therapist did not consider him to be the bad guy. Mark may also have developed a defensive way of reacting from a lifetime of having the blame put on him, starting in childhood and continuing into his current relationship. Mark did mention his childhood was dysfunctional.

Mark may also just be one of those people that love to argue and always have to be right. Such behavior tends to be reinforced in our society. Indeed, individuals with this attitude tend to be favored by businesses and find themselves promoted to positions of power within the company. They get a lot of pleasure out of "winning", and proving the therapist wrong in front of their partner could be seen as the ultimate prize. However, when Mark threw down that gauntlet in front of the therapist, the therapist wisely chose not to pick it up. It's not an easy thing to do, but by refraining from arguing with Mark or appearing bothered by his statements, the therapist robbed Mark of the satisfaction of his condescending statements. If the therapist continues with this strategy, Mark's negative behaviors should decrease over time.

The first time you encounter a couple like Mark and Sarah, you're really going to have to fight the temptation to just take the easy way out and tell the couple that you can't work with them or that they are not compatible. It is not unheard of to hear of an inexperienced therapist telling a couple they should end the relationship based off of just one session. One of my successful, although initially quite difficult, couples told me that they had seen a couples counselor previous to me and that the counselor had such a difficult time with the couple that halfway through the first session he told the husband "I think you should divorce the bitch!" I had a hard time believing a therapist could be that unprofessional at first, but after hearing so many similar stories over the years, I have to believe it is true. Do not be that therapist!

An inexperienced therapist would probably look at this particular case and assume that couples counseling just isn't going to work for Sarah and Mark. They may suggest seeing them both in individual counseling until tempers can be controlled or even suggest they end the relationship. However, that is not the therapist's judgement to make. Both Sarah and Mark have said that they want to try couples counseling. Sarah even said over the phone that she would like to work towards the goal of marriage! Obviously this is a couple that, despite contradicting behaviors, is very devoted to one another and must love each other very much as well.

Based on the information gathered during the session, problem behaviors in this relationship include: Frequent arguing, feelings of mistrust, putting all of the blame on the other person and not recognizing one's own contribution to the problem, poor communication, emotional outbursts, and misunderstandings. Although Mark disagreed, we can assume on average that they experience these symptoms roughly once a day. Based on this, goals for the relationship are to learn and utilize conflict resolution skills and communication skills, resolve negative feelings resulting from past infidelity, and decrease overall frequency and intensity of symptoms to one time per month.

You should feel proud of yourself, you just got through one of the hardest sessions in couples counseling. If you can hang in there, you should find that the sessions start to become easier. By the end of the tenth session, you should feel a deep sense of satisfaction, like you just climbed Mount Everest. Although it is sometimes hard to sit through in the beginning, couples counseling is rewarding work.

Session 1 outline

Step 1: Build Rapport

Step 2: Gather Information

- Occupations
- Who they live with
- Medications and medical conditions
- Psychiatric history
- Trauma history
- Presenting problems or concerns
- Frequency of problem behaviors

Step 3: Educate clients about the process of couples counseling

- Get a firm commitment for 10 sessions

Step 4: Express confidence that the relationship can be saved

- Normalize their experience
- Let them know that you can help
- Highlight the good points of the relationship

Chapter 3

Second Session: Reveal Potential

The point of this session is to shift the couple's mindset from what's wrong with the relationship to what the couple could become. To be honest, this is my favorite session. The couple is assigned a writing assignment to do in session, and then the therapist processes what each partner wrote afterwards. There's no right way or wrong way to do the assignment and I've noticed that each couple puts their own spin on it. The results of the assignment are often very interesting and insightful.

Step 1: Review progress

It might seem unlikely that there would be any progress after just one session, but you would be surprised how quickly couples counseling can act as a "wake-up call" for some couples. It's not unusual to hear that couples are on their best behavior now that they are being held accountable to a therapist. No one wants to get "told-on" to the therapist and look bad. If the couple does have good news, provide positive reinforcement for the progress they've made. Again, express confidence that their relationship can improve even further through continued counseling, and skip to Step 2.

Sometimes when you ask for an update of the past week clients have bad news to report. They may have experienced a major blow-up or crisis of some sort and are now looking to you to help avert the crisis. Although you had planned to do the writing assignment today, a crisis or major problem trumps that. It may take the entire session to deal with the crisis, which is why I say couples counseling lasts ten to twelve sessions. Sometimes an extra session or two is necessary to deal with a crisis or devote extra time to learning a new skill that the couple is having difficulty grasping. Some couples breeze right through the ten sessions with no problem, while others require a few extra sessions.

There are many crises that can pop up during couples counseling. Between one session and the next, one partner may have admitted to having an affair, or worse, the other partner discovers the affair. There could have been a falling out with the in-laws. Or there could have been a fight that resulted in both partners saying especially nasty things to each other. You may even encounter couples that separate or break-up during counseling despite agreeing to wait until the tenth session (you may need to remind them of the promise they made not to break up during counseling). There may be some disagreement if the couple actually broke-up if they then chose to come to their next session together, but what's important is if the break-up feels real to the couple.

As someone who is probably inexperienced with couples counseling, dealing with a crisis may sound scary to you. The good news is that if the couple has experienced a crisis in their relationship and still returned to couples counseling the following week, then they probably want to move past it, they just need a little help from you. The steps to dealing with a crisis are actually quite simple. They don't require anything especially advanced from you other than your ability to remain calm under fire.

Step 1: Let the couple tell the story of the crisis. This may result in some arguing between the couple like it did in the first session. Respond in the same way. If the arguing becomes intense, do not be afraid to call a timeout. You might have to call a time-out several times. Reiterate to the couple that you think it is important for them each to tell their side of the story, but that that can't happen if people are interrupting and yelling. This is going to be uncomfortable at times, but as the therapist, you have to keep the situation under control. If you allow the arguing to get bad enough that one person walks out of the room, it is highly unlikely that that person will ever come back. Try to keep arguments from escalating in the session.

Step 2: Reflect, validate, express empathy, and work towards a solution. After one person has been allowed to talk, follow up with your essential therapist skill of reflecting, validating, empathizing, and working towards a solution. This was discussed previously in regards to dealing with difficult clients, but I'm going to briefly explain it again to make sure you got it. First you reflect or paraphrase in your own words what the other person had told you. This lets them know that you were listening. It also gives them the chance to correct you in case you got it wrong or misunderstood. You then validate their experience by saying something like "I can see how someone would feel that way." The therapist then expresses empathy for their situation by saying "I'm sorry you feel so hurt right now." And finally, you ask for a possible solution by saying something like "what would you like to do about this?" The therapist acknowledges their response and then turns to the other person for their side of the story. Wash, rinse, and repeat.

It sounds simple, but this is actually a very powerful technique. In today's world, people aren't used to having another person listen to them and understand them so fully. Especially if someone has spent the past several years in a relationship with someone who doesn't listen, to finally be understood is a powerful experience. But it doesn't end there. The therapist then does the same thing with the other partner. The person witnesses their partner also being listened to and having their ideas validated. In doing so, the therapist is communicating that there is more than one solution to a problem, and that no one's right and no one's wrong. Each person is shown equal respect by the therapist.

Step 3: Problem Solve. At this point, each person has had a chance to speak and share what they would like to have happen to solve the conflict. You are now going to demonstrate to the couple the art of compromise. In the past, your couple has solved problems where one person would be the winner and the other the loser. You are going to demonstrate to them that there is a way to solve a problem where both people win. If possible, try to incorporate both of their suggested solutions. If that can't be done, create a new solution that avoids "punishing" any one person. You want both of them to be able to live with the solution.

Of course, not every problem can be solved. The other person may just be looking for an apology and an acknowledgment from the other person that they could have handled the situation better. My personal policy is if I do something wrong or make a mistake, I admit to it quickly and ask the person I have wronged how I can make the situation better, but most people are not like this. Most people have a hard time admitting to the mistakes they've made, especially early on in couples counseling. Because of this, you might want to ask both partners how they could have handled the situation better and ask them to each apologize to the other person for their contribution to the problem, rather than expect that a client will intuitively know to do this without prompting from a therapist.

Step 4: Moving Forward. The session is wrapped up by asking each partner what they've learned from this situation and if there are things they can do to prevent this from happening again in the future. The couple is then asked if they can move past this event in order to make progress in the relationship. Most couples will say that they feel they can move past it. That is the reason that they are here in counseling after all. Some may express some uncertainty about their ability to let-go, but that may simply be them putting their partner "on notice." In my experience, simply having come to today's session shows a willingness to move forward. The couple could have sent you an email saying they've dropped out of counseling and will be getting that divorce after all, but they chose to try to work it out instead.

Here is how a crisis intervention session would look in practice:

Therapist: It's great seeing you two again. Since last time I saw you, have there been any progress or obstacles you would like to talk to me about?

Sarah: Actually, yes. I'm glad you've brought this up because something major happened this week.

Therapist: Please, tell me more about that.

Sarah: I discovered that Mark put up a profile on a dating site.

Mark: I put it up a long time ago but then forgot about it. It was a mistake from a long time ago!

Sarah: It's one of those dating sites that you have to pay for each month. How could you have forgotten about it?

Mark: I set up automatic payments and you know I'm not as OCD about my monthly spending as you are. We've already talked about this!

Therapist: Mark, I'm going to ask you not to interrupt while Sarah is talking. I know it's hard when you feel like you're being accused-

Mark: She's always accusing me!

Therapist: You're going to have a chance to tell your side of the story in a moment, but for now I need to understand where Sarah is coming from. Okay?

Mark: Fine.

Therapist: Sarah, please continue.

Sarah: One of my friends is single and she's a member of the same dating site. She came across his profile and then told me about it. She thought the profile looked pretty recent.

Mark: I made that profile two years ago and then forgot about it!

Therapist: Mark, I'm going to need you to overcome the tendency to interrupt while Sarah is talking. This is important. You will have a chance to speak in just a moment.

Sarah: I can't say for sure if it's recent because as soon as I confronted Mark about it, he quickly deleted the profile before I got a chance to look at it.

Mark: You told me to delete it!

Therapist: ::ignores Mark:: Sarah, it sounds like it must have been awful for you to find out about this dating profile, especially from a close friend. I'm sure it must have been uncomfortable for her to tell you about it as well.

Sarah: She was horrified.

Therapist: It sounds like this also opened up an old wound for you with Mark's affair. I can see how something like this would stir up lingering feelings of mistrust. It must feel really painful to have these kind of doubts about someone you love.

Sarah: ::eyes fill up with tears:: That's exactly right. It is really painful to feel this way. Mark is the love of my life, and to have this kind of betrayal really hurts.

Therapist: What do you think should be done to make things right again?

Sarah: Well, I'm glad that the profile got deleted. If there are anymore profiles, I think he needs to be honest and get rid of them all immediately. To be honest, I think he needs to spend less time on his computer too, and apologize to my friend for putting her in such an uncomfortable position.

Therapist: Mark, I'd like to hear your side of the story now.

Mark: Look, I've made mistakes in the past and I've owned up to those mistakes. I know I've messed up, but I will not be accused by her every day for the rest of my life! Like I said, that profile was made two years ago and I forgot about it. Cheryl is mistaken if she thinks it is more recent and quite frankly I think she should mind her own business. I never met anyone from the website or even messaged anybody. It was a mistake.

Therapist: It sounds like you're saying that when that profile was made you were at a different phase in your life, and looking back you wish you had never done it.

Mark: Of course.

Therapist: It must have been horrifying for you when you realized you never deleted it and Sarah's friend had seen it.

Mark: It was one of the most embarrassing moments of my life.

Therapist: It was probably horrifying for Cheryl too.

Mark: I know. I'm going to apologize to Cheryl and explain to her that the profile was from a long time ago.

Therapist: Good. I hear what you're saying about feeling like you're always being accused by Sarah. It's not a good feeling, especially when you feel that you should be past that by now. Is there anything you can think of to do that would ease her mind?

Mark: I'm tired of trying to get her to trust me. It's up to her now.

Therapist: What are some of the things you've done in the past to try to get her to trust you again?

Mark: I've tried just talking to her. I also spend all my waking moments with her. I work 50 hours a week and then spend the rest of my time with Sarah. I don't have time to cheat on her even if I wanted to, and Sarah knows that!

Therapist: I think talking to each other is good. I also think it was good how you agreed to apologize to Cheryl. What about Sarah's suggestion to spend less time on the internet and maybe do more fun things together instead?

Mark: I think we already do a lot of fun things together. The problem is that Sarah never tells me what she wants to do until after the fact to guilt trip me. Not everything in this relationship is my fault.

Therapist: Mark, I hope you don't think that I hold you completely responsible for the problems in this relationship. I want you both to know that I don't take sides. I'm sure you will agree that you both have contributed to the problems in this relationship.

Sarah: Of course. I know you're not supposed to take sides.

Mark: I hope I haven't come off as too defensive.

Therapist: Do you think you both can move past this for the sake of making progress? I see a lot of potential in this relationship, and I really do mean that.

Sarah: I'm willing to forget about it so long as Mark follows through.

Mark: ::nods::

Therapist: Good. Next time I'd like it if we could do a little writing in session. It's an exercise that will help you reveal the potential in your relationship. Sounds good?

Mark: I like to write. Sounds good.

Therapist: Good. I'll see you next week. Thanks for coming.

The Internet has made it so much easier to get in trouble in our relationships. Having a partner discover another partner's online dating profile is a problem I hear about a lot. The times I have had a chance to speak with the offender about it in private, many have admitted to doing it just out of curiosity. They are interested to see if someone would even be interested in them and that is all. For some it is a self esteem booster. It feels good to have someone email them asking for a date, especially if they don't get any attention from their partner. They have all denied using it as a tool to meet people to have an affair. Most people choose to have an affair with someone they already know rather than a random person they met online. Of course, that doesn't mean it's okay to be on a dating site when you are already with someone, but I think it helps to understand the offender's motives.

In this scenario, the therapist allowed Sarah to give her side of the story first since Sarah was the first one to bring up the problem. As usual, Mark became defensive, but the therapist handled it well. The therapist allowed Sarah to fully express her feelings, something that she probably wasn't able to do before given Mark's tendency to interrupt when he feels threatened. Just being able to express herself and be understood by another person, seems to be something that was deeply satisfying for Sarah. It seems to have been enough to allow Sarah to let go of the dating profile fiasco.

The therapist chose not to reprimand Mark for interrupting for a third time because the therapist suspected that given Mark's rising tension, a third reprimand may have caused him to storm out of the office. In which case, the therapeutic alliance probably would have been unable to be repaired and the couple would have most likely dropped out of therapy. Verbal reprimands were also not working. They just took the attention off of Sarah and put it on Mark. By ignoring Mark and keeping the attention on Sarah, the therapist effectively silenced Mark's inappropriate behavior in this instance.

Whether Mark is lying or not about the recentness of the profile is unimportant. The therapist still had an obligation to validate and emphasize with his feelings as had been done for Sarah. This allowed Mark to drop his defenses enough to agree with Sarah's requests. Not all couples are going to come in with a conflict they want you to mediate, but it does happen from time to time. This does not mean that the couple is "bad" or "incompatible" if they bring a lot to therapy. That is why they are here, after all. I once had a couple that it took twenty sessions because of a number of conflicts that surfaced during the course of therapy. They also needed an extra session to really master the communication skills I was trying to teach them. However, when all was said and done, they had created a marriage that one could be envious of. I consider them to be one of my greatest successes and in the end found the experience of working with them to have been very satisfying.

Step 2: Explain the writing assignment

Barring any conflicts, you are now ready to explain to the couple what you will be doing in today's session. Hand each person a notepad and pen and tell them that you want them to imagine what their perfect relationship would be like. It's okay for there to be a fantasy aspect to it since there's no such thing as a "perfect relationship." You aren't looking for a novel or essay, just some phrases or words that describe your ideal relationship. Some of them may be descriptive of how the relationship currently is, and that's okay too. A list of at least ten items is preferable. Some people will come up with very large lists, while others will only make it about halfway to that goal of ten items.

Although this sounds pretty straight forward, sometimes people can get confused about the assignment. It may help to give an example of some of the things you are looking for. Some of the most common things people write on their lists are "have sex every week; have a partner that helps out with the housework; love and support each other; have a clear budget and stick to it; never argue." Once people hear a few examples, that usually gets the ball rolling and people start writing. This activity usually takes between ten and twenty minutes for the couple to finish writing.

Step 3: Process the list

After the couple have finished writing their list of ten or more things they'd ideally like to be descriptive of their relationship, the therapist has them take turns reading their list out loud. The listening partner is asked to put a checkmark next to any items on their list that is the same as the other person's. They don't have to be worded exactly the same to get a check mark, but something that is basically the same, or the same "in spirit", is okay too. Clients are often amazed to find how many check marks are on their lists. If I see a lot of check marks, I point it out to the couple and will make a comment about how great it is they are on the same page about what they want in the relationship.

While a list is being read, intervene if any items on the list are vague or subjective. You are looking for specifics. If a client writes "have more sex" on their list, ask them "specifically, how often would be ideal for you?" The point of this is to help the client translate the fantasy into a workable goal. It is also helpful because the listening partner will have a better idea of what exactly the other person wants. In couples like these, very rarely do the partners actually tell the other person what they want. They assume that the other person can read their mind or should just know after being with them for so long. Unfortunately, life doesn't work that way. You can't expect people to fulfill your needs unless you express them clearly. That is what this assignment is all about.

By intervening and asking for more clarity, you are helping your clients practice stating their needs in a clear and concise manner. Ideally, you want to be able to define the items on the list behaviorally, in a similar manner to when you did the intake. With one couple I worked with, the wife put on her list "to be treated with respect." The husband was shocked to hear this because he honestly thought that he did treat her with respect. I asked her to describe to me the type of behaviors that he could do that would be respectful, but she said she couldn't define "respect" in that manner. I asked her "If I set up a video camera in your home and I caught your husband being respectful on tape, what would I see?" Framed this way, she was then able to come up with a list of behaviors more specific and defined. At the next session, she happily reported that her husband had started treating her with much more respect. He had wanted to treat her with respect all along, he just needed to know how to do it.

Sometimes couples will use the assignment as an opportunity to take a jab at one another. They'll write something on their list that they know the other person feels insecure about, for example "a wife that will go to the gym" or "a husband who's not afraid to ask for a raise at work." The person writing it knows the other person is going to blow-up as soon as they hear it, but they chose to write it anyway, and then an argument follows. For many of our couples, this is the only way they know how to relate to one another. The idea of having a shared responsibility to change doesn't exist and they have little concern for the other person's feelings. Fortunately, that will be changing in future sessions, but for now you should be doing what ever you can to discourage arguments.

If you indulged the couple arguing in the past, try not to do it now. You really want them to be listening while the other is saying what they want in the relationship. Interrupting, criticizing, or degrading their partner needs to be discouraged during this exercise. It is as easy as saying "Sarah, please stop criticizing Mark's list. We'll get to yours in a moment. For now I really need you to listen to what Mark is saying." If the couple are behaving themselves, give as much positive reinforcement as you can. You want to try to increase those positive behaviors for future sessions.

Step 4: Assign homework

The couple now gets assigned their first homework assignment. Their homework is to go home and create a new list together and then bring it with them to the next session. I have them bring home the list they made in today's session as a guide and tell them the easiest way to start is to first write down the things on their list that have a check mark next to them. If there are things on their original list that the other person didn't include but that they want to be in the final copy, it's up to that person to find a way to compromise.

People usually find this to be an easy and enjoyable assignment. The idea is to have the couple practice expressing their needs in a straightforward manner while also expressing some hope for the future that they could achieve an ideal relationship. You want the couple to get used to doing this outside of the therapy office. However, the whole homework assignment is useless if the couple waits until five minutes before their next appointment to do the assignment.

Before I started giving guidance to couples about when to do the assignments, I would often catch them sitting in their cars outside of my office hurriedly doing the homework assignments before their next appointment. At that point, the whole assignment was wasted. Now I advise my clients to do homework assignments in a day or two and educate them that the point of homework is to allow the concepts they learned in therapy to carry over into their regular lives. Waiting until the last minute to do homework prevents that. Homework helps them to maintain steady progress throughout the week.

Second session vignette

Therapist: Welcome back! How has everything been since last time I saw you?

Mark: I would say everything has been basically the same since last we saw you.

Sarah: Yes, just the usual. Nothing big has happened.

Therapist: I was wondering if you would be willing to do a writing assignment today?

Mark: Sure. I consider myself to be a rather good writer actually.

Sarah: Sounds fun.

Therapist: ::hands them each a notepad and pen:: Good! I bet you guys will be good at this. I'm not looking for an essay or anything like that. Just a list of at least ten items or phrases describing your ideal relationship. It's okay for it to be unrealistic or pie-in-the-sky. Obviously a "perfect" relationship doesn't exist, but this exercise is meant to get you thinking, to reveal your potential as a couple.

Sarah: So...what exactly are you looking for on our lists?

Therapist: However you want to interpret it is okay. It seems that every couple puts their own spin on the assignment. I just want you to imagine your ideal relationship and describe it to me in short bullets. Some of the things you come up with may actually describe how things currently are. If there are parts of this relationship that you consider to be ideal, it's okay to put them on your list. If it helps to have some examples, in the past clients have written things like "show each other more affection, stop yelling, support one another, go out on dates, show respect for one another" etc.

Sarah: Oh okay, I think I've got it.

Therapist: This assignment usually takes people between ten and twenty minutes. Afterwards, I'll have you take turns reading your lists out-loud. Try to resist the urge to look at what the other person's writing. Okay?

Sarah: Okay

Mark: Got it.

Therapist: ::fifteen minutes have passed and both partners seem to be done writing:: It looks like you both were able to come up with a lot of things for your lists. That's great. Who wants to go first?

Sarah: I guess I will.

Therapist: Mark, while Sarah is reading her list, if you hear anything that is the same as something you wrote on your list, or the same in essence, put a checkmark next to it. If you hear something that sounds really good and you wish you had put it on your list, you can add it to your list and put a checkmark next to it. Sarah, I want you to do the same when Mark reads his list. I may interrupt you guys while you're reading your lists in order to get more clarity. Sarah, you can go ahead if you're ready.

Sarah: Okay, here goes. I put on my list that an ideal relationship would have better communication, trust-

Therapist: Tell me more about "trust."

Sarah: I feel like I can't believe a word Mark says-

Mark: It was two years ago!

Sarah: Even now, I feel like he lies to me.

Therapist: What is happening now, nevermind what happened two years ago because it sounds like you can move past that, but what is happening now that makes you feel like there is a lack of trust in the relationship?

Sarah: It's hard to think of a specific example...

Therapist: An example would be helpful. You have all the time

you need to think.

Sarah: Well, just the other day, I caught him in a lie. He had assured me that the parking ticket was paid, then when I went to renew my license I was told I couldn't because there was an outstanding parking ticket. I was so angry. I reminded him to pay the ticket, it was his fault that we had gotten it, and several times he assured me that he had paid it. Now I find out that it had interest and fees piled on because it never got paid.

Mark: I forgot! I paid you back didn't I? You got your license renewed. I don't know what the big deal is.

Therapist: Did this feel like a "big deal" to you, Sarah?

Sarah: Yes.

Therapist: Why?

Sarah: Because it feels like I can't count on him for anything! It feels like he doesn't care. He knew I cared a lot about having a parking ticket and he just blew it off even though he knew it was important to me. It's obvious that he didn't mind paying the fees and what-not, but it was important to me! Just like when he cheated on me two years ago, he wasn't thinking about my feelings then either.

Mark: Oh come on, that's not fair! I've explained myself to you several times.

Therapist: But have you really listened?

Mark: Of course I listen to her.

Therapist: What do you hear her saying right now?

Mark: That she thinks I don't care about her. But I do plenty of things to shows I care for her, like when I took care of the crack in her windshield she didn't want to pay for-

Therapist: I'm sure that you care for Sarah. Just having you being here in couples counseling shows how much you care about her, but she's feeling like she can't trust you when it really matters, and we can't argue with how someone feels. It helps to acknowledge a person's feelings and then ask how you can make things better. It doesn't mean you agree with the logic behind those feelings, just that you can understand it. This is the only way to move forward.

Mark: I guess I can see her point of view. I just thought that after two years we had moved past all of this. And I really don't think it's fair to say I'm not there for her when she needs it most. She struggled to think up one example of why I'm not trustworthy. I can think up one hundred examples of why I am-

Therapist: I believe you Mark. It's not necessary for you to prove yourself here. Again, you can't argue with someone's feelings. You can only acknowledge those feelings and then ask how you can help her feel better. It has nothing to do with being right or wrong. What do you think you could do to help her feel better right now?

Mark: I don't know. That's why we're here!

Therapist: Could you ask her? Try asking her "what can I do to make you feel more like you can trust me? I want you to feel like you can rely on me for what's really important to you."

Mark: What can I do to make you feel like you can trust me?

Sarah: I need you to listen to me. I need you to really hear me when I say something's important to me. I want you to keep me in the loop if you're going to be working late or want to do something with your friends.

Mark: To keep tabs on me.

Sarah: No, not to keep tabs on you. Because I worry about you when you're two hours late from work and not answering your phone.

Therapist: So it sounds like you're just asking for Mark to follow through when you tell him something is important and to be kept up to date if he's going out or is going to be late. Do you think you could shoot Sarah a quick email or call if you're running late, Mark?

Mark: That wouldn't be a problem.

Therapist: Good. Although Sarah, I might suggest that if something is urgent to you, that sometimes it's best to just do it yourself.

Sarah: Yes, I'm learning that.

Therapist: I do get where you're coming from though. What else is on your list?

Sarah: To be in a committed marriage, have both of us spend more time with my family-

Therapist: Specifically, how much time is preferable?

Sarah: My mom likes to throw these big Fourth of July BBQs and a holiday party every December. Mark has only ever gone once.

Mark: It's been more than once!

Therapist: Why is it important to you that Mark goes to these get-togethers?

Sarah: Well, everyone else comes with their boyfriend or girlfriend, so it's awkward when it's just me. Everyone asks "Where's Mark?" and I feel like I have to make an excuse for him because I don't want them to think he doesn't like them.

Therapist: Why else is it important to you?

Sarah: My mom's parties are an important family tradition to me. I have great childhood memories about going to them and they're just a lot of fun. I want Mark to be a part of those memories too. I want him to be a part of my family.

Therapist: Mark, tell me why you avoid going to her family get-togethers.

Mark: Sarah has a great family. I like them, I really do, but it's awkward for me because I don't know everybody and people just talk about "old times" so it's impossible for me to be a part of the conversation.

Sarah: That's not true. I'm sure if you tried to include yourself people would be welcoming. He just stands in the corner and doesn't try to talk to anybody.

Mark: I stand in the corner because the minute we get there, you wander away and leave me stranded. You have to introduce me to people and help get the conversation started.

Therapist: So it sounds like you would be more amenable to going to these parties if Sarah stayed with you while you were there.

Mark: Yes, but the parties are also really long. They start around noon and don't end until well after midnight. That's not enjoyable for me.

Therapist: Yes, I can see how that would be really tiring. What about if you compromised? What if you agreed beforehand on a set time you would leave the party by? Then would you be willing to go?

Mark: If Sarah stayed with me during the parties and we stayed for a maximum of four hours, then yes, I would go.

Sarah: Could I stay longer if I wanted to?

Therapist: Let's ask Mark.

Mark: It would be okay for her to stay so long as I was allowed to leave guilt-free after four hours.

Therapist: It sounds like we have a deal. What else describes your ideal relationship?

Sarah: Not being so quick to anger, expressing more appreciation... What I mean by that is if he sees I've cleaned the whole house, I'd just like him to say thank you.

Mark: I always say thank you when you clean! The problem is that you clean so rarely. I feel like I do most of the housework and when do I get any appreciation?

Sarah: I clean the whole house twice a week and wash most of the dishes every night. You just don't notice.

Therapist: I think Sarah is saying she just wants a little extra appreciation every now and then. In return, she'll also express appreciation for the things you do.

Sarah: I also wrote "be more affectionate with one another." We spend a lot of time with each other, but we aren't really affectionate. Even when we watch TV together at night, I'm sitting on one couch and he's on the other couch with his computer. We rarely cuddle.

Therapist: Are you saying that you would like it if you guys cuddled on the couch while watching TV together?

Sarah: Yes. We don't have to cuddle the whole time. But I would like it if we sat next to each other and he wasn't on the computer. Then we could talk during commercials and I'd feel more like we were spending time together.

Therapist: Does that sound like something you both could try?

Mark: Yes, and just for the record, I'm rarely on the computer while we watch TV together, but I guess I can never go on the computer if that is what it takes to make Sarah happy.

Therapist: Sarah, please continue.

Sarah: "say yes' more often." It seems whenever either one of us makes a suggestion, we're so quick to say no to the other person. I'd like it if we would listen to each other's ideas and say yes more often.

Therapist: A good rule of thumb is to give three yes's to every one no. You don't need to keep a score board, but just try to keep a mental note of how many no's and yes's you've given.

Mark: Don't worry, she'll keep track.

Sarah: The last thing on my list is "support each other's careers."

Mark: What?! We do support each other's careers. I thought that was something we do very well!

Sarah: I know. The therapist said we could include things on the list that we currently do so long as we considered it to be ideal.

Mark: Oh!

Sarah & Mark: ::laughs together::

Therapist: Sarah, thank you for sharing your list. Would you like to share your list, Mark?

Mark: I don't have as much stuff on my list as Sarah's... I wrote "not to be blamed for everything, not to have a forceful statement be misperceived as anger"-

Therapist: Unfortunately, we can't control the way people perceive things.

Mark: You said this was supposed to be our idea of the ideal relationship. In my perfect relationship, I can talk however I want without being misunderstood.

Therapist: You're right, Mark. The purpose of the assignment was to describe your ideal relationship. That's true. But what if I told you I could teach you how to communicate in a way that would eliminate misunderstandings?

Mark: That sounds nice in theory, and I understand you have lots of pearls of wisdom to contribute here, but I'm pretty set in the way I communicate.

Therapist: Learning a new way of communicating is like learning any new skill. It feels weird at first and takes a little more effort, but it becomes second nature with time. In fact, I'd think you'd be surprised how quickly you'd get used to it. Of my clients that practice communication skills daily, most report that after just two weeks they aren't even conscious that they are doing it anymore.

Sarah: Just two weeks, huh?

Therapist: If you're willing to stick with it, you can make a lot of changes.

Mark: We'll see.

Therapist: Since you both mentioned communication on your lists, how about we devote all next session to just learning some of these communication skills?

Sarah: Yes, I'd like that.

Mark: I'll follow through with all your suggestions, but I'm telling you it's not as easy as you make it sound.

Therapist: If the communication skills don't work for you for whatever reason, we can try something else, but I hope you would give it a solid effort because these skills really do work. What else is on your list?

Mark: "To be able to come home and relax without being attacked."

Therapist: It sounds like you need some time to relax after coming home before dealing with any issues. Did I get that correctly?

Mark: Yes. As soon as I walk in the door she starts yelling at me.

Sarah: Because you're three hours late and haven't picked up your phone!

Therapist: I think we came to an agreement that Mark was going to call you if he's going to be late, so maybe that won't be much of an issue anymore. But if there are important issues that need to be discussed, when would be a good time to do it?

Mark: I'd like it if we could have an implemented "quiet time" for an hour after I walk in the door. During that hour, no one's allowed to yell at me, make demands, or nag me to do anything.

Therapist: I think that sounds reasonable. What do you think, Sarah?

Sarah: Okay, I could do that.

Mark: I also wrote "no more nagging, and more time to be intimate" and that's it.

Therapist: Specifically, how often would you like to be intimate with Sarah?

Mark: Currently we are only intimate about once a month. I would really like it if it was more like two or three times a week.

Sarah: It's hard to be intimate with Mark when I spend so much time being mad at him.

Therapist: Well, I think that's why learning better communication skills are so important. You'll learn how to discuss important issues without it turning into a fight.

Sarah: I'd like that.

Therapist: I noticed that you each had similar things on your lists. It's good that you're both on the same page. I also thought that most of the things on your lists were very doable.

I was wondering if you would both be willing to make a list together as homework and bring it in with you next time.

Mark: Just a combination of both of our lists?

Therapist: Sort of, but I want everything on the list to be things that you both agree with. It might mean compromising.

Sarah: Okay. We can do that.

Therapist: It's best if you work on the assignment in a day or two. Sometimes people wait until the last minute to do homework assignments, but that defeats the whole purpose. I want you guys to be able to think about and discuss your relationship throughout the week, not just during counseling.

Mark: Okay

Therapist: Great! Will I be seeing you guys next week?

Sarah: We'll see you then.

Therapist: Have a great week. Bye.

To the inexperienced therapist, it probably looks like Mark and Sarah haven't made any progress. You may also feel that Mark's defensiveness is getting in the way of therapy. Mark certainly is defensive. Even his list had a defensive quality to it. Mark was quick to defend himself after nearly every statement on Sarah's list, including an item on her list that was meant to be a complement to him! So, you may now be wondering how it's possible for there to be any progress.

Mark is the most vocal member of the couple and tries to steer the therapist's attention to how he's a victim in this relationship and isn't capable of learning new skills despite the fact that he has a Masters degree in engineering. But if you reread the vignette, only reading the exchanges between the therapist and Sarah, you will see that Sarah is actually making some progress. Her list was very vague in the beginning, but after a few clarifying questions from the therapist, Sarah modified the later items on her list to be more behaviorally specific. On one of her items, she said "It seems whenever either one of us makes a suggestion, we're so quick to say no to the other person. I'd like it if we would listen to each other's ideas and say yes more." She reworded it so that it didn't have any blaming language in it and acknowledged that it required her to change also. Sarah may have discovered how to ask for positive change in her relationship without triggering Mark's defensiveness.

Mark doesn't seem to have made any progress yet. That's okay, it's only the second session. The good news is that Sarah seems to be making some changes. It may seem that in couples counseling it wouldn't be a good thing for just one person to change. We want both people to change, and having only one person change may make it seem even more obvious that Mark and Sarah aren't right for each other. The good news, is that it only takes one person to change for both of them to change as a couple. According to Systems Theory, couples are part of a system whereby if one person changes, the whole system changes (Elliot & Saunders, 1982). So anytime one person changes, the whole system changes.

Mark may not be ready to admit that he needs to make some changes in his interpersonal styles in intimate relationships, but fortunately Sarah is. The changes in Sarah's behavior will inevitably cause a change in Mark just by default. Seeing that change in Sarah and how much more enjoyable it makes the relationship, may help Mark feel more trust in the process of couples counseling. I wouldn't count Mark out yet. He may be slow to get going, but Mark could still turn into the biggest vehicle for change in this relationship.

Crisis intervention outline

Step 1: Let the couple tell the story of the crisis

Step 2: Reflect, validate, empathize, and work towards a solution

- Practice active listening and unconditional positive regard

Step 3: Problem Solve

- Ask partners how they would like to solve the problem
- Brainstorm possible solutions
- Suggest a compromise if necessary

Step 4: Moving Forward

- Get a commitment from partners to move forward

Session 2 outline

Step 1: Review Progress

Step 2: Explain the writing assignment

- Ask couple to each make a list (at least 10 items) of changes they would like to see in the relationship

Step 3: Process the list

- Have partners take turns reading the list aloud and put check marks next to the items on their list that are the same or similar.
- Therapist intervenes to clarify items that are vague and to help client define them in behavioral terms.

Step 4: Assign homework

- Therapist assigns couple homework assignment of creating a new list together and bring it with them to next session.

Chapter 4

Third Session: Communication Skills

This is one of the most important sessions in couples counseling. It is also the most difficult. You will be teaching a lot of communication skills in this session, and some couples may need an extra session devoted to learning these important skills in order to really grasp the concepts in today's session. Fortunately, you don't have to teach the couple all the different communication skills out there (there are many), just the ones that you see would be most helpful for this particular couple. Some couples may just need to grasp the core concepts of communication skills, while others will need a lot more work.

If you really want to master communication skills, I recommend reading the book "How to Win Friends and Influence People" by Dale Carnegie. The book is a classic and taught me many useful communication skills that I have utilized in both my personal life and professional life. Although the title makes it sound like the book is just for learning how to network, the book is actually great for couples too. I often recommend the book to couples if they seem interested in learning more about communication skills.

Another reason why this is a difficult session is because it is when most clients drop out of therapy. I have found that in using this program, about 80% of the couples I work with are successful in couples counseling, while the other 20% drop out of counseling prematurely. Of the couples that drop out, this is the session where most choose to do it. It was surprising to me at first because it seemed that learning communication skills is what helps couples the most, and aren't people always saying that they want practical solutions from therapists? Then I realized that the third session is also where it really becomes clear to people that they have to change. Previous to this session, they may have still been holding on to the fantasy that I was going to tell them that only the other person needed to change. In this session, there is no doubt: it takes two to tango.

The thought of change can give people anxiety and people react to anxiety with avoidance. If couples counseling is causing anxiety, the way to avoid it is by dropping out or firing the counselor. This used to be deeply upsetting to me, but now I recognize that it is part of the process. In the end, it is the couple's choice if they want to change, and there is nothing I can do to force them to make the "right" choice. Sometimes couples decide to get a divorce rather than make necessary changes. Sometimes they just drop out of therapy and continue being miserable for a few more years until they are ready to make the real changes. Sometimes they try going to a different therapist and have a better or worse experience depending on their readiness to change.

Many of the couples that drop out of counseling prematurely eventually do come back. For many of these couples, they tried working it out on their own and found they just don't have the skills necessary to do that or tried going to one of those couples counselors that do take sides and realized that wasn't what they needed after all. I think the reason why they chose to come back is because I have long given up on trying to guilt couples into staying if they don't want to. If a couple tells me they want to drop out of counseling, 1. I remind them that they made a ten session commitment and no counselor can save a marriage after just three sessions, but that 2. they are free to drop out at any time, and 3. they are also free to come back at any time in the future. I make dropping out painless but also leave the door open for when they are ready to come back.

Although relationships may be our expertise, only the couple knows specifically what's right for them. As part of their process towards change, they may need to take a break from therapy for a while and try other methods. If you feel responsible for the couple dropping out of therapy, I recommend getting some supervision from an experienced couples counselor and seeing if there is anything you could have done differently to keep the couple in therapy. If you are following the sessions in this book, avoiding taking sides, and offering plenty of positive reinforcement, then the odds are there was nothing you did personally to harm the couple. The sad reality of the situation is that the relationship was dysfunctional before the couple met you and will continue to be so after they've left you. If it is revealed that you made a mistake in counseling, make a promise to yourself to not make that mistake again and move on.

Step 1: Review homework

Last session you assigned the couple to make a new list of statements describing their ideal relationship and asked them to bring it with them to the next session. Not following through with this would give the message that homework is not important or the couple is not important enough for you to remember what you did last session. If the couple forgot to bring it, ask them to bring it to the next session. Reviewing homework shouldn't take longer than ten to fifteen minutes. In this case, you are just going to ask the couple to read the list out loud and you may need to ask for more clarity on certain items like you did in the last session. Most likely, the items on the list are not going to need as much clarifying as last time since now they have a better understanding of what you are looking for.

Step 2: Have the couple argue

This may sound counterproductive, but the next step is to actually have the couple argue. Yes, up until now we have been trying to discourage this, but it is important to observe the couple argue for a few minutes so that you can make some mental notes on what communication deficits they are experiencing. By the third session, the couple may still go into arguments easily. Just asking them how the past week has gone may turn into an argument between the couple. If they do not start arguing on their own, you can ask the couple what was something that they argued about recently that was never resolved. Ask them if they would be willing to attempt to resolve that issue now. The couple may feel weird about arguing on command at first, but you would be surprised how quickly they forget their inhibitions about arguing in front of a therapist and fall into their usual patterns of speaking with one another.

Allow the couple to argue about the issue as long as necessary in order for you to gather some information about their communication styles. At this point you probably already have a good idea of what is lacking in their communication style, so it shouldn't be necessary to let the couple argue for more than ten minutes. Arguing raises blood pressure and releases stress hormones in the brain (University Of California - Irvine, 2002), including the "fight or flight" response (Kemeny, 2003), and because of that we should only allow the minimum amount of arguing that is necessary. If you decide that you are going to wait until the couple stops arguing on their own you might be waiting all day. Call a time-out and ask the couple to take a few deep breathes.

Now the therapist provides their "assessment" on the couple's communication skills. Most clients have never heard their arguing broken down this way and are fascinated by your report. Instead of telling them what they are doing wrong, you're going to tell them what they are doing right. Remember, it is easier to increase positive behaviors then to decrease negative ones. You may have noticed that their arguing has gotten better since the first session. You have been giving them a lot to think about the past three weeks and I am sure it has rubbed off on them in some way. If you see progress, say so! Giving positive reinforcement for progress, even if it's only a little progress at the moment, is one of the most effective things you can do to cause positive change in the relationship.

So what do you do if the argument is so hateful and so toxic that there is simply nothing positive to report? The first time I had this happen, I was at such a loss that I didn't know what to do. I had always been able to find something that was positive, but not this time, so I panicked and made up something. To my surprise this actually worked. The couple nodded in agreement and started doing those positive behaviors I had said they were already doing, even though prior to that moment they had never done them before. Since then, I have done this paradoxical technique often. I have found it is a great way to get a couple to start using a communication skill that is sorely needed.

Although most people are unaware of their own arguing, you don't want to say anything too out of the ordinary. If a couple yells and screams at each other, it wouldn't be good to say "One thing you two do well in your communication is that you talk to each other in a calm respectful manner." If you're too far off the mark, you run the risk of the couple realizing you're trying to use some kind of reverse psychology, or worse, they think you're a complete idiot. The ones I use the most are: you try to define the problem, you try to calm the other person down if you see they are getting upset, you can tell if you've gone too far, you maintain eye contact, and you know when to slow things down.

Of course, I don't want you to rely on just the examples above.

Really dig deep and find something positive to report about their communication style. Become familiar with the communication skills I'm going to teach you later in this chapter. Most people already know and use a few of these already. If you catch one of them being used in an argument, point it out and offer positive praise. It's easier to increase the behaviors they already do well then try to teach them new behaviors that feel completely foreign to them.

Step 3: Educate the couple on "the four horsemen"

When I was trying to learn how to conduct couples counseling, John Gottman's books were among the few that I actually found helpful. The problem I found with a lot of other so-called marriage experts was that their methods and techniques were just based on their own personal opinions and values. Gottman's techniques were based on actual research, research that he had conducted himself over many years. Psychology is afterall a science, so our methods should be based on science, not faith. For that reason, John Gottman is one of my favorite relationship experts.

After many hours of observing couples at his "Love Lab" at the University of Washington, Gottman discovered that he could predict with a very high rate of accuracy whether a couple stayed married or divorced based on the presence of what he later came to call "the four horsemen": criticism, contempt, defensiveness, and stonewalling (Gottman & Levenson, 2000). The couples you work with may show all four or none of the four horsemen while in your presence. It is important to educate them about all four anyways since they probably act differently at home than they do in the therapy office. I educate my couples about the four horsemen, not because I'm trying to predict if they're going to divorce, but because I want them to avoid using these communication failures going forward.

I always have a stack of index cards within reach. This is so I can write down any important concepts that I really want the clients to remember. You want to write down the four horsemen onto index cards for each member of the couple to help them remember. You'll be covering a lot of important information in this session and you don't want your couple to forget everything they've learned as soon as they walk out the door.

Criticism: It is important to understand that criticism is different than complaining. According to Gottman, complaining is fine and should even be encouraged, but criticism needs to be avoided like, well, the four horsemen of the apocalypse (Gottman & Silver, 2000). When you complain, you are describing a specific behavior that you didn't like. When you criticize, you are saying it is your partner you don't like. One targets a behavior, the other target's your partner. Here is an example of a complaint:

> Sarah: I noticed that the grass has gotten really long. You agreed to mow the lawn as one of your chores and it bothers me that it hasn't been getting done regularly. Do you think you could get it done before dinner?

And here is an example of a criticism:

> Sarah: You agreed to mow the lawn when we divided up the chores and you haven't been doing it. You always let me down. You're so lazy.

See the difference? One shows consideration for the person's feelings, while the other doesn't. A complaint is also more effective than criticism in eliciting change from others.

In my life, I prefer to do things the easiest way possible. I think most people are like this as well. So if I'm trying to get my husband to change a behavior, I want to do it in such a way that requires the least amount of effort from me as possible. If I criticize him about not mowing the lawn, it may get him to mow it more often, or my nasty tone may trigger an argument that lasts for twenty minutes and puts me in a bad mood for the rest of the day. Complaining, as opposed to criticizing, resolves the matter in two minutes tops and no one feels angry or hurt afterwards. Sounds like a win-win, right? The problem is that being critical feels good in the moment and that is very reinforcing. You have to show the couple that the long-term gains from speaking with consideration for the other person's feelings is better than the short-term gains of blowing off steam.

If you really want to help your client get a new concept, you have to have them actually practice it in the session. Using role play and role reversal, have your clients practice giving complaints and making positive requests for change. The formula is as simple as saying "I feel upset because (give complaint). I would like it if we could (make request for change)." Although there is nothing complicated about this, for many of our couples this way of speaking is so out of the ordinary that they require a few practice runs before they feel confident enough to implement it in real life.

Contempt: Of the four, Gottman considers contempt to be the most destructive to a marriage. Having contempt in a relationship means feeling resentment, disrespect, and even hostility towards the other person. Contempt may also be disguised as "humor" that is condescending and insulting towards the other person. Contempt may also manifest as facial expressions or sneers. We've heard Mark express contempt towards Sarah during the vignettes. He has also made some condescending remarks to the therapist.

There is no formula, script, or easy treatment for contempt. According to John Gottman, the cure for contempt is creating a culture of appreciation within the relationship (Gottman & Silver, 2000). When people feel contempt for their partner, it is because they are making that classic cognitive error called "discounting the positive"(Beck, 2011). Whenever their partner does something good for them, they sort of brush it off as something the other person has to do or is expected to do, so it gets discounted. The problem is that the negative things their partner does doesn't get the same treatment. Every negative thing gets stored and cataloged into conscious memory until it seems that the partner is the cause of all of their misery.

We'll talk more about cognitive errors, unrealistic expectations, and distortions in Chapter Eight. For now, there is no easy trick for dealing with contempt. It simply must be eliminated. You can start by educating the couple about contempt and pointing out things they said or did during the argument that were of a contemptuous nature. Ask them how they think that made the other person feel. Point out the logical fallacies of using words like "always" or "never" when describing their partner and encourage them to discontinue expressing contempt towards their partner as much as possible.

Defensiveness: People become defensive because they think it will make the situation better. If they feel they are being attacked or treated unfairly, they try to convince the other person why they are wrong and hope that will somehow end the argument. Gottman's research found that despite the common misconception that defending yourself will make the situation better, it actually makes things much worse. He found that becoming defensive caused both individuals' blood pressure to raise and that the argument lasted significantly longer (Gottman, Coan, Carrere, & Swanson, 1998). I have noticed that in observing couples argue that the two people tend to just say the same thing over and over again. Sometimes word for word. They repeat themselves because they assume the other person isn't listening. Becoming defensive makes it seem that you haven't listened or ignored what the other person said. Just saying, "yes, I understand" can stop an argument cold. Suddenly both people calm down and the argument is over in two minutes rather than two hours. Try it in your own life. The next time your partner complains, resist the urge to get defensive. Admit to your mistake and ask how things can be made better. I think you will be surprised how good it feels and how quickly matters get resolved.

Gottman encourages couples to take more responsibility for the problems in their relationship as a cure for defensiveness. According to Gottman, you are always at least 30% responsible for any given problem. Couples should ask themselves, "what have I done to contribute to this problem?" rather than be so quick to assign 100% of the blame on the other person. Although this can be difficult for some people, couples should be encouraged to openly admit to their part of the conflict to their partner. It's not an easy thing to do, but can have a powerful effect on a relationship.

Stonewalling: Stonewalling is when one person refuses to respond during an argument or simply walks away. This is most often done by men and the women who are the recipients of the stonewalling find it infuriating. According to Gottman, men are more likely to feel "flooded" during an escalating conflict so they react by tuning out the other person. I think that stonewalling is another one that starts with good intentions. We've all heard the advice "just walk away" or "just ignore the bully." The person may think that by simply not responding, the conflict will end, but it actually just results in making their partner even angrier.

Another way people stonewall is by avoiding necessary complaints. Their partner is doing something that bothers them but they think "No, I won't say anything. I'll just let it go to avoid conflict." They are doing this with good intentions, but the problem is that they don't actually let it go. They let it build up in their psyche until it one day comes pouring out of them in a mixture of criticism and contempt. Couples should be educated on the importance of airing complaints as soon as they experience them rather than let it build up. Frequent complaints, said in a controlled respectful manner do not harm relationships. Instead they lead to more positive change, more appreciation for your partner, and less contempt and stonewalling.

Step 4: Teach basic communication skills

Depending on the couple, it may take an entire session just to get through the four horsemen, if that is the case, end the session by assigning the couple to practice the new skills they learned during the week. Follow up at the beginning of the next session by asking how they did practicing the new communication skills. It may require that you briefly review the four horsemen again. Be sure to give positive reinforcement for effort.

You are now ready to teach your couple the basics of good communication. There's an almost endless number of communication skills and I've chosen to only include those that have been shown in the research to be effective. Even still, you might not find it necessary to teach your couple all of these. Some they may already do on their own, while others may require giving examples and using role playing to really help the couple get it. The first two below are also thanks to John Gottman's research (Gottman, Coan, Carrere, & Swanson, 1998).

Avoid harsh start-ups: In Gottman's research he found that the way a conversation started was a strong predictor of how it would end. If a conversation or discussion started "harshly", it inevitably ended harshly as well. He found it was very rare for someone to use a harsh start-up and then have the other person in turn calm them down and have the discussion end on a positive note. Starting a conversation with a criticism or harsh tone of voice is more likely to cause the other person to react just as harshly, if not up the ante.

The idea here is that by always taking those few extra moments to make sure you use a positive start-up, you can cut down on the amount of arguments significantly just with this one communication skill. The only problem is that clients have to feel motivated enough to use a positive start-up. Do not underestimate the immediate satisfaction of using a harsh start-up. The sad reality is that it initially feels good to let off some steam on your partner. A positive start-up doesn't feel good until moments later, when the matter has been effectively resolved. Clients are going to have to be willing to practice positive start-ups a few times in order to see the long term rewards of doing so consistently.

Use repair attempts: Repair attempts are what you do to try to calm an argument if you see it's getting out of control. If you were unable to avoid using a harsh start-up, using a repair attempt may be able to make things more positive again. Some couples use humor to repair an escalating disagreement. Others will agree with some of the points their partner has made in order to repair the fight. While some couples decide to call a timeout until they have both calmed down.

There are no right or wrong repairs, just what works for the individual couple. When educating the couple about repairs, I simply ask the couple what works for them. I may have noticed the couple attempting to use repairs in some previous arguments. If I have observed them use repair attempts, I bring it up and we discuss how effective they think it was. Sometimes a couple is so lost in the cycle of poor communication that they don't know what they could use as a repair. In that case I tell them to ask their partner outright what they think would help calm them if they are in the middle of a heated argument, or I make a suggestion for a repair based on my assessment of their communication deficits.

The second part of this is for the couple to be able to identify when things are escalating and when a repair would be useful. A lot of couples have described to me feeling like arguments go from zero to sixty in a matter of seconds. It seems like things get out of control so quickly, it's too late for them to try to use a repair. In this case, the therapist will have to help the couple break down their arguments step by step and be sure to identify triggers along the way. It's amazing that most couples know how to push each other's buttons, but few know how to repair things after those buttons have been pushed.

Be clear and be considerate: This is one that could just be described as common sense, and yet is lacking for so many of the couples we see in counseling. In observing your couple argue, you may have noticed how unclear they are about what they are actually arguing about. There have been many times where I simply could not understand why a couple was arguing or what they were even arguing about. In the second session, you demonstrated to the couple the importance of being clear and specific when stating their desires. Anything on their lists that were vague or confusing, the therapist asked clarifying questions. You can teach the couple the importance of being clear by using their lists from the second session as an example. Remind them how by making their lists more specific they made it easier for their partner to know specifically what they needed to do in order to please them.

Some people are very resistant to speaking more clearly or specifically. Many times people have said to me things like "after all these years, he should know what I mean!" You can't expect your partner to be able to read your mind. If you do, they will inevitably disappoint you time and time again. The interesting thing is that we don't have these kinds of expectations when it comes to our friends or coworkers, people we've known for possibly longer than our partner. So why is it that we become enraged that our partner can't anticipate our needs? Mind-reading is a nice fantasy, but far from the reality of human capability.

The next step is to be considerate. Ways that a couple can be more considerate include expressing more positives, letting your partner know that you are listening even if you don't agree, reserving judgment, apologizing, and showing consideration for their feelings when expressing negatives. Being considerate also means being more aware of the tone of voice they use while arguing and how that makes their partner feel. Sometimes clients don't realize how harsh or inconsiderate they sound while arguing. Try pointing this out gently.

Avoid blame: When discussing a problem, the couple should be careful to avoid assigning blame. Remember what John Gottman said, you're always at least 30% responsible for a problem in your relationship. Sometimes this can be tricky because if a partner is used to being blamed a lot, they can become hypersensitive to it and perceive blame where there is none intended. Due to this, it might take a while for the other person to get used to the new "no blame policy" and stop being so sensitive. Sometimes clients need to be coached in how to make a complaint without any blaming language in it.

Ways to eliminate blame including making more "I statements", asking for increases rather than decreases in behavior, and accepting partial responsibility for the problem. The couple should practice making complaints in a calm and respectful manner.

Have "couple's meetings": Depending on how hurtful arguments have become, the couple may have begun avoiding talking to each other. It makes sense that if something causes you pain that you would avoid it, but if the couple follows through on your communication recommendations, starting now, communications should be a lot less painful and maybe even enjoyable. You want to encourage the couple to have increased communication so that they can have ample opportunities to practice all of the skills they learned today. My way of doing this is to encourage the couple to have regular "couple's meetings."

Just as the name implies, this meeting is for the couple only. Meetings should take place in private and preferably after the children have already gone to bed. In-laws or friends should not be privy to the information that is exchanged during a couple's meeting. Meetings don't have to take place on the weekends, but I think it is best to make them a regular part of the week day routine. I think daily or almost daily meetings are important because it encourages the couple to talk about the relationship regularly rather than wait until one of them explodes.

In the beginning, the focus of the meetings will probably be more on the serious side since the couple has been putting off having these discussions for so long. However, eventually they will get to a point where they have resolved any lingering issues and most meetings will be of an enjoyable or casual nature where they just share thoughts and feelings with one another about the day. Not every meeting has to be a serious discussion. Meetings are also an opportunity to have loving exchanges with one another, and isn't that what being in a relationship is supposed to be about?

As a therapist, I love it when towards the end of therapy couples report to me that their couple's meetings have become very casual and chatty and that they mostly spend the hour just joking around with one another. That's when I know that I have succeeded as a couples counselor.

Step 5: Assign homework

This week's homework assignment is pretty straight forward. The couple is to attempt to have daily couple's meetings at which time they will practice utilizing the communication skills they learned in today's session. You may find that the couple is resistant to having daily couple's meetings at first. Remember, in the past talking with their partner has been a painful event and people have a tendency to want to avoid pain. If they are unable to agree to daily meetings, see if they will agree to at least three meetings over the course of the following week and then slowly build your way up to nearly every day.

Some people may just have a problem with the term "meeting." If the idea of a "meeting" sounds too regimented or fills your client with work-related anxiety, see if they will agree to just talking with their partner everyday and practice using the skills during these talks. Rename them "couple's talks" and move forward. Sometimes just changing the terminology can make people feel a lot better about an activity.

Third session vignette

Therapist: So how did the homework assignment go?

Sarah: I tried to do it with Mark on Friday, but Mark refused to.

Mark: Because I know how she is. The second I slip up and violate something on that list, Sarah is going to rub it in my face.

Sarah: Oh for God's sake! I don't do things like that.

Therapist: Maybe I was unclear about the assignment. It wasn't meant to be a behavioral contract but just an opportunity for the two of you to imagine what your ideal relationship would be like. No one was going to be held accountable to it.

Mark: Look, I know how she is. She watches and waits for me to slip up so she can rub it in my face and I'm not going to play that game anymore.

Sarah: When have I ever done that?

Mark: Just last week I had agreed that I would go to your mom's Fourth of July and Christmas get-together. I sacrificed two of my favorite holidays to spend time with your family. I thought that was pretty generous of me. Then your mom invites us to have dinner with her next Thursday night and I can't go because of a trip I had planned with my friends and you flip out on me and accuse me of breaking my promise!

Sarah: I didn't flip out!

Mark: You yelled at me about how you couldn't depend on me for anything! I agreed to go to her block parties, not every single invitation for dinner.

Sarah: My mother has helped us out so much-

Mark: But I need to have time with my friends! If you can't give me time with my friends then I don't know what to say.

Sarah: What? You're going to say it's over?

Therapist: I'm going to call a timeout now. I want you two to take some deep breaths and try to calm down...I've been observing your arguments and I've noticed that there are actually some things you do very well. I've noticed that both of you will ask clarifying questions if you don't understand the other person, you maintain eye contact with one another, you don't sneer or use disrespectful body language, and you both attempt to define the problem when you argue. Those things are very good foundations for communication skills.

Mark: I've received communication skills training at work and consider myself to be very good at it.

Therapist: I can tell. This will probably be easy for you. We had decided last time that we would devote today's session to learning communication skills. Is that okay with everyone?

Sarah: Yes, we really need to work on our communication.

Mark: I think me and Sarah already know all this stuff and I don't want to waste your time.

Therapist: I feel that we can always improve our communication. There are so many communication skills out there, the odds are good you haven't learned all of them, but I'm just going to teach you guys the ones that have been proven to be effective in the research on couples. Like learning any new skill, it can feel weird and unnatural at first, but with practice you'll forget you're even using them. Are you willing to give it a chance?

Mark: I guess so.

Therapist: Great! Now, there are four major communication errors I want you two to try to avoid. I'm going to write them down on an index card to help you remember. The first one is "criticism." You want to try to avoid criticizing your partner whenever possible. No one likes how it feels to be criticized and criticism will often trigger an argument or fight. The cure for criticism is complaining. When you criticize, you attack the person, whereas when you complain you are simply bringing notice to a behavior or situation that is bothering you. An example of a criticism is "You never visit my mother! I can't depend on you for anything!" An example of a complaint is "I wish we could visit my mother more often. I feel bad that we cancel so much. Can we pick a day the week after you get back from your trip to invite my mom out for dinner?" Mark, do you think you would have reacted differently if Sarah had phrased her complaint in the same way that I just did?

Mark: Probably.

Therapist: It's hard to get angry and defensive when a complaint is phrased like that.

Sarah: That's true.

Therapist: A formula you will want to remember, which I'm also going to include on the index card, is "I feel upset because (give complaint). I would like it if we could (make request for change)." Or using the same example, "I feel upset because we haven't seen my mom in a while. I would like it if we could see her the week after you get back." Do you think you guys could practice that?

Sarah: Sure.

Therapist: The second thing you want to avoid is becoming defensive. All being defensive communicates to your partner is that 1. you aren't listening and 2. you're right and they're wrong.

Mark: But what if you are right? I mean, sometimes you're just right and you can't have the other person believing something about you that's wrong.

Therapist: Research has been done on the effects of becoming defensive during an argument and they've found that becoming defensive causes both people's blood pressure to go up and the argument continues for much longer than if the person had simply said "I understand where you're coming from. What can we do to make this better?" It doesn't mean you have to agree with the person, just see where they are coming from.

Mark: That all sounds very good in theory, but if someone is wrong, I'm going to correct them.

Therapist: No one is ever 100% to blame and there's always more than one solution to a problem. Something that's important to remember is that you are always at least 30% responsible for every problem in your relationship. Keeping in mind how you've contributed to the problem, and taking partial responsibility for it, can help you to become less defensive.

Mark: Now, something that I think is important for you to

know is that me and Sarah are not sure if you're the right couples counselor for us.

Therapist: You are free to leave at any time, but I must remind you that you did initially agree to ten sessions and no therapist can "cure" years of relationship problems after just three sessions. It's going to take a lot of commitment and effort from both of you. If it's okay with you I would like to continue talking about the four major communication errors. Being able to identify and avoid them will help you guys a lot in improving your communication and arguing less.

Sarah: Yes, I'd like that.

Mark: Please continue.

Therapist: The third communication error is "contempt." Contempt is a lot like criticism, but harsher. It's when you express resentment or disgust towards one another. The cure for contempt is appreciation. There is good and bad in everyone, and turning your attention to all the good things your partner does can help reduce feelings of contempt for that person. If you catch your partner doing something good, point it out and express appreciation. That can go a long way towards repairing a relationship. The final communication error is "stonewalling." Stonewalling is when you stop talking to your partner. This usually happens when communication breaks down to the point that you are afraid that anything you say will result in a fight.

Sarah: That sounds like us.

Therapist: I think it happens with good intentions. You see your spouse do something that you don't like and you think "I wont say anything. I'll just let it go." But then it just piles up until eventually you explode and it becomes a fight.

Sarah: That's definitely me.

Mark: You shouldn't do that. You should tell me if something bothers you.

Therapist: The cure for stonewalling is more complaining. If you are upset about something, don't try to just ignore it because that backfires in the end. Just make sure you complain instead of criticize.

Sarah: Okay.

Therapist: ::Hands them both an index card with the four horsemen written on it:: It's best to put these somewhere that you will see them often, in order to remind you.

Mark: The computer desk sounds like a good place.

Sarah: I'm going to put mine in my purse so I can look at it at work.

Therapist: Those sound like very good places. I have a few more essential communication skills I would like to teach you guys. These have been shown in the research to be very effective.

Sarah: Good.

Therapist: One of the most effective communication skills you can use is to avoid harsh start-ups. The research has shown that the way a conversation begins is predictive of how it ends. In other words, if a conversation starts negatively, it is going to remain negative. So one of the simplest things you can do is to start a conversation positively or at least neutrally. One way to do this is to start a discussion with a complaint instead of a criticism, or mention positive things before mentioning things that could be perceived negatively.

Mark: What if the other person started the conversation negatively? Are you just supposed to hope that everyone else will remember to avoid harsh start-ups?

Therapist: If you find the conversation is starting to go to a dark place, you can attempt to repair the conversation. What do you think is something you can do or say to Sarah to help her calm down if you the argument is escalating?

Mark: I don't know, that's why we're here.

Therapist: You could try asking Sarah.

Sarah: It's hard because it feels like I get angry so fast, I'm not sure what I would suggest Mark do.

Therapist: Hmm, do you think it would be helpful if Mark refrained from debating with you and tried to see your point of view?

Sarah: Yes! I agree with that completely! That's just what I need from Mark.

Therapist: What's something you think you could do to help Mark calm down if he's getting upset?

Mark: There's nothing she could do. Once I get in that frame of mind there's no going back.

Therapist: Well, that's what we're hoping to prevent. We want to try to come up with some things Sarah could say or do to help you from going into that frame of mind.

Sarah: I don't think I can come up with anything.

Therapist: Well, Mark has mentioned several times that he feels blamed a lot. I think refraining from using accusatory language, taking partial responsibility for your contributions to the problem, and expressing appreciation could do a lot to keeping the conversation positive. If worse comes to worse, I think you guys could call a timeout, go for a walk or cuddle on the couch for a few minutes and then start over.

Mark: Yes, I think it would be helpful if either one of us could just call a timeout and then started over if necessary.

Therapist: I think that would be a good idea. I think it would also be good to make it a part of your daily routine to have a couple's meeting. It doesn't have to be every day, you can skip weekends if you want, but most days would be preferable. Just a time each day that you have scheduled to talk about the relationship. This way important issues get dealt with daily instead of being left to fester over time. At first, most meetings will probably be more serious in nature since there have been a lot of issues that have gone neglected over the years, but eventually you will get to a place where meetings are just an enjoyable time to talk about the day and have meaningful conversations. Does that sound doable?

Sarah: Yes! I really think that would help our relationship a lot. We have so many things we need to talk about. It would be good to have a reserved time each day just to work on those issues.

Mark: I'm certainly willing to try it, although the thought of having a stressful argument every night is not appealing to me.

Therapist: If you follow the communication skills we discussed today it shouldn't be stressful or an argument, but I can understand why you would be hesitant.

Sarah: I think it'll be a lot better now.

Therapist: Is this something you can agree to?

Mark: Like I said, I'll try.

Therapist: Good. Well, I hate to do this to you guys but our time is up. Will I see you next week?

Sarah: We'll see you next Wednesday.

Therapist: Bye. Enjoy your weekend!

This session was off to a rough start but ended well. Like a lot of clients, the thought of having to change scared Mark. Your first question during the vignette may have been "why did Mark refuse to do the homework assignment but had no problem making the list in session? What's the difference?" When Mark made his list in session, everything on his list were changes he wanted Sarah to make. Making a combined list with Sarah meant admitting that there were changes they both needed to make, and it was implied that it was expected that Mark would start making efforts towards those changes. Although Mark tried to put the blame on Sarah for why he didn't do the homework, this was really about Mark's unwillingness to change. This was the therapist's first sign of trouble and it was why the therapist chose not to make more of an issue out of Mark's refusal to do the homework assignment.

The therapist then allowed the couple to argue for a few minutes but cut them off when it was clear that things were starting to get out of control. Mark was implying that he would break up with Sarah and that angered her. If the argument had been allowed to continue any longer, one of them may have walked out of the office, or worse, actually broken up. The therapist should always intervene if a couple mentions divorce or breaking-up during an argument, no matter how casually or passive-aggressively. The odds of you being able to repair the session after something that toxic are slim.

During the therapist's assessment of what the couple does well during arguing, the therapist said three things that were true of the couple and one thing that was not. The therapist said the couple asks clarifying questions, maintained eye contact, didn't use disrespectful body language, and attempted to define the problem. Asking clarifying questions was something that Sarah learned in the previous session and was starting to utilize, so that was given positive reinforcement. However, one thing that was sorely lacking was that the couple were not defining the problem when they argued. By delivering this next to three things that the couple already did in their communication, the couple will be more likely to try defining the problem in their next discussion.

The therapist also did not disagree with Mark's statement about being an excellent communicator. For all we know, Mark may be very good at communicating while he's a work. It's just when he's interacting with his partner that there are these communication problems. The therapist also used the opportunity to give Mark positive reinforcement and thus encourage him to use the skills he learned in his work trainings. However, things took a turn when the therapist discussed the four horsemen.

Mark's defensiveness is definitely his biggest communication deficit and something that is getting in the way of him achieving his ideal relationship with Sarah. Deep down, Mark knows this and has a lot of anxiety about giving up this part of his personality. When the therapist mentioned defensiveness as being something that needed to be avoided, Mark went on the attack and basically threatened to fire the therapist. A more detailed case history would reveal that Mark has a history of firing helping professionals once they make it clear that a problem can't be solved simply by taking a pill or having other people change. Of course, firing a professional doesn't solve the problem but it does help Mark avoid the anxiety of self responsibility in the short term.

The therapist was faced with two choices: 1. address Mark's threat to fire the therapist and in turn make the session about Mark and his unwillingness to change, or 2. move past this quickly and get on with the session. The therapist chose option 2 because arguing with Mark and bringing light to his insecurities would only make him more resolute, and more justified, in firing the therapist. Don't fall for this trap! The only way to make Mark a believer was to have a really good session. There's no doubt that Mark will be pleasantly surprised by how well his first couple's meeting goes and think "hey, maybe there's something to this couples counseling thing after all."

Seeing the enthusiasm from Sarah towards the end of the session helped Mark to lighten up a little and he even offered something to the discussion instead of just trying to argue with the therapist. Despite Mark threatening to fire the therapist, the therapist was able to turn the session around and help it to end on a good note. The important thing is to remember your mission as a couples counselor. Even if Mark had chosen not to come back next week, at least he and Sarah would have left counseling with some better communication skills. If the therapist had instead become defensive and angry towards Mark, the couple would have only left with a bad feeling towards couples counseling and that probably would have been the last time they tried to work on their relationship.

You should feel proud of yourself. You have just gotten through the three hardest sessions in couples counseling. Now that the couple has some clearly defined goals and are beginning to learn the skills necessary to make those goals a reality, you should start seeing some progress in your couple. It is a beautiful sight to see a couple transformed, and I think you will agree that it made the first three difficult sessions worth it.

Third session outline: communication skills

Step 1: Review homework

- Couple reads aloud their shared list
- Therapist critiques or offers insight about list if necessary

Step 2: Have the couple argue

- Therapist observes couple have an argument and then provides positive reinforcement for what they do well while arguing

Step 3: Educate the couple on "the four horsemen"

- Criticism
- Contempt
- Defensiveness
- Stonewalling

Step 4: Teach basic communication skills

- Avoid harsh start-ups
- Use repair attempts
- Be clear and be considerate
- Avoid blame
- Have couple's meetings

Step 5: Assign homework

- Therapist assigns couple to practice communication skills during daily couple's meetings

Chapter 5

Fourth Session: Couple's Dialogue

An exercise called "couple's dialogue" is part of a therapy that was founded by Harville Hendrix (Hendrix, 2007). In Susan Johnson's Emotionally Focused Couples Therapy, she describes a similar way of having a dialogue that is taught to the couple by the therapist (Johnson, 2004). Both are related to Rogerian, Gestalt, and Person-Based therapeutic methods. What I like about the couple's dialogue is that it is basically the same skill that therapists use with their clients to help the clients feel understood and connected with their therapist. By teaching this skill to your couple, you are teaching them to be their own couples counselor. With time this will allow the couple to become more independent from the therapist to the point where they will no longer have to rely on the therapist. In other words: successful therapy.

Hendrix became interested in providing couples counseling after experiencing his own divorce and coming to the painful realization that there were things he could have done to prevent the dissolution of his marriage. Like me, he found that his graduate training as a therapist left him poorly prepared to work with couples. Over time and through much trial and error, Hendrix became a mostly self-taught couples counselor and founded his own therapy form, called Imago Therapy.

The basic premise behind Imago therapy is that we tend to fall in love with people that have the same negative traits as our parents, usually the opposite sex parent. According to Harville Hendrix, we do this in order to have the opportunity to heal childhood wounds. The hope is that by recreating these childhood wounds in our adult relationships, we can heal them. This partially explains why people who grew up in dysfunctional homes tend to choose dysfunctional partners and can never seem to learn their lesson. We go into relationships with a hidden agenda of finding that one person that can make us whole. For a lot of obvious reasons, this inevitably causes disappointments and problems in our relationships.

When I was first starting out as a couples counselor, Hendrix's book "Getting The Love You Want" was recommended at a training. I promptly read the book and started implementing it in my counseling practice, but like other therapists, I ran into a few problems with Imago Therapy. The core of Imago Therapy is based on the concept that we choose partners that possess the same negative traits of our parents. In my own personal life, I felt that this could be true of a couple of boyfriends I had in the past, but was definitely not true of my husband. I really tried to find those traits my husband shared with my parents, but couldn't find any. The same was true of the men my sisters married. Hendrix does note that there are a few exceptions to the rules, so I just figured that my sisters and I were the exceptions, but I ran into this problem again and again when I started working with my clients. For a few of my clients, it seemed a possibility that their partners shared the negative traits of their parents, but I found a majority of my clients strongly denied this.

My second problem with Imago therapy was that it was so rigid. The therapeutic interventions Hendrix has created are very scripted and he insists that couples follow the script exactly. Therapists utilizing Imago Therapy are also urged to follow a script, causing clients to complain that talking to their Imago therapist is like talking to a robot. Although some clients like having specific scripts or formulas to follow, my experience has been that many respond by rebelling against the controlling nature of these scripts.

After trying Imago therapy with many couples, I found that it did improve my success rate, but about half of the couples I worked with either dropped out of therapy or did not stay together. My success rate was better, but still not where I would like it to be. I started modifying Hendrix's techniques and combining them with work done by other theorists, much like Hendrix had originally done to create his own system of couples counseling. In the end, I found Hendrix's ideas interesting but not practical for the problems I was addressing. I created a modified version of his "Imago Dialogue", combining it with elements from Susan Johnson's Emotionally Focused Therapy, and ultimately making it simpler.

In my own modified version, I have toned down the psychobabble and made it less rigid. I also make it feel more familiar for my clients by using it myself with them from the very first session. I describe this in Chapter 1. Finally, I added a fourth step, which is problem-solving. It seemed to me that Hendrix's techniques were very good at allowing couples to express themselves, but then what? Something was missing, and it was solving the problem. Without adding that final step, I found that clients were often complaining "I feel like we have very good conversations about our problems but we don't end up doing anything about it. What's the point of talking if nothing gets resolved?" By allowing each client to say what they want to do to solve or prevent the problem, they received a sense of closure and satisfaction.

Step 1: Review homework

The couple's homework assignment from last session was to practice using the communication skills you taught them at daily or near daily couple's meetings. It's important to review how they did so you can 1. provide positive reinforcement for success and 2. correct any errors in utilizing the communication skills. Last session you covered a lot of information and it is possible that your couple got confused about some of the concepts you covered. Correct any misconceptions that are revealed while reviewing the homework. Don't forget to ask how successful they were at avoiding the four horsemen or if they were able to practice using repair attempts, being more clear and considerate, and avoiding blame and harsh start-ups. If the couple seems to have forgotten about these, you may need to review them briefly again.

Step 2: Teach the couple how to have a couple's dialogue

In my version of the couple's dialogue, the four steps are Reflecting/Paraphrasing, Validation, Empathy, and Problem Solving. I described this in the first chapter, but I will describe it briefly again here. In Reflecting, you paraphrase or repeat what your partner has said in your own words. You then validate them by saying something like "I could see how you could feel that way." You then express empathy by saying something like "That sounds really frustrating." And finally you attempt to solve the problem by saying something to the effect of "What would you like me to do about this?" You don't have to say it exactly the same way as I did in the examples. Clients are encouraged to use their own words in order to make it feel more natural to them, so long as they are still going through all the steps. I've often been impressed with the way my clients have modified the couple's dialogue to better fit their needs.

Unlike Hendrix's version, you do not need to make an appointment or ask permission to use the couple's dialogue. I found that making an appointment was one of my clients' biggest complaints about using the dialogue. Now I just tell my clients to use the dialogue as a way of responding when your partner is upset about something or coming to you with a concern. At this point, your couple should be having at least weekly couple's meetings, and those meetings are a great place to practice this technique.

Because this technique has multiple steps, I always make sure to write it down on an index card to give to the couple I'm working with.

Step 3: Practice, practice, practice

For a couple whose primary mode of communication with one another has been yelling, blame, criticism, and defensiveness, the couple's dialogue can seem like a foreign language and many couples are going to be skeptical of using it. It is unrealistic to expect the first time they practice this method to be outside of the session. Due to this, the couple's dialogue will be practiced several times in session.

The therapist will first role play with each partner to make sure they get it before letting them practice it as a couple. When deciding which partner I'm going to use first for my role play, I tend to choose the most cooperative person to go first. In the case of Mark and Sarah, that person would be Sarah. This allows the more resistant partner to be able to observe the method a few extra times before attempting it with the therapist themselves.

After you have picked the partner that will go first, explain to them that you are going to role play having a couple's dialogue with them. Ask them to think of a recent argument or issue they had with their partner. They will then pretend that you are their partner and tell you about something that is upsetting them. After they have finished giving you their message, you then go through the steps of the couple's dialogue. Make sure to use your regular voice and mannerisms. Although the client has been instructed to present the message to you as if you are their partner, do not mock the other person by pretending to be them. You are there to teach them the method, not show-off your acting skills.

The next step is that you switch positions. Now the therapist is the sender and the client is the receiver. When it's my turn to be the sender, I will either choose to say something I have heard the other person complain about in session or choose to complain about something that most couples face, such as how housework isn't being done. I think that complaining about how the other person didn't do their chores is something that a lot of couples can relate to. After the therapist is done speaking, the client practices reflecting, validating, empathizing, and problem solving the therapist's message. It is unlikely that the client will get it right on their first try, so provide some feedback and try it again until they get it right.

The other client has now witnessed the couple's dialogue being done with their partner at least twice, so they will probably have an easier time with it. The therapist gives the other client the same treatment the other partner received, being able to role play being both sender and receiver with the therapist. Now that both partners know the method, they are ready to practice it with each other. I usually ask the couple to bring up a new topic, maybe something that has been bothering them for a while that they haven't had a chance to discuss yet. Now the couple gets to experience just how effective this method is with dealing with a real-life problem. If necessary, the therapist can intervene to make sure the couple is doing the dialogue correctly.

Step 4: Do you want to be right or do you want to be happy?

For many of the couples we work with, at the core of their dysfunction is a belief that they are right and their partner is wrong. The beauty of this method is that it removes that from the equation. Nowhere in the dialogue does the other person express agreement, only that they can understand the other person's view and are willing to consider their solution to the problem. You may have heard the saying "do you want to be right or do you want to be happy?" It speaks to the universal truth that you are sometimes better off being "wrong" than "right." What good is it to be "right" if your spouse resents you for it? Was it really worth it to beat down the other person's spirit until they agreed to let you go on that shopping spree? Is that really "winning"?

If you are dealing with a couple who are currently caught in a power struggle like Mark and Sarah are, you may find it's important to remind them of this saying. I have often been surprised by the power of this saying while a couple is in the midst of insisting that one of them is right. You may also need to remind them that being in a functioning relationship is not about finding what is right for the individual, but what is right for the couple.

Fourth session vignette

Therapist: How are you?

Sarah: We're doing well, actually.

Mark: This past week has been one of our better weeks.

Therapist: How have the couple's meetings been going?

Mark: We only did it once and I think only having a meeting once a week is the perfect frequency for us. Having a meeting every night would be too stressful for me and I need to be able to wind-down after work.

Therapist: If I'm not mistaken, I think you wrote on your list that you would like time to settle down after you come home from work.

Mark: You are correct.

Therapist: Has Sarah been letting you do that?

Mark: Yes, she's been great about letting me relax for an hour or so after I get home.

Therapist: So it looks like your ideal relationship is becoming a reality. That's great to hear. Was the couple's meeting stressful?

Mark: Yes, it went well actually, but I think having one every night would be too stressful.

Therapist: So the idea of couple's meetings are stressful?

Mark: Yes.

Therapist: I can understand that. Hopefully the idea of couple's meetings will become less stressful after you've had a few more good experiences and you'll feel comfortable having them more often.

Sarah: I hope so. I think the meetings are very helpful.

Therapist: It's great that you guys have been experiencing some progress. I was wondering if you would be open to learning how to have a "couple's dialogue"?

Sarah: What's that?

Therapist: It's sort of the final piece of the puzzle in improving you and Mark's communication. It's a way of responding to your partner so that they feel completely understood and connected to you. Previous couples I have worked with have had a lot of success with it.

Mark: We can give it a try.

Therapist: Great! There are four steps to having a couple's dialogue and I'm going to write them down on this index card to help you remember them. After I explain them we're going to practice them in session to make sure you understand. Okay?

Sarah: Got it.

Therapist: When your partner tells you about something that is bothering you, I want you to reflect back, or paraphrase in your own words, what they just said to you. For example, if I complained to Mark about how he wasn't washing the dishes in a timely manner, Mark might reflect me by saying "It sounds like you're annoyed because the dishes keep piling up." Now, if that's not what I'm saying, I'd try to explain myself again, and Mark would reflect me again. The next step is to validate what the person is saying. Validating doesn't mean you are agreeing with the person, just that you can understand where they are coming from or that you can see how they would feel that way. To validate me, Mark might say "I can see how that would be frustrating." The third step is to offer empathy. Whether you agree with it or not, your partner is hurting and that makes you feel hurt too, right?

Mark: Right.

Therapist: So you offer empathy by saying something like "I'm sorry you feel so frustrated by the dirty dishes." The last step is that you try to solve the problem. Now, not every problem can be solved and maybe I'm just venting, but either way you should ask "What would you like us to do about this?" In this case I might say "Can we have a new policy where we make sure all the dishes get washed before bed?" If that doesn't sound feasible to you, you can make a counteroffer. But that is a couple's dialogue in a nutshell. The reason why I love this technique so much is that I've noticed that when people are arguing, they are basically just saying the same thing over and over again. The argument continues because neither one thinks they are being heard. This dialogue lets the person know they are being heard, so a problem ends up getting solved in five minutes instead of five hours, or never.

Sarah: Interesting.

Therapist: ::Hands Mark and Sarah each an index card with the steps written out:: I'd like to roleplay this technique with both of you. How about we try it with Sarah first?

Sarah: Okay.

Therapist: Sarah, I'd like for you to think of a complaint or something that has been upsetting you lately. Maybe you've tried talking to Mark about this before, but you didn't feel understood or validated by him. I'm going to pretend to be Mark and go through the steps of the couple's dialogue.

Sarah: Okay. Umm... Well, we got into an argument a while ago about his friends...

Therapist: Tell it to me as if I'm Mark and you're bringing it to me for the first time.

Sarah: It bothered me that when we went to the bar with your friends the other week, that your friend Tom bought a round of beers for everyone except me. He didn't even bother asking if I wanted anything. I feel that I have always been courteous to Tom and welcomed him into my home on numerous occasions.

Therapist: It sounds like you felt disrespected or neglected by Tom because he bought a drink for everyone but you, even though you've been so nice to him in the past. I can see how that would make you feel unappreciated. I feel bad that my friend made you feel sad. What can we do about this?

Sarah: I don't know if there's anything that can be done, I just wanted you to know that it made me feel sad. Maybe next time you could just say something like "Hey, maybe Sarah wants a drink too" to remind them.

Therapist: Okay, I'll try to remember that next time.

Sarah: I would appreciate that.

Therapist: Sarah, thank you for participating in the role play. How did it feel to be part of a couple's dialogue?

Sarah: I thought it was weird at first, but it felt pretty good actually to have someone listen to you and validate you.

Therapist: Good. Now, I want to do another role play, but this time I'm going to be the one to be complaining to you about something and I want you to validate me. It's okay to look at the index card if you have to.

Sarah: Okay.

Therapist: Sarah, I'm upset because I got the credit card statement in the mail today and we somehow managed to spend over $2,000 this month. A lot of it was at stores that you like to shop at.

Sarah: It sounds like you're mad because we went over budget this month. I can see how that would bother you. I'm sorry that you feel that way. What would you like me to do about that?

Therapist: Could you try to go lighter on the credit card this month to make up for last month?

Sarah: Yes, I can do that.

Therapist: That was great, Sarah. Mark, what do you think about what me and Sarah have been doing?

Mark: I can see how it could work in certain situations.

Therapist: Would you be willing to try a role play with me?

Mark: Alright. I don't know if I'm going to be as good at it as Sarah is.

Therapist: Don't worry, I'll coach you through it if you need me to.

Mark: Okay.

Therapist: I want you to pretend that I'm Sarah and there's something that has been upsetting you lately. Tell me what has been bothering you.

Mark: Well, Sarah can be difficult with the way she-

Therapist: Tell it to me as if I am Sarah.

Mark: Oh okay... Well, Sarah... it really upset me how the other day when my sister called you were really nasty to her on the phone-

Therapist: Let's try it again with a more neutral tone of voice and without the blaming language.

Mark: How else would I say it?

Therapist: You might want to try "sometimes I don't like the way you talk to my sister."

Mark: Okay... Sometimes when my sister calls you can be rude to her on the phone-

Therapist: Better.

Mark: And that bothers me because then she complains to my mother about it and I get put in the middle.

Therapist: It sounds like the problems I have with your sister are causing problems between you and your mother. I can understand how that would bother you. I'm sorry that the relationship I have with your sister has made things difficult for you and your family. What would you like to do about this?

Mark: I don't know, maybe not be so rude to my sister on the phone?

Therapist: What if you told your sister to call you on your cell phone instead of the house phone so that I wouldn't have to talk to her? In the meantime, I'll try to be more polite towards her when I do have to have contact with her.

Mark: I guess I could live with that.

Therapist: Great! Me and you just compromised. So, how did it feel to do a couple's dialogue?

Mark: It felt okay, but I'm not sure that it would work in real life.

Therapist: Me and you are going to practice one more time and then I'm going to have you and Sarah try it.

Mark: Okay.

Therapist: This time I'm going to be the one to complain about something and you're going to reflect and validate me. You can look at the index card if you need to. Okay?

Mark: Sure.

Therapist: I feel sad because we don't go out like we used to. We used to go out on such fun dates, but now it seems like you just go out with your friends and I get left home alone. I miss having fun with you.

Mark: You're saying you want us to go out on more dates. I can understand why you would want us to do that. What do you want to do about it?

Therapist: Don't forget to express empathy.

Mark: I'm sorry you feel sad that we don't go out more.

Therapist: I would like it if we could go out on Friday nights.

Mark: That could get expensive.

Therapist: They don't all have to be expensive dates. Some Fridays we could just go for a walk in the park.

Mark: Okay, that sounds fair.

Therapist: That was great, Mark. Do you think you are ready to try it on each other?

Sarah: Yes. Let's see how it goes.

Therapist: Because I want this to be a real-life test, I want you to each think of something that has been bothering you but you haven't talked to the other person about it yet. Or maybe you've tried talking about it in the past but it's always turned into an argument.

Mark: That's a hard one.

Therapist: Then we'll let Sarah go first to give you time to think. Sarah will tell you about something that's bothering her and you will reflect, validate, emphasize, and problem solve with her. Okay?

Sarah: I think I can think of something.

Therapist: Sarah, we'll wait until you are ready. Take all the time you need to think.

Sarah: Mark, Monday I wanted to have a couple's meeting to talk about our trust issues and you refused to talk about it. I want to be able to talk about it now-

Mark: I don't think this is what the therapist had in mind.

Therapist: Part of the process of having a couple's dialogue is that you can't interrupt the other person. Let's let Sarah finish.

Mark: ::sighs::

Sarah: Whenever I try to talk to you about the affair you get angry or change the subject. I feel like I can't move on because you've never let me really talk to you about the way it has hurt me.

Mark: It sounds like you feel frustrated because I don't want to talk about the affair. I can see how that would bother you. I'm sorry that you feel like you've never gotten the chance to talk about it. What would you like to do about it?

Sarah: I would like to have more couple's meetings.

Mark: We can talk about it at the next meeting, but I really don't feel like I could handle having more than one a week.

Sarah: Okay, but I want the next meeting to be devoted to this topic.

Mark: Fine.

Therapist: Great job, guys. It's your turn, Mark.

Mark: Sarah, I don't like it how whenever I go out with my friends you act like I'm sneaking off to have an affair. I can't live my life like that. I need to be able to see my friends without feeling guilty or accused by you. It was a mistake that I'm never going to repeat again. I've learned my lesson and not a day goes by that I don't regret it. You know I hate talking about it, so that's all I'm going to say.

Sarah: ::wipes a tear from her eyes:: It sounds like you're saying you don't want to have to feel guilty when you go out with your friends. I can understand how you would feel that way. I'm sorry I make you feel bad. What would you like to do about this?

Mark: I'd like to stop talking about the affair. It happened two years ago, it's time to move on.

Therapist: I think not talking about it is what has caused these problems to have persisted for so long.

Mark: Then what am I supposed to suggest?

Therapist: Maybe you could suggest you be allowed to have a "guys night out" once a week where you can have fun with your friends guilt-free.

Mark: Sarah, I don't want you to make me feel guilty just because I'm going to go out with my friends.

Sarah: I could agree to one night a week that you can spend with your friends.

Mark: I think Saturday night should be "boys night."

Sarah: Okay.

Therapist: You guys are really good at this! How did it feel to solve two things that had been really bothering you quickly and without conflict?

Mark: I think it works well in theory, but in order for it to work you basically have to admit to being wrong, and what if you're not wrong?

Therapist: That's the beauty of this technique; no one is right or wrong. You are just acknowledging the other person's feelings, which isn't an admission of guilt, and then seeing how you can help them feel better.

Mark: Yes, but what if you are RIGHT?

Therapist: Mark, I think you are a very intelligent person who knows what is right when it comes to you, but the question is "what is right for you as a couple?" and you need Sarah's input in order to answer that.

Mark: But, I mean, sometimes I just know that I'm right but she's insisting on doing something else.

Therapist: There's always more than one solution to a problem and you have to put into consideration what's right for Sarah, not just you.

Mark: No, what about when I'm right and I know I'm right.

Therapist: Do you want to be right or do you want to be happy?

Mark: ::long pause:: Well, I guess that's just it then.

Therapist: Sometimes it's better just to be "wrong" even when you're really "right." If it means being able to move forward and be in a happy relationship, I'd rather be wrong.

Mark: Hmph.

Therapist: I'd like for you guys to do a few couple's dialogues during the week. It feels strange at first, but if you do it consistently, after about two weeks it'll feel like second nature to you.

Sarah: Okay.

Therapist: You guys did really well today. Will I see you next week?

Mark: We'll see you then.

Therapist: Take care.

Despite threatening to fire the therapist in the last session, Mark chose to come back this week. Judging by his report, it is because he has experienced some improvement in the relationship after implementing the communication skills he learned during the last session. It is still unclear if Mark is a "believer" in couples counseling now, but he has certainly become easier to work with. In today's session, Mark was more cooperative and less argumentative. Both Mark and Sarah are starting to show some improvement in their relationship skills.

Because the couple have made some progress in counseling, they were more open to the concept of the couple's dialogue, which can sound very strange to someone who has never heard of it before. The therapist made the couple's dialogue more approachable by having used it on the couple during previous sessions and by providing positive reinforcement while the couple attempted to learn it. It is important to establish a feeling of trust so the clients feel safe enough to role play with you and try new things.

You will find that a lot of the couples you work with have one or both people that just have to be right. Dr. Phil McGraw refers to these people as "Right-Fighters." They would sooner end their marriages then see their spouse's point of view. Most of us will accept that there are two sides to every story and more than one solution to every problem, but not right-fighters. Mark could be described in this way, but when the therapist asked "do you want to be right or do you want to be happy?", Mark's sudden silence seemed to indicate it gave him something to think about. He may not have agreed with the therapist right away, but the therapist just planted a seed that will hopefully grow into Mark accepting more influence from Sarah.

Communication skills are things that you may need to continuously reinforce throughout your sessions with the couple. Always remind them that the tools are there if they need them. If the couple you are working with start an argument in future sessions, say "let's start over, but this time let's avoid using a harsh start-up" or "let's have a couple's dialogue." Now that they know the skills, you can better intervene and coach them through disagreements in session. But you should also notice a steady decrease in arguing during sessions. The "dark days" of couples counseling are coming to an end and you will find your couple easier to work with here on out.

Fourth session outline: couple's dialogue

Step 1: Review homework

Step 2: Teach the couple how to have a couple's dialogue

- Write on an index card the four steps
- Reflecting, Validation, Empathy, Problem Solving

Step 3: Practice, Practice, Practice

- Therapist uses role-play and role-rehearsal with each partner
- Couple then practices with each other

Step 4: "Do you want to be right or do you want to be happy?"

Chapter 6

Fifth Session: Problem Solving & Compromise

This session marks the halfway point in therapy. By now the therapist should have a brief history of the couple's problems, have discussed their hopes and dreams for the future, briefly touched upon their individual needs in the process, and have had multiple sessions devoted to communication skills. I want you to take a few moments to reflect on how your clients must be feeling about couples counseling at this point. They've been able to make some progress in counseling and have sharpened their communication skills, but are they feeling fulfilled yet? Probably not. For the past four or more sessions you, the therapist, have been running the show. Today's session is your opportunity to give some of that power back to the couple and allow them to feel like they are being heard by you and that their individual concerns are important to you.

It's important to understand that today's session wouldn't have been possible earlier in counseling. Allowing the couple to lead the session before they had developed basic communication skills would have resulted in chaos. You will notice that the couple is now more capable of discussing their problems in a calm respectful manner. If not, you can always say "let's have a couple's dialogue" or "remember to avoid defensiveness", but overall you will notice a decrease in negative behaviors in therapy.

In the previous sessions you have had the opportunity to act as a moderator or arbitrator when the couple has presented any problems to you. You have also probably helped the couple solve some of these problems. What's different about this session is that you are going to be teaching the couple how to solve their problems on their own. This is an important step in having the couple become their own marriage counselor. Although the problems couples present to us are usually easily solved, if the couple has to rely on the counselor to solve every problem, you can not say that counseling has been successful for that couple. The point of counseling is not to foster a lifelong relationship of dependency, but to show the couple what they can become by learning and implementing the same skills the therapist possesses.

Step 1: "What problems are you currently experiencing that haven't been addressed yet in couples counseling?"

By now you should be in the habit of reviewing the couple's compliance with the homework. Ask if they encountered any difficulties while using the couple's dialogue on their own, how it felt to use such a different way of responding to one another, etc. If the couple complains that it feels stilted or contrived to talk in this manner, remind them that it takes about two weeks of using communication skills consistently before it feels natural. Make sure to provide plenty of positive reinforcement for improvements made by the couple.

After reviewing the homework, I like to ask the couple something like "So what would you like to work on today?" This always catches the couple off guard and they may even show some signs of panic at being responsible for their own treatment. Nine times out of ten, the couple will say "I don't know", and that's okay because I always have something planned for each session. The reason why I ask this question is because I want to communicate to the couple that I want a more active participation from them moving forward. The ball has been thrown in their court and I'm going to expect more from them than "I don't know. That's why we're in counseling" from here on out. That response is not going to fly anymore. Now that we are about halfway through counseling, I'm going to expect the couple to slowly begin to shift towards becoming their own counselors.

Since the question "what do you want to work on today?" usually won't result in anything useful for today's session, I ask a follow up question like "What problems are you currently experiencing that haven't been addressed yet in couples counseling?" That is a question that couples have an easier time answering. I'll usually hear a sigh of relief from the couple that the responsibility is off of them for possibly one more session. Unless your couple's problems were purely due to poor communication (highly unlikely), there are still some problems that haven't been being addressed through couples counseling. Now is the time to address them.

For a lot of the couples we work with, prior to seeing a couples counselor, they probably asked their friends and family for advice on how to handle the problems in their relationship. As I said earlier, a lot of these problems are straightforward and have simple solutions. The odds are good that their friends and family gave them reasonable advice for solving the problems, but something then got in the way of the couple following through with the advice. For most of our couples, what got in the way were poor communication skills, unreasonable expectations, and an unwillingness to compromise. Those obstacles have now been being worked on in counseling and should be on their way out the door for good, making our couple more likely to follow through on solutions successfully. However, instead of just rehashing the same advice they have been getting from their friends, we're going to take it one step further and help the couple learn to find the solutions on their own.

Step 2: Help the couple to find the core "themes" in their arguments

You may find that your couple is still unable to find some problems to work on in today's session, or that the problems they do volunteer are so vague that it's not really workable. If after having sufficient time to stop and think up some problems that haven't been addressed yet in counseling your couple is still unable to come up with anything useful, it is now up to you to help them to identify the problems in their relationship. After years of communicating in a dysfunctional manner, it is not unusual for a couple to simply not know what exactly the problem is, they just want to stop fighting. I have often listened to a couple arguing in my office and wondered "What the hell are they even arguing about?" I can only imagine how they must feel about it. You are now going to help them figure that out.

The way the therapist goes about identifying problems in the relationship is by identifying the core "themes" of the arguments (Halford, 2001). I'm going to list the core themes of arguments in a moment so that you know what to look out for, but in the meantime, you can get the ball rolling by asking the couple "What are some things you have disagreed about recently?" We're not looking for ancient history here, those problems have probably already been solved on their own, but rather things that the couple have disagreed on within the past two weeks or so.

If a couple tends to be unclear when arguing, it can be difficult to decipher what exactly is at the core of the disagreement. Let's do an example. I was working with a husband and wife of two years and the husband told me that one of the things he disagreed with his wife about was their second refrigerator. The wife was unemployed but contributed to the household by keeping the house clean and cooking extravagant meals every night. The husband said he was fine with this arrangement and loved coming home to a clean house and a good meal. So what's not to love? The problem was that cooking large meals every night created a lot of leftovers. She hated to throw out the food and convinced her husband to buy a second refrigerator to put in the basement and keep the leftovers in. Although he apparently agreed to buy the refrigerator, he now complained about it. The wife retorted "It's in the basement. It's not taking up any room. You don't even ever see it. What's the problem?"

The husband would then respond "It's ridiculous to have a second refrigerator when it's just the two of us in this family!" The wife obviously didn't think it was ridiculous to have a second refrigerator and it wasn't in the way, so what was the real problem?

Remembering the core themes, I asked the husband, "Is it the cost of having a second refrigerator that's bothering you?"

"Yes, there's just the two of us living in this house but we have the budget of a family of five."

"Tell me more about that" I asked. It was then revealed that the wife had a borderline shopping addiction that she felt too ashamed to talk about in the earlier sessions, but that now that she had gained more trust in the therapeutic process she was more forthcoming than she had been in the beginning. I guided the couple through the problem solving process and in the end the couple decided to reduce their budget, discuss purchases over $100 before committing to buy, and the wife got a part time job working in an office. An unintended side effect of the wife getting a part time job was that she had less time to cook and the couple found themselves having more "leftover nights." The extra refrigerator ended up being donated to a family member that really needed it.

The core themes of arguments

Couples may not argue about the same thing every time, but they certainly do argue about the same types of things. It's amazing how many times couples can argue about the same type of thing over and over again and not even realize it. Identifying the core theme of arguments is essential to breaking this cycle. I've included what I have found to be the seven most common core themes of arguments in relationships. Become familiar with these so that you can more readily identify them when your clients describe their recent disagreements.

Trust vs Mistrust is probably the easiest one to identify. People more readily state "you don't trust me!" in disagreements if the other person is trying to keep a short leash. In getting to the heart of the problem, try to find out what is getting in the way of trust. Does the person have baggage from previous relationships? Unresolved childhood issues? Or did the other person do something to betray their trust such as by having an affair? If one partner did betray the other, ask what it would take to win that trust back again. Is what they are asking for feasible? This is where problem solving and compromise come in.

If the lack of trust is due to an affair, a lot of times the cheating spouse has a hard time adjusting to the fact that now their life has to be an open book. Previous to being caught, the adulterer experienced the full range of privileges afforded to an adult, including being able to come and go as one pleased and having privacy. However, that is a privilege and not a right. When you violate the most sacred tenement of marriage, being faithful to your partner, you essentially throw away that privilege and then have to earn it back. No adulterer wants to hear this, but that is the only way to rebuild trust in a relationship. This means coming home on time, telling your spouse where you are if they call, keeping your spouse in the loop about your social activities and giving your spouse vetoing powers about certain activities that have in the past lead to cheating (such as trips without your spouse, going to clubs, drinking parties, etc) and having no more secrets.

Of course, you can never keep a tight enough leash on a person to prevent them from cheating if they really want to. But allowing the victim spouse to have a sense of control is important to alleviating their anxiety and feeling some relief. As time goes on, the spouse releases some of that control and sees that it is okay to not be in control all the time. They then experience less anxiety and more feelings of trust over time. One of the common reactions I deal with from adulterers is their belief that their spouse should be "over it" by now. They were willing to be an open book for a month or two after they got caught, but after that they were shocked to hear that their spouse didn't want them to go to the club with their friends (which is previously where they were orchestrating affairs). The cheating spouse does not get to decide how long it takes for the other person to feel safe in the relationship again.

Appreciation, or Reality vs Expectations, can take many forms in disagreements. Most often it has to do with problems over the division of labour. One person feels they are doing more than their fair share of work and not receiving any appreciation from their partner, while the other doesn't understand why they have to express appreciation because they feel the other person is only doing what is expected of them. Each of their expectations cloud the reality of how much the other person contributes to the relationship. This causes problems.

The easy answer is "just split up the work 50/50" but it is rarely that simple. The couple needs to look at how many hours they each work and how they both contribute financially. If one person is paying the majority of the bills, it probably isn't fair that they should also be doing the majority of the housework and childcare. Certain things such as work schedule, other ways the person is contributing to the relationship, and domestic skills should also be put into consideration. One should also put into consideration the preferences of each individual. For instance, if the wife just has to have a clean bathroom and doesn't like the way her husband cleans the bathroom, cleaning the bathroom should be her chore.

I find it helpful to make up a list of all the chores and approximately how much time it takes to complete each chore. Creating a list of all the chores along with the time it takes to complete them can also help to shed light on the reality of the situation. Someone who's never cooked dinner before may have no idea just how long it takes or how tiring it can be. The fact of the matter is that over time we come to expect certain things from our spouse and eventually take it for granted. We would never take a friend for granted, and yet we often do this to our spouse. You may have heard that behind every good marriage is a solid friendship with their spouse. Indeed, couples in good marriages will often describe their spouse as being their best friend. This may be connected to expressing more appreciation and understanding towards your partner.

If a couple is confused about what they should express appreciation for versus what should just be expected, teach them the friendship rule. The rule goes, if it was a friend instead of your spouse that did the thing for you, and you would express appreciation to the friend, then express appreciation to your spouse. It seems to me that all anyone wants is to feel loved and appreciated by their partner. If all it would take to make your partner feel that way is a few simple words, why wouldn't you do that for the person you love?

Respect vs Disrespect is similar to Appreciation. The difference is that this theme usually has to do more with years of nagging, name-calling, using foul language towards your spouse, emotional abuse, or making fun of your partner. Like most adults, I do swear in the privacy of my own home and amongst friends. I've even swore at the cat. But one thing I will not do is swear at my husband. Some clients will try to minimize their actions by saying things like "But that's just our style. We're adults. We can swear if we want to." I completely get the whole "We're adults and we can swear if we want to" thing, but it is never okay to swear at your partner. It is so disrespectful and I have zero tolerance for such things.

The next one is making fun of your partner. Usually this starts out as light-hearted teasing but then it goes too far and someone gets their feelings hurt. This is another one that people try to minimize as well. Regardless of their intentions, this behavior is causing problems in the relationship and should be stopped. There are some couples that have the type of relationship where they can have light-hearted teasing and they both enjoy it. That's a whole other ball game. It's different if one partner is consistently getting mad or having their feelings hurt. Any behavior that is causing the other person pain should be stopped.

Nagging is on the list of disrespect because it involves treating another person like they are an idiot or child. It is not the behavior of two people who are in an equal relationship. I once worked with a couple that brought up the problem that her husband would put his dirty clothes on top of the hamper instead of inside of the hamper. She saw this as being disrespectful towards her since she considered it to be just as much work to put the laundry inside the hamper as on top of the hamper. She felt that he did it intentionally to annoy her, which he denied. This resulted in her going into a screaming rage every time she saw the clothes on top of the hamper and the rages would last between thirty minutes and an hour. The husband offered problem solving the situation by simply getting rid of the lid on top of the hamper so that he wouldn't be able to pile the clothes on top of it. This seemed like a reasonable solution to me, but it was unacceptable to her. For her, it wasn't about the laundry. She believed that he didn't respect her because she was a housewife and didn't have a career like he did. He pointed out that he found her nagging to be disrespectful. He worked long shifts as a surgeon and was responsible for making life or death decisions. He said he respected her role in the family but did not appreciate coming home after being in surgery for twelve hours to be scolded and yelled at for leaving his shoes in front of the door.

In this case, both partners felt disrespected by the other and needed to find a way to compromise. The wife came to realize that she was spending thirty minutes to an hour yelling at her husband about something that would only take her thirty seconds to fix on her own. He realized that it was also quicker to just do something the first time rather than get nagged about it later. They both decided that the solution to this problem was to express more respect, understanding, and appreciation for each other.

Unity vs Discord happens when couples have disagreements about what it means to be in a relationship / marriage or to act like a team. Arguments about unity vs discord usually have to do with other people interfering with the marriage (meddling in-laws, boundary-crossing friends, etc.) or not being unified strongly enough (not acting as a team while parenting, disagreements about the kids, etc.). The problem is not having clearly defined boundaries in the relationship.

When I was planning my wedding I came across a poem that read "a son is a son until he takes a wife, but a daughter is a daughter for the rest of her life." At first glance it just seems cute, but there is a deeper meaning here about the role of in-laws in a marriage, that there is perhaps a need for a son to separate himself from his parents when he becomes married. Although traditionally men have been more vocal in complaining about their mother-in-laws, the research actually shows that wives have a much harder time dealing with in-laws than husbands do.

A psychologist at Cambridge University, Dr. Terri Apter, examined twenty years worth of research regarding the relationship married couples have with their in-laws. She discovered that the husband's mother is far more meddling than either of the wife's family members. She then conducted a large survey and found that although 60% of women described their relationship with their in laws to be very stressful, only 15% of men said the same (Farouky, 2008). Proving that yes, wives do have a more difficult time with their husband's family.

So what causes in-laws to meddle in the first place? According to

Apter's research, problems occur because the mother feels she is being replaced by the daughter in law and fears her son loves her less now that he is married. Daughters are better at reassuring their parents that they still love them and are more likely to visit as well, which is why there is less friction between the daughter's parents and her husband. Apter's research suggests that part of the problem could be solved by the son being more reassuring that even though he is married, he still loves and treasures his mother. And of course, it wouldn't hurt for him to visit her every now and then.

The most common way that in-laws meddle is by criticizing or telling the spouse what to do. This intrusiveness can take on a whole new level if there are also grandchildren. No one likes how to be told to parent their kids and this kind of meddling can cause major conflict. It can be just as troubling for the spouse whose parent is doing the meddling. They can feel just as trapped, helpless, and frustrated as their partner in this. Something that is important to understand is that although the person may know that their parent is causing problems, your mother is still your mother. It can be a very uncomfortable feeling to be pushed from either side.

In trying to deal with the pressure of dealing with a family member that is interfering in one's relationship, a person can make some well-intentioned mistakes. The first mistake is that they will try to reassure their parent by taking their side. They may even bad-mouth their spouse to their family since it seems to please them. Of course, you should never say anything negative about your partner to your family because they are far less forgiving of your partner than you are. You may be able to forgive the fact that your partner isn't consistent with timeouts with the kids, but your mother will make it her personal mission to teach your spouse the proper way to discipline a child and now things have gotten worse. The second mistake is that the person will try to minimize the things that their meddling family member does. Instead of validating and empathizing, they disregard what their partner says by trying to minimize or deny the negative behaviors of their family member. All this accomplishes is to enrage your partner.

There really is only one solution to this problem, and that is to become a more unified couple. As hard as this sounds, the partner whose family is meddling needs to take a stand. I am not advocating "cutting off" anyone, and actually that almost always backfires, but I am advocating setting strong boundaries. This means that it is not okay for the other partner to be criticized by their in-laws, even if they are not around. The in-laws must not be allowed to try to influence the marriage either. And of course, having strong boundaries goes both ways. The couple should keep personal matters between the two of them and not give family any "ammunition" to use against the other person.

In-laws aren't the only ones who meddle. Sometimes people have friends that can damage the relationship as well. If a friendship predates the relationship, sometimes a friend can feel threatened when they see that the "newcomer" has more influence over their old friend. And that's when trouble starts. The friend feels insecure about being replaced so they fight back by sabotaging the relationship. If they are questioned, they completely deny it and try to make the person believe that actually it is the significant other who is trying to sabotage their friendship. It's not always this insidious. Sometimes the friend just expects that things should go on like they did in their friend's bachelor/bachelorette days. The solution here is to agree as a couple what are the proper boundaries in the relationship and then to make it clear to the friend that crossing boundaries will not be tolerated any longer.

Having stronger boundaries with friends can mean different things to different people. Perhaps in your bachelor days it was fine to have a friend show up at your house with little notice and "crash" at your place. For many couples, it would be considered inappropriate to consider this practice once a significant other has moved in with you. Doing favors for friends like loaning money, giving rides, and agreeing to hang out without talking to their partner first can be seen as a boundary violation by some couples. If you are working with a couple who is dealing with this problem, discuss with them what their personal views are on boundaries with friends. Once they have decided on what are appropriate boundaries, talk with your couple about how to enforce these boundaries. Hint: It involves being able to say "no" to friends.

Conflicts over parenting and kids also fall into the Unity vs Discord theme. Children learn pretty quickly how to manipulate their parents and if their parents are not unified in their parenting, the children will take advantage of that. Couples may disagree how to parent and have different parenting styles, but they must agree to a specific set of rules and consequences within their own home. I feel that if one parent sacrificed their career to take on the role of full-time parent then that person should have more of a say in the parenting since they interact with the child more often. The other parent must be willing to back up their parenting decisions (barring abuse of course) while in the presence of the child, and then discuss any disagreements in private.

Closeness vs Distance becomes a conflict in relationships when one person wants to spend more time with their partner while the other wants more independence. Often this comes out in arguments where one person states "you spend more time with your friends than you do with me!" The closeness seeker reacts by making the distancer feel guilty for spending time with friends, causing the distancer to seek even more independence. They fall into a trap whereby they each worsen the other's behavior.

The solution is simple, the couple needs to come to a compromise about how often the other person is allowed to go out or seek their own individual pursuits guilt-free. I have always thought it was a good arrangement to have Saturdays be a day for friendships or individual activities while Sunday be a day reserved just for the couple. This way both are given equal time and there's a chance to pursue activities with friends that your partner doesn't necessarily enjoy doing. For example, if he wants to go on a ski trip with his buddies, she can go on a shopping trip with her girlfriends. But in order for this to work, the closeness seeker must have enough of his or her own life to keep him or herself satisfied on Saturdays. I have often found that closeness-seekers don't have their own friendships and have a lot of issues about doing things alone. This may be something that needs to be discussed in counseling in order for the couple to move forward.

Finances, or Short-term vs Long-term Security. There seems to be two types of people in this world, spenders and savers. Spenders could also be described as short-term strategists (they'd rather spend the money now while they know they can use it rather than wait until some unforeseen future where they could die or be too old to enjoy their money) and savers described as long-term strategists (they want to save the money now while they can instead of living in poverty when they are too old to work). There are pros and cons to each strategy and who am I to say which strategy is better? It becomes a problem when a saver finds themselves in a relationship with a spender and they can't agree on how to allocate their money. This is a scenario I see often in couples counseling. This differing in spending habits causes a lot of conflict in the relationship.

Another thing I've noticed about couples who fight about money is that they don't want to talk about their finances with each other. But since not talking about money isn't going to solve the problem, I use our time together in the therapy office as an opportunity to get

them talking about this very important subject. I will ask the couple
to write down how much money they bring in each month and where
it all goes. The couple will then compare each other's spending in
a non-judgmental manner and start drawing up a budget. Creating
a budget is a simple but time consuming process. You may want to
assign it as homework depending on how much time you have available
in the session. I will outline the steps to making a budget below:

1. What is your monthly income and expenses? You want
to be specific. If you use a credit card or debit card for all your spending, it will be easy to look up online where all your money goes. If you
use cash for everything, this will be a little tricky. Specifically, how
much do you get paid? How much goes to the rent/mortgage? Utilities? Groceries? Eating out? Car/transportation? Entertainment
(movies, cable bill, internet, music subscription, etc)? Health (insurance premiums, prescription co-pays, gym membership, etc)? Other
miscellaneous spending?

2. Which of these expenses are absolutely necessary? You
want to make a separate list of necessary expenses (rent, utilities, groceries, health insurance, car) and unnecessary expenses (new clothes,
eating out, cable, internet, gym membership). You can then prioritize
your unnecessary expenses and maybe start to see how they could be
reduced or eliminated. This is your potential savings.

3. Start making cuts. One of my clients was shocked to find
that she was spending $400 a month on new clothes. She realized that
if she cut that down to $100 a month, in a year's time she could afford
to take that trip to Ireland she had always wanted. Cutting back is a
matter of priorities and people can become very possessive about their
spending. It works better if each person agrees to give something up
rather than just put all the pressure on the spender to cut back.

4. Make a leaner budget and stick to it. The couple now
needs to decide how much money can be spent in each category and
it needs to be something they can both live with. This may involve
compromise, but whatever it is that they decide on, they need to stick
with it. I think it is important that they budget each of them having
"fun money" that they can do whatever they want with. I think that
it is important that each person have their own money that they can
make guilt-free purchases with and not have to explain themselves to
their partner. Remember, the whole point of creating a new budget
is to eliminate fighting over money. Keep that in mind during this
process.

5. Now that you have created a leaner budget, you need

to decide what to do with the money you are saving. One couple decided to only spend money on the necessities until they had paid off all of their debt. Another couple reserved 20% of their income and decided to use half of it to pay down debt and put the other half in a retirement fund. Some couples may be able to save more while others less. The important thing is to carve out enough savings to help the saver feel more secure, but not so restrictive that the spender feels penniless.

Sex, or My Needs vs Your Needs is the final core theme on my list. Couples often have disagreements about the frequency or the quality of the sex they are having. Typically the argument is in regards to frequency. In extreme cases, it is not uncommon for me to be told by a couple that they haven't had sex in years. According to some experts, the definition of a sexless marriage is having sex less than once a month, but for these couples, sex ten times a year would sound like heaven. Estimates are that about 16% of couples are in a sexless marriage (Donnelly, Burgess, Anderson, & Dillard, 2001). How does this happen? I have a few theories.

Sexless relationships usually don't start out that way. Often the partner with the greater sexual desire (usually the man) starts out as the initiator. The partner with the lesser desire (usually the woman) gives in more often to the initiator in the beginning phases of the relationship for the sake of securing the relationship. However, as time goes on and the relationship changes (such as after becoming parents) she says no more often. Being repeatedly rejected causes the initiator to initiate less often or not at all. Eventually, the couple settles into a sexless routine of working, eating, and sleeping. The woman feels it is not her place to initiate sex and the man feels less motivated after repeated rejections. Soon months without sex turn into years.

I believe that contrary to tradition, the partner with the least sexual desire should be in charge of initiating sex. This way no one has to deal with the sting of rejection. A lot of times just switching up the routine can help. If a couple complains that by night time they are too tired for sex, I suggest they try initiating sex on a weekend morning. I might also suggest that the couple break up their routine by going on an "adventure" such as a weekend getaway without the kids or if they are more daring, trying something like a nude resort. Problem solving ways to decrease stress, criticism, or a boring routine can help bring intimacy back into a relationship.

Some people will try to convince you that they don't need to have sex in order to have a great relationship. I disagree. The science has revealed that during sex, the chemical oxytocin is released in our brains. Oxytocin has been referred to as the chemical of love. It makes us feel more bonded and in love with our partners (Curtis & Wang, 2003). Without oxytocin, the best you can have with someone is a really good friendship. This is why regular sex is vital to relationships. In addition, sex has been shown to relieve stress, boost our immunity, and increases our self esteem (Doheny, 2011).

The "my needs vs your needs" conflict isn't always in regards to sex. People have other needs they expect their partner to fulfill and when that comes in conflict with their partner's needs, the couple has a problem. You can't expect your partner to fulfill all your needs, but I have found that couples in counseling often do. If their partner doesn't enjoy doing all the same things that they do, they assume that their partner is either being stubborn or isn't the right person for them. The reality of the situation is that men and women are simply too different for anyone to ever find an opposite sex partner that has all the same desires that they do (this isn't to say that gay couples are immune to conflict; they aren't). I believe that this is what same-sex friends are for. It is important to schedule some time away from your partner in order to pursue the needs that you are unable to fulfill as a couple. Contrary to popular belief, I do not think that it is healthy to spend all your free time with your partner.

Step 3: Teach the couple how to problem solve

Now that you have identified some problems to work on, you are ready to teach the couple how to solve problems. This is another multi-step process, so it is a good idea to write these steps down on an index card for each partner to refer back to while they are still learning the steps. You've probably already helped the couple do some problem solving and resolve many conflicts that had come up in previous sessions. The difference is now you are going to teach them how to solve the problems on their own. They may still need your help in session, but they should be encouraged to apply the steps on their own outside of therapy as well.

1. Define the problem. I mentioned earlier that defining the problem is an important communication skill. If your couple is still having difficulty with this, finding the core theme of their arguments can help them to better define the problem. For instance, if one person complains "I don't like the way he treats me or the way he talks to me", the theme is probably "respect vs disrespect" and the problem is that they don't treat each other with respect.

2. Finding common ground; what do you both agree on? Using the same example of respect vs disrespect, both clients will probably claim that the other treats them with disrespect while denying any responsibility on their part. Playing "the blame game" in not productive to finding common ground. You are not looking for any one person to take full responsibility for the problem, but you are looking to find mutual agreement about the problem. Most likely they have both contributed to the problem in their own way. It doesn't matter who started the cycle of mutual disrespect. To solve the problem, you just need to find something that they can both agree on. Can they both agree on a behavioral definition for disrespect? Can they both agree that teasing and swearing are disrespectful behaviors? Try to get the couple to at least agree upon the basics.

3. Each person proposes several different solutions. The couple now brainstorms several different solutions. I have found that three possible solutions from each person is a good place to start. The reason why you want to brainstorm several solutions instead of just one is to show people that there is more than one solution to a problem. People will also feel less attached to their solution and less defensive if they propose several. Some possible solutions to our disrespect problem is to propose a no-swearing rule, a no-teasing rule, implement the "friendship rule" (if you wouldn't treat a friend that way, don't treat your spouse that way), and express more appreciation and understanding for one another.

4. Weigh the pros and cons of each solution. Before deciding which proposed solution you should pick, try weighing the pros and cons of each solution. For instance, lets say a couple was having a problem with a meddling in-law. One of the proposed solutions would be to "cut off" their relationship with the in-law. At first look, the pros of cutting off the in-law look great. The in-law would be out of their life, so no more problems, right? However, looking at the possible cons of this solution reveals it creates more problems than it solves. Cutting-off the mother in-law will most likely just make her even more against her son's wife than she was before and possibly turn the entire family against them. Weighing the pros and cons carefully revealed that it was not such a good solution after all.

5. Decide to try one or more solutions as an "experiment." You don't have to just pick one solution and have that be the final say.

Ideally you want to treat it as an "experiment" where you will give one or more proposed solutions a trial run and at the end of a given period of time, re-evaluate your solution. The couple may have come up with several different solutions that appear to be equally effective. Why not try out a few of them and see how it goes? This type of thinking will take the couple even further from a "right or wrong" mindset and lead to more flexible decision-making down the road.

6. Review the effectiveness of the solution. As I mentioned earlier, you want to think of these solutions as an experiment where you can review their effectiveness later. How long you wait before evaluating effectiveness depends on the situation. Just keep in mind that you want to wait long enough to give the proposed solution a fair chance. You also want to agree ahead of time on how long the waiting period should be. When time's up, have a couple's meeting with your partner to evaluate the effectiveness of the solution. Did it solve the problem? If not, try implementing another solution off of your list or come up with a whole new list now that you have a better understanding of the problem.

Step 4: Teach the couple how to compromise

Compromise has been referred to as an art. It is similar to problem solving, but is more focused on the aspect of give and take in decision making. It's about asking "what do we both want?" instead of "what do I want?" Most people know what they want and are capable of making the "right" decisions when it comes to themselves, but problems arise when the other person in the relationship is just as capable and self-focused. Now they each feel they have the "right" solution if only the other person would listen. This is the opposite of compromise because it means that only one person can win. When you compromise successfully, both people win.

Some clients have a very hard time with compromise. They just can't accept that there is more than one solution to a problem or that it's possible for both people to win. It's true that it does mean that you can't always get exactly what you want, but life doesn't work that way anyway. Even kings have to compromise. Unlike problem solving, there are no specific steps to take, you simply negotiate until both people are happy. Let's look at some examples of compromising.

A couple is trying to decide on what movie to watch this Sunday.

He wants to see the latest horror movie while she wants to catch the latest romantic comedy. Horror movies give her nightmares and romantic comedies put him to sleep. They decide on a third option that they both want to see and decide that they will see the horror movie and romantic comedy separately with their friends next Saturday. Another couple is trying to decide where to go on vacation. She wants to go lay on a beach all vacation while he would rather visit a big city. Neither one of them hates the other's preference, but would just prefer their vacation idea more. They decide that they will do a beach vacation this year and a city vacation next year. A third way couples can compromise is by meeting each other halfway. Going back to the vacation example, the couple could have also decided to compromise by going to a big city that also has a beach, such as Miami. They could spend the days relaxing on the beach but then spend the evenings exploring the city. This would be considered a successful compromise because both people win.

You may argue that not every matter can be compromised. For instance, what if one person wants to have a baby while the other wants to never have kids at all? What if one person wants to move to a foreign country and start a new career there but the other person needs to stay in this country for their own career? There's no way both people can win in those situations, right? I have helped couples work through both scenarios and can tell you that they are not necessary deal breakers. The first step is to walk the client through the pros and cons on if their partner did agree with their plans and they went through with it. I have found that many people have misconceptions about the reality of parenting or life overseas. Usually they are only thinking about the pros and don't think about all the cons and extra hardships that go along with it.

Often when a person wants to completely change their life (move far away, have a baby, go off on an long-term adventure) it is because they are not happy with their current life right now. Some need of theirs is not currently being fulfilled. Luckily I have found that there are multiple ways of fulfilling one's needs and they don't involve completely changing your life. Ask the couple or individual, "what need would this fill that is not being fulfilled the way your life is currently?" Sometimes people are just looking for a way out of an unfulfilling career. Sometimes people just need to shake up a boring routine or need some small adventure.

Before a couple makes the decision to end a relationship over something like this, they should try it out first. For the couple that is in disagreement about having a baby, I would recommend that they try babysitting a friend's baby over the weekend. The person who wants to work overseas could sign up for a short term volunteer mission in that country. After trying it out, the couple can then meet and evaluate how that went. The next step is to try shaking up their routine either through having more adventures or applying for a new career here at home. The couple then evaluates how that feels as well.

Although those two examples may have sounded like "deal breakers" at first, I was still able to help the couple live with their differences through applying the same methods of problem solving and compromise. This is not to say that every problem can be solved. Some simply can not. There are certainly relationships out there that have ended because the two individuals had two very different life paths that couldn't be compromised. However, I will still do my very best to help the couple try to stay together since that is the help they have come to me for. If a compromise cannot be reached and the couple does decide to part ways, the goal of counseling then becomes to help the couple split amicably. But it is never the therapist's decision if a couple should stay together or separate.

Step 5: Assign homework

Because you have to provide a lot of education during this session, you probably only had enough time to solve one or two problems during today's session. If there were any other problems that were identified that you didn't have time to get to today, assign the couple to work on them independently at their next couple's meeting. Make sure that the couple knows that problems will continue to pop up from time to time in their relationship and may require weekly problem solving. The good news is that you do get used to it, and then life gets so much easier.

Fifth session vignette

Therapist: How have you been this past week?

Sarah: Not bad.

Therapist: Did you two get a chance to practice the couple's dialogue at your meetings?

Mark: We've tried it a few times but one of us ends up forgetting a step in the process.

Therapist: Keep practicing, it will get easier with time. How did it feel to communicate in this manner?

Mark: To be honest with you, my problem with it is how unnatural it feels.

Therapist: That's a common complaint I hear about this exercise. The cure for that is actually to practice the couple's dialogue more. After about two weeks of practicing consistently, that "weird" feeling goes away.

Sarah: See! That's what I was telling you.

Therapist: The good news is that you are halfway there to making this a natural part of the way you communicate. It's not just a good skill for relationships either. Having good communication skills is great for everyday life as well. One of my clients told me that the communication skills I taught him helped him a lot at work as well.

Mark: Okay, I'll keep trying. Like I've said, I'm willing to do whatever it takes.

Therapist: That's great to hear. It shows too. I've seen such a positive change in the way you two interact with each other now. It's great to see.

Sarah: We think so too.

Therapist: So what would you like to work on today?

Mark: It's up to us to pick today's topic of discussion?

Sarah: Oh wow, I wasn't prepared for that...

Therapist: We're about halfway done with counseling and I wanted to make sure we're working on the things you want to work on.

Mark: Well, I think the way you've organized the sessions have been good so far.

Therapist: What problems are you currently experiencing that haven't been addressed yet in couples counseling?

Sarah: I think we still have a hard time talking to one another.

Therapist: Tell me more about that.

Sarah: Although the arguing has gone down a lot, we still argue about some things.

Therapist: Tell me about some of the things you guys have argued about lately.

Sarah: It feels like Mark is able to do plenty of fun things with his friends, but when it comes to spending time with me, he doesn't have the time. Or he makes up some other excuse why we can't do things together, but he never says no to his friends.

Mark: It's true that I have been spending a lot of time with my friends lately, but it hasn't always been that way. My friend Dave just got out of the Navy and we've been catching up.

Sarah: It's been nearly every weekend for the past three months. And when you go out it's not just for a few hours, it's all day. You leave around early noon and don't come home until after midnight.

Therapist: Sarah, what do you do while Mark's gone with friends?

Sarah: I don't do anything. Sometimes I'll try to go for a long walk or maybe do some shopping but it gets boring. I basically don't do anything. I don't have a lot of girlfriends I can do things with. I lost a lot of friends because of the problems I was having with Mark. They didn't want to deal with the drama anymore, which I can understand.

Therapist: That sounds very difficult, and very lonely. It must be hard having to rely on Mark for socialization when he also has a responsibility to maintain his relationships with his friends.

Sarah: It's true. I do feel lonely a lot.

Therapist: Mark, what do you think about what Sarah is saying?

Mark: I can see where she is coming from. I feel bad knowing that she is stuck at home while I'm out having fun, but it's like you said, I have a responsibility to my friends as well. We can't seem to agree on a solution either.

Therapist: The past couple of sessions when a problem has come up, I've guided you through the process of problem solving and compromise. You have done very well with that and I think that it is something that will come easily to you once you learn the steps. Is it okay if we work on learning how to compromise and problem solve today?

Mark: Sure.

Therapist: Great. Systematic problem solving involves six steps, so I'm going to write them down on an index card to give you something to refer to.

Sarah: Good. I've found having a cheat-sheet to be really helpful.

Therapist: I'm glad to hear that the index cards have helped you. So, the first step in problem solving is to "define the problem." In this situation, what is the problem that you are trying to solve?

Mark: That I go out with my friends too much..?

Sarah: I don't think it is really a matter that you go out too much, I just feel like I'm not getting equal time with you.

Therapist: So maybe the problem could be defined as "not making enough time to do things as a couple"?

Sarah: Yes, I think that's it. I don't care that he spends time with his friends, I just want equal time.

Therapist: If it's okay with you Mark, I'm going to write down that the problem is that equal time is not being made to do things as a couple.

Mark: That's fine.

Therapist: Okay, now that we've defined the problem, we can move on to step 2. Step 2 is to try to find some common ground. In other words, what do you both agree on?

Mark: I'll agree that I've been spending a lot of time with my friends lately and I could stand to cut back a little. I can see why she would feel neglected. The problem was that in the past we were fighting so much that I would avoid going home as much as I could.

Sarah: I think we're in a better place now where we can spend time with each other without it turning into a fight.

Mark: Agreed

Therapist: So it sounds like you're willing to spend less time with friends in order to make more time to do things as a couple.

Mark: Within reason, of course. I'm not going to sacrifice my friends completely.

Sarah: No, I understand that you need time away from me to recharge your batteries. That's okay, Mark. It wouldn't hurt for me to try to make some new friends either.

Therapist: Good, it sounds like you guys actually agree on a lot. I knew you would be good at this.

Mark: Thanks, we've been really trying.

Therapist: I can tell. You've both made a lot of progress.

Sarah: Thank you.

Therapist: The third step is to brainstorm solutions. I don't want you to just propose one solution and then debate back and forth until one person gives up in exhaustion. Although that's commonly what people do, you know personally that that approach doesn't work. Instead, I want you to try to come up with as many possible solutions as you can. You'll want to come up with three good ones each.

Mark: Well, I guess we could have a date night. . .

Therapist: Good. I'm going to write that one down.

Sarah: Maybe limit activities with friends down to once a week?

Therapist: I'm going to write that one down as well. Good job, Sarah. Mark, what other solution can you think of?

Mark: Maybe Sarah could make more of an effort to reconnect with some old friends so she doesn't feel so lonely while I'm with my friends.

Sarah: Forming new friendships is going to take time, but I suppose I could try to plan things with my sister while Mark goes out with his friends.

Therapist: You guys are coming up with some great ideas. I'm writing all of these down.

Sarah: Maybe Mark could try to include me sometimes when he goes out with his friends. It doesn't have to be every time, but I would like to be included every now and again.

Mark: We could possibly have a dinner party where I invite my friends over and also their wives or girlfriends. It would be an opportunity for Sarah to meet my friends and also possibly form new friendships with my friends' significant others.

Therapist: These are all really great. I'm impressed. Any other ideas?

Sarah: No, I don't think I can come up with anything else.

Mark: I think that's everything.

Therapist: Okay, the fourth step is to look at the pros and cons of the proposed solutions. What would be the pros and cons of having a date night?

Sarah: The pros would be spending more time together, I'd feel less lonely and would probably feel more receptive to sex if we were doing romantic things together.

Mark: A con would be that it could get expensive going out on dates every week.

Sarah: It doesn't have to be expensive dates. Sometimes we could go hiking or do other things that are inexpensive or free. You know I'm not high maintenance. Also, don't forget about how much money you spend with your friends. A beer tab can get expensive.

Mark: I guess if it didn't have to always be expensive dates then that would be fine.

Therapist: What would be the pros and cons of limiting activities with friends down to once a week?

Sarah: A pro would be that it would free up more time for us to spend together and I would spend less time feeling lonely during the week.

Mark: A con would be less time with friends, which may make my friends feel a little annoyed with me, but like I said, it wouldn't be a bad thing to decrease it down to once a week.

Therapist: Would it be helpful to have a designated day for friends and then a designated day for spending time as a couple? I usually recommend people reserve Saturdays as a "friends day" and make Sundays "couples day", but you can do it however you want.

Mark: I think that sounds good actually. Then when Saturday comes around there isn't anything to argue about since it's already expected that I'll be seeing my friends.

Sarah: And I'll have Sundays to look forward to.

Therapist: You just have to be flexible enough to tweak it in case there's a holiday or special event that falls on one of those days.

Sarah: I think we can do that.

Therapist: Good. What about the pros and cons of Sarah trying to reconnect with old friends?

Mark: I think that would really help Sarah a lot.

Sarah: It's easier said than done.

Therapist: What would be the worst that could happen?

Sarah: Well, I guess the worst thing that could happen would be I would get rejected.

Therapist: Hmm, rejection is really hard for a lot of people but it's the chance you have to be willing to take to make friends. Do you have any other friendship opportunities? Maybe ones that pose less of a risk for rejection?

Sarah: There are a few women I work with that would probably be willing to do things as friends. We already get lunch together sometimes so I don't think it would be a difficult transition to go from doing lunch together to going shopping on a Saturday.

Therapist: That sounds like a good idea. Do you think you could try inviting them to do something together for next Saturday?

Sarah: Yes, I could give that a try.

Mark: I think that would be really good for you, Sarah.

Therapist: What are some pros and cons for sometimes including Sarah with your friends?

Mark: My friends and I sort of have a "guys only" rule. It's not just me, my friends don't ever invite their girlfriends either. I also doubt that Sarah would enjoy the things we do.

Sarah: I liked the dinner party idea and just occasionally hanging out as a group.

Therapist: We've gone through the pros and cons of all the solutions and it seems that the solutions that you guys liked the most were to have one day a week that you can spend with friends but also one day a week for spending time as a couple, for Sarah to try to make some new friends and do more things with her sister, and have a dinner party or the occasional get together that would also allow Sarah to meet new people and feel more included. Now you don't have to pick just one solution. You can pick several if you want.

Mark: Well, in that case, let's try all of those.

Sarah: Yes, they all sound good to me.

Therapist: The last step is to re-evaluate the effectiveness of your solution. You want to treat this as an experiment. If in a couple of months from now you are still feeling lonely or neglected you can try other solutions.

Sarah: Okay.

Therapist: When do you think would be a good time to evaluate the effectiveness of your solution?

Mark: Maybe we could do an evaluation after our first date night and just see how it goes. After that we could check in every month or so to make sure Sarah feels happy with the arrangement.

Therapist: Does that sound good to you, Sarah?

Sarah: Yes, I think so.

Therapist: Good. You guys did a great job problem solving today. Do you know what to do if you can't decide on a solution?

Sarah: No, not really. I think that's a problem of our's.

Therapist: If you find yourselves in a situation where you just can't come to an agreement, it is helpful to change your focus from "how can I get what I want" to "how can we both get what we want."

Mark: You're talking about compromise.

Therapist: Exactly. Compromise is about finding a way for both people to win. It also sometimes means giving up something in the process. Mark compromised earlier when he suggested having the dinner party. Sarah also compromised when she agreed to do this rather than expect to be included when Mark does things with his friends. You both didn't get exactly what you wanted, but you came to a solution that you could both live with. That is the art of compromise.

Sarah: Oh, I see.

Therapist: I actually noticed a few other instances where you both have compromised. You are actually really good at it.

Mark: I've had to take some trainings on compromise for work, so I'm very familiar with it.

Therapist: So I guess it's just a matter of implementing it into your regular life with Sarah. What other problems in your relationship haven't been addressed yet?

Sarah: We also have some financial disagreements. I want to put away more savings so that we can buy our own house, but Mark disagrees.

Therapist: Mark, are there any problems in the relationship that you've experienced that haven't been addressed yet?

Mark: I feel like we don't have sex often enough. That is one problem that hasn't been addressed at all yet.

Therapist: Yes, I remember that you had put that on your list for your ideal relationship. Do you think that you could work on these two problems this following week during your couple's meetings?

Sarah: We could give it a try.

Therapist: I'm sure you'll see that so long as you follow the steps there really isn't anything too difficult about it. You guys are actually really good at this and I'm sure I'll get a good report about it next week.

Mark: Okay, we'll see you then.

Therapist: Take care.

Compare this session with the first and second session and it's easy to spot the progress. Neither one of them raised their voices, interrupted, or was disrespectful. Furthermore there is also some evidence that the couple is starting to internalize the communication skills they've learned in counseling. Several times during today's session the couple validated and expressed empathy for the other person almost absent-mindedly, as if it was the natural thing to do. This is a very good sign.

As a therapist, it always feels good to see progress like this but you may also be wondering what else is there left to do with this couple? We're only halfway done but they are already showing tremendous progress and seem to have transformed as a couple. Traditionally, those are signs that it is time to terminate therapy. However, if you were to discontinue therapy at this point, we risk having the couple slowly slip back into their old ways. More permanent changes need to be made with this couple, including changing the way they think about relationships in general.

Fifth session outline: problem solving & compromise

Step 1: "What problems are you currently experiencing that haven't been addressed yet in couples counseling?"

Step 2: Help the couple to find the core "themes" in their arguments

- Trust vs Mistrust
- Appreciation, or Reality vs Expectations (example: division of labour)
- Respect vs Disrespect
- Unity vs Discord (example: meddling in-laws, kids, parenting disagreements)
- Closeness vs Distance
- Finances, or Short-term vs Long-term Security
- Sex, or My Needs vs Your Needs

Step 3: Teach the couple how to problem solve

1. Define the problem
2. Finding common ground; what do you both agree with?
3. Each person proposes several different solutions (3 is a good number)
4. Weigh the pros and cons of each solution
5. Decide to try one or two solutions as an "experiment"
6. Review the effectiveness of the solution

Step 4: Teach the couple how to compromise

Step 5: Assign Homework

- Continue to solve problems and compromise during couple's meetings

Chapter 7

Sixth Session: Bringing Up the Past (in a Good Way!)

There's a park near my home where couples often enjoy going for walks. I love going for walks at this park and observing the couples. It is easy to identify the couples that are new in the relationship. Couples that have been together for many years often don't hold hands anymore and rarely talk to each other. They just walk the familiar paths and enjoy the scenery in silence. Couples that are new in the relationship talk almost constantly, smile, and laugh with one another. They seem so interested in what the other has to say and demonstrate excellent communication and listening skills. They often take a seat at a bench and cuddle. It is truly a beautiful sight to behold. The early years of a relationship are grand.

I don't believe that we are doomed to eventually become the couple that has stopped listening to one another or that it's not reversible once it gets to that point. I actually believe that if a relationship was once good, it has the ability to be that way again. They've proven that they have the ability to have a mutually satisfying relationship, they just need some direction to bring it to that point again. In John Gottman's book "The Seven Principles for Making Marriage Work", he asserts that one of the best things a couple can do is talk about their early years together to help unearth those positive feelings they felt for each other at the beginning of their relationship.

So far in counseling, the couple has been focusing on the negative aspects of their relationship and you have been helping them to decrease those negatives. Hopefully the couple has made some progress in doing that and has been experiencing some relief. There is however, something missing. Just making a relationship tolerable isn't the purpose of counseling. As therapists, we want to help the couple restore the relationship back to when it was at its best, which was most likely during the early years of the relationship. To do this, we are going to need to take a break from focusing on the negatives and instead focus on when the relationship was at its most positive.

Step 1: Ask the couple how they met

If the couple has already mentioned to you how they had met, ask again. It's interesting to hear how the story changes in later sessions compared to the beginning stages of therapy. When people are in a bad phase of their relationship, the story of how they met may take on a more negative twist. The couple will tend to selectively remember the bad aspects. Now that the couple is in a better place, the story should take on a more charming and romantic tone. I love hearing the stories of how two people met and fell in love. I especially love observing the reactions of the couple while they tell it. There is often a lot of laughing, smiling, and playful touches. In a lot of ways, they begin to resemble the newly in-love couples at the park.

After the couple has told the story of how they met, I follow up by asking each of them, what made this person so special? We meet thousands of people during the course of our lives, what made this person different? What made you fall in love with the other person? Try to pinpoint that moment that they fell in love. By doing so, you remind them why they are together and why they should continue trying to work on this relationship. Remind the couple why it's not so easy to just split up and find someone more compatible.

For most couples, their best years together were in the beginning of the relationship, during the courtship phase. If the couple you are working with has children, ask them to describe their relationship in the beginning, before the children were born. Most couples take great delight in talking about their early years together. While they are describing their early years together, listen for elements such as they spent more time together having fun, they put each other first, they really listened to one another, they were open to receiving feedback from the other person and allowed the other person to influence them, and make a mental note of these elements. They will be important later in the session.

Step 2: Specifically, how were things different then from now?

Now I want you to help the couple make a comparison of their life back then to how it is now. If you ask the couple "how was your relationship different back then to how it is now?", the couple will probably say something vague like "We were just happier back then. We had less responsibilities and had more freedom." You don't want to let them off the hook that easily. Remember when you had the couple create a list for their ideal relationship and then you helped them turn the items on their lists into behavioral terms? You want to do that sort of thing again.

Being specific and defining things behaviorally helps the couple turn a vague memory into a road map for change. It makes it easier for them to identify the elements and behaviors of those early years together that made them the best years of their lives. If the couple is still confused about what you are looking for, you can say something like "Earlier, when you were describing your life together before the kids were born you mentioned that you would make sure to go out at least once a week. Can you give me more examples like that of how your life together was different back then?" Usually giving an example or two is enough to get the ball going.

Ask the couple, "how were things better then?" Again, you are looking for specific behaviors. In a lot of ways, this exercise is similar to the one you did in the second session, when the client generated a list describing their ideal relationship. Their early years together may not be describing an ideal relationship by any means, but it is describing their relationship back when it was at its very best. Although it's a worthy task to strive for an ideal relationship, and I myself continually strive for this in my own life, the ideal is not always possible to obtain. The early years, however, we do know is possible. Unlike the ideal relationship, the couple has already achieved a good relationship together. The early years are proof that the couple has it in them and can achieve this again if they can identify the necessary ingredients for recreating it. That is what we are trying to accomplish in this session.

We don't want to focus on the past to the point where all the progress that has been made in therapy or through "living life's lessons" is ignored. That's why I follow up with a second question "how are things better now?" Again, we want specifics. Perhaps the couple is better at solving problems now. Maybe they are better off financially now that they have had time to advance in their careers.

After so many years of being together, maybe the couple has a better understanding of one another than they did in the beginning of the relationship. Have they overcome a lot of struggles together? If they have, remind them of this and point out that makes them a stronger couple than couples that are just starting out. If they have children together, it is often wonderful to prompt the couple to discuss what a good parent their partner is.

You have now spent some time talking to the couple about both the good and bad of their early years together and at present. If we could combine the positive things from the beginning of the relationship with the positive things the couple is doing now, we might still not have achieved the ideal relationship, but we'd be pretty close. The beauty of this exercise is that it does not require the couple to learn any new behaviors. These are all things that the couple is either doing now or have done in the past.

Step 3: How can romantic elements from the beginning of the relationship be incorporated into the current relationship?

During the courtship phase of the relationship we take pains to nurture the relationship and impress our date. We cook special meals for our partner, hurry home from work to have optimal amounts of time to spend together, clean up the home extra good if they are coming over, laugh at all their jokes, and support their dreams. We go the extra mile, sometimes to ridiculous heights. Although these things are a nice treat every now and then, most people don't expect their spouse to be a "Stepford wife." Part of having a mature relationship together is also not expecting your partner to spend as much money on you as they did in the beginning. We're not looking to incorporate the over-the-top things the couple did to try to impress one another, but the small positive caring behaviors they did in the beginning. Unlike lavish gifts and expensive vacations, It's the little things we do for each other that shows we care.

Although romantic getaways and ironing your husband's socks are lovely gestures, unless you win the lottery you can't do those things on a daily basis. You should still try to squeeze in those really special things every now and again, but what about the little things? In the beginning of the relationship, the couple didn't just go out to fancy dinners and shows, they also did little things every day to show each other that they cared. Some examples of those things are turning on the coffee maker in the morning for your spouse, picking up their favorite snacks when you go to the grocery store, going for long walks and holding hands, greeting them at the door when they came home from work, surprising them by doing one of the chores off their list, making their favorite meal, asking about their day and really listening, taking an interest in their interests, telling them that they look attractive and meaning it, showing appreciation, saying "I love you" often, and many more.

Getting couples to incorporate caring behaviors into their daily lives is not a new strategy in couples counseling. In 1980, Richard Stuart wrote a book called "Helping Couples Change." In the book he describes a technique called "caring days." He instructs the couple to each make a list of about twenty small caring behaviors they would like for their partner to do and to then have their partner do five of these caring behaviors each day. In 1988, Harville Hendrix published a book called "Getting the Love You Want" which advises couples to make a similar list of caring behaviors they would like their partners to do and then have those partners do about three caring behaviors a day. Instituting caring behaviors in this manner has been found to be helpful in the research (LeCroy, 1989) as well.

If you would like, you may have your couple do a similar exercise where they write down a list of little caring behaviors and then prescribe that they do these caring behaviors for one another on a daily basis. I have found with the couples that I work with that although they are happy to create these lists in session, there's something about writing these things down on a list that takes away the whole "caring" element from it. Isn't the whole idea of caring that you are putting thought into your behaviors? There seems to be very little thought into reading something off of a list. I have also found that over time people became bored with doing the same list of caring behaviors over and over again. Making a list is easy and effective in the short term, but in the long term it fails.

So instead of having my clients make lists (although you are free to try it if you like), I simply ask them "What are the things you do currently to show your partner that you care?" Sometimes people can be very surprised by this when they realize just how many things their partner puts a conscious effort into to show that they care. It can be a very enlightening experience. I then ask each person, "What were the little things your partner did back in your early years together that they don't do now that made you feel loved? What were the little everyday things that showed you they cared that you wished they would do again?" This can be very enlightening for people in relationships. There are many things that will come up that the person thought didn't matter to their partner anymore. It will get them thinking and bring more into conscious awareness how they can better please their partner. Lastly, I ask each of them "Based on what your partner has said, what caring behaviors are you willing to start doing again?"

This isn't to say that the caring behaviors they are currently doing should be replaced completely by old ones. Rather, we want to meld the two together as much as possible. If the couple has other ideas of how romantic elements from the past can be incorporated into the present relationship, listen to your clients. My clients have often come up with excellent ideas that I would have never thought up on my own. Those ideas may not work for other couples, but if it'll work for this couple, encourage them to use their own ideas. Remember, they're really the experts when it comes to their own relationship.

What I believe makes this exercise better than making a list is that it encourages the couple to better voice their desires and listen to each other. This exercise also encourages the couple to be on the lookout for things that would please their spouse, rather than just relying on a list posted on the refrigerator. It inspires more communication, more listening, more thought, and more awareness about their relationship. Communication, listening, thoughtfulness, and awareness also happen to be among the essential elements of a successful relationship.

Step 4: Assign homework

If you guessed that the homework assignment is to incorporate more caring behaviors, you are right! But there is a twist. The couple is also to keep a record of the daily caring behaviors that their partner does for them. They will then bring their record to the next appointment and read it outloud during the therapy session. They are not to show eachother their records until after the session. The purpose of this homework assignment is not only to hold them accountable to start implementing caring behaviors, but also to get them in the habit of noticing the little things they do for eachother and appreciating it.

Sixth session vignette

Therapist: How have you been this past week?

Sarah: We've had a good week.

Therapist: Did you get a chance to practice solving problems and compromising during your couple's meetings?

Mark: We found a way to compromise on our vacation plans. Sarah brought up a third option that suited both our needs. It was great.

Sarah: I think we're doing a lot better.

Therapist: That's great to hear. You two have made a lot of progress.

Sarah: Thank you.

Mark: Things have gotten a lot better and I wanted to thank you for the excellent work you have been doing these past few weeks. It has really made a difference in our relationship.

Therapist: Thank you, Mark. I appreciate that, but you two have been doing a lot of hard work also.

Mark: Well, I don't think we could have done it without you.

Sarah: Absolutely.

Therapist: Well, it's good that you two are doing so well right now. But I was thinking, you never told me how you both met.

Mark: We met at a bookstore.

Therapist: Tell me more about that.

Mark: Well, we were both browsing in the science fiction section of the store and I noticed that she was looking at a book by one of my favorite authors and I couldn't help myself, I just had to tell her about what a good author he was. So we got talking some more and then we decided to go have some coffee at a nearby cafe. It's usually not my style, but it's hard to find a woman that attractive who's also into science fiction.

Sarah: It's also not like me to go get coffee with some stranger.

Usually friends would set me up on dates, but Mark was different.

Therapist: What made Mark different from the other guys you had dated?

Sarah: He was just so passionate. I loved the enthusiasm he showed for things. There was an energy to him that I wish I possessed.

Therapist: So, being with Mark completed you?

Sarah: Yes. That's exactly it. I felt like a whole person when I was with Mark.

Therapist: Mark, what made you fall in love with Sarah?

Mark: Like I said, Sarah is a very beautiful woman, so I think that helped. But also, I fell in love with her gentleness, her kind loving nature. Sarah is truly a good person. I also admire her patience, something which I lack.

Therapist: Could you describe your early years together?

Sarah: We used to have so much fun. Sometimes we would just go out for long drives and talk for hours. I loved doing that.

Mark: Sarah used to laugh at all my jokes and I felt very charming when I was around her. I always felt a little awkward around women, but not with Sarah.

Sarah: Moving in together was nice too. Remember how you used to make pancakes almost every morning?

Mark: Mmhm

Sarah: Mark used to make these nice breakfasts every morning and then we'd go for a run to burn off the extra calories.

Therapist: It sounds like the memories you share of your early years together are something that you both really cherish. When you compare your relationship back then to how it is now, how were things better then?

Sarah: .I think we put more thought into how we treated each other. We were more careful about each other's feelings.

Mark: We definitely put in more effort.

Sarah: We did more for each other.

Therapist: Couples often mention to me that they were more careful about each other's feelings in the beginning of relationships and that they did more to try to make the other person feel special.

Sarah: Yes, exactly. We cherished each other's company more. Now we take it for granted.

Therapist: Well, I don't see why you can't start cherishing each other again. I don't think it's inevitable that we come to take each other for granted. If you want, you can take the things you liked about the past and start doing those things again. Of course, there's good and bad in everything, so it would be wrong to glorify the past. In what ways are things better now?

Sarah: Hmm...

Mark: I think we've grown more as individuals and as a couple.

Therapist: Tell me more about that.

Mark: For one thing, we communicate better now.

Sarah: We're not as broke as we were back then either.

Mark: We've created a comfortable life for ourselves where we are able to pay our bills and go on nice vacations.

Sarah: We definitely have the means to do more fun things if we want to. The strange thing is that we did more back then even though we have more money now.

Mark: Well, to be honest, I've been meaning to have more fun with you.

Therapist: So there were good things in the past and some good things in the present. If we could combine the two together, you would have the type of relationship people are envious of.

Mark: How do you suggest that we combine the two?

Therapist: What are things you enjoyed in the past that you would like to enjoy again? What are elements from the beginning of the relationship that you could incorporate into the present?

Sarah: I miss going on dates.

Mark: We could start doing that again.

Sarah: I want us to hold hands and kiss in public.

Mark: Okay. We could do that.

Therapist: What are some of the little things you do for each other to show that you care?

Sarah: Mark likes a tidy home, so I've started cleaning more often for him.

Mark: It's generally Sarah's job to cook, but I take over for her sometimes because I know that she likes that. I've also been saying "I love you" more often.

Sarah: I take really good care of Mark when he's sick. I make sure he's comfortable so he'll get better sooner.

Mark: That's true. Sarah is really good about taking care of me when I'm sick.

Therapist: Mark, what are some caring behaviors that Sarah did in the beginning of the relationship that you would like her to do again?

Mark: Sarah used to do crazy stuff like iron my bed sheets and cut the crust off my sandwiches. I don't need her to do stuff like that again, but Sarah used to do a lot of things that showed me that she was thinking of me like email me a link to an article she read online, rent comedies that she thought I'd like, things like that.

Therapist: Those sound really nice. Was there anything else Sarah did that made you feel loved?

Mark: She was definitely more affectionate. She would touch me a lot. Sarah would give me a lot of compliments, which I loved. We'd have long discussions about the books we were reading.

Therapist: Thank you, Mark. Those were great. Sarah, what

are some caring behaviors that Mark did in the beginning of the relationship that you would like him to do again?

Sarah: Mark used to buy me little gifts. I miss that. It may sound petty, but I like getting gifts every now and then. He used to tell me I was beautiful and take me places where I could have an excuse to dress nice. Mark used to give me a lot of back massages which I really enjoyed. Mark used to let me pick out where we would go for our dates and not complain if it was a place he didn't like. He would make me a mixed CD of music he thought I would like. We were affectionate in public. We would act silly, like sit on the swings together in the park.

Therapist: Those sounded great, Sarah. I can see why you fell in love with Mark. Do you think you guys could start doing those things again in addition to the other progress you have made?

Mark: Yes, I think so.

Sarah: It'll be fun to do those things again. I'm looking forward to it.

Therapist: Something I would like for you guys to do is to keep a daily log of the caring behaviors you notice your partner doing for you. Write them down in a notebook or on a piece of paper and bring them in with you next time. In the meantime, you can't look at each other's logs, okay?

Sarah: Sure.

Mark: Not a problem.

Therapist: Great! I'll see you guys next week.

Surprised to see Mark go from threatening to fire the therapist to thanking the therapist for excellent work? It's really not that unusual to see this much of a change in couples counseling. People tend to start counseling feeling skeptical of the process and against anything that involves owning up to their flaws and making changes, but once they experience how life changing it can be, they become believers. It seems that Mark and Sarah are now therapeutically aligned with the therapist, meaning the rest of the counseling process should continue without conflict.

It seems that this couple had already started to implement some caring behaviors without prompting. Some couples intuitively want to start putting more effort into pleasing one another once things start going better in the relationship. However, there is always more that we can do. Anytime you can encourage a couple to talk more with each other about their needs and how they can be fulfilled, that is a good thing. Often couples just expect that the other person should just know what they want and what they are thinking and that they shouldn't have to tell them. These kinds of expectations hinder progress, but we'll be talking more about expectations in the next chapter.

When things don't go as planned

Every now and then you will encounter a couple whose relationship was never good, they met under horrible circumstances, but for some reason fate kept them together. Although these couples are rare, you should still be prepared for how to handle them because there is nothing worse than having an entire session planned around bringing back the romance from the early years and you discover that the early years were nothing you would want to repeat again. Before you start to panic, have this alternate session planned in case you find yourself with one of these couples.

Step 1: Ask the couple how they met. This session is going to be similar to the original session planned. You are still going to ask the couple to tell the story of how they met. In some cases, the story of how they met may still be semi-romantic. If it is, cherish that memory with the couple. The story of how they met may be sweet, but maybe what happened afterwards isn't. However, not all the stories you hear are sweet and romantic. Some relationships form almost on impulse. For example, they met each other online and then quickly moved across the country to be together, the relationship starts out as a one-night stand but then she gets pregnant, or they met while still married and use the affair as an excuse to leave an unsatisfactory relationship. Since relationships like these don't have a "courtship phase", you cannot draw upon the early years of the relationship for inspiration.

You do not need me to tell you that it is not good to start a relationship this way, but some relationships do, and some of them end up in couples counseling. I think that in these cases it is important to reserve judgement. Most of these clients are ashamed of how their relationships began and had plenty of people in their lives tell them that they were crazy for doing it. It is not our role as therapists to put down these clients or scold them. What's done is done. We can only help them move forward. These couples deserve just as much of our help as the couples that met in more traditional ways. Furthermore, I have witnessed many of them flourish into great couples by the end of therapy.

Continue to ask the couple some questions about the beginning stages of the relationship. If they met under unusual circumstances, why did they choose to remain in the relationship? What was their life like at the time that made these circumstances desirable? What was the hope they had for the relationship back then? There must have been some force driving them. Perhaps that has changed over time, but it is still important to understand the reasoning at the time for being in such a relationship.

Once you have an understanding of how they met and why they chose to continue the relationship, ask the couple to describe their early years together. For those couples that met by traditional means but their relationship quickly deteriorated, this is where you will deviate from following the sixth session outline to following this alternative session outline. For those that met under unfortunate circumstances, the odds are very high that the relationship continued to suffer. Remember when we discussed "harsh start-ups" earlier? A relationship that deteriorates almost immediately or one that begins under unfortunate circumstances is the ultimate harsh start-up, and like how a conversation that starts negatively is likely to continue negatively, the same is true for these relationships.

It is common in these situations for the couple to say something like "actually, these past few weeks in therapy have been the happiest time in our relationship." Obviously when a couple says that, you can't then say "how can we incorporate those positive things from the beginning of the relationship into your current relationship?" Although there probably was something positive about the relationship back then, searching for those few positive elements and bringing them into the current relationship would have a very small impact on the couple. With only ten or twelve sessions available to us, we only want to use techniques that will have a big impact.

Step 2: How has this "rough start" affected your relationship? Beginning a long term relationship negatively has a lasting effect on a couple. Often the couple had no idea what they were getting into, but the dream or fantasy of the relationship compelled them to take these risks. When the couple discovers that the dream was a lie or a delusion, they feel cheated. Instead of taking a look at their contribution to the problem, they blame their partner for not living up to the fantasy. Clients often report feeling trapped, pressured, or manipulated by their partner into the relationship. If one or both partners are feeling resentful towards the other for the relationship, it is important to remind them again of the motives they discussed earlier. Remind them that it was their own decision to remain in this relationship.

It's important to let the couple vent any resentments they may be feeling. This is also another opportunity to practice having a couple's dialogue so the partner can help validate those feelings and process them. If a relationship has baggage, the only way to get rid of it is to unpack it. Of course, no one likes unpacking baggage, but it is the only way to truly get rid of it. Venting and having a good cry can do a lot for helping a couple move past those lingering feelings of resentment. We'll deal more with resentment and forgiveness in the ninth session. For now we are just planting seeds.

If the couple is able to put any kind of positive spin on the way this rough start has affected the relationship, give the couple positive reinforcement. With some thought, most things can be positively reframed. What new opportunities were discovered thanks to this relationship? Did they learn anything from this experience? Have they become less judgemental towards other couples? If any dreams were realized in this relationship (such as becoming a parent), emphasize those achievements.

Step 3: Implement caring behaviors. Unfortunately, this couple never got to have a courtship phase, or if they did, it did not last very long. Fortunately, it's not too late. Having a courtship phase is very important to a relationship. It sets a foundation that the couple can look back upon and remember in tough times. You can start the conversation by asking the couple what they think courtship means. It is entirely possible that they have never experienced courtship and that you will have to teach them what it means to court someone.

Discuss with the couple the caring behaviors that are typically seen during courtship and ask them how they would feel about doing these same behaviors. Ask them if they would be willing to go on dates with one another and basically "start over." Completely starting over in the relationship won't be possible if the couple already lives together or has children together. If their lives are too entrenched to truly start over, they can still go through many of the same motions that beginner couples go through such as going on regular dates, paying extra attention to one another, and being on their best behavior.

Now that you have described examples of some of the caring behaviors that are typically seen during the courtship phase, have each partner take turns naming several caring behaviors they would like their partner to implement. Then, just like for the regular session, ask the couple to repeat what caring behaviors they would be willing to do on a daily basis for their partner. The couple now has an idea of what the courtship phase in a relationship looks like and how to implement it in a way that would please their partner.

Step 4: Assign homework. The homework assignment for the alternate session is the same as the regular session. In addition to continuing their couple's meetings, the couple is now asked to keep a daily log of their partner's caring behaviors or other things they did during the week that pleased them. Again, this is not only to hold the couple accountable to actually do the assignment but to get them in the habit of noticing all the caring things their partner does for them.

Alternate session vignette. Although we have been using Mark and Sarah for all of our sessions thus far, for our alternate session vignette I thought it would be wise to use a different couple in order to avoid confusion. Our imaginary couple for this vignette is Steve and Julie. Steve and Julie have attended appointments every week and have made a lot of progress since learning some new communication skills. However, the therapist is about to learn that they are not your standard couple. Rather than panicking, the therapist is able to address the harsh start-up of their relationship and also teach the couple to start implementing caring behaviors, which was the original intent of the session.

Therapist: How have you been this past week?

Steve: We've been doing really well. Learning to problem solve has really helped us in parenting our son.

Julie: Yes, parenting as a team has made things so much easier. I think our son likes this new approach better too. The other day he came up to me and said he was happy that we don't argue anymore.

Steve: Yeah, things have definitely improved.

Therapist: It sounds like you guys have had a lot of success in applying the problem solving skills to real life and parenting as a team. It's not the easiest thing to do at first, but it's so worth it in the end, right?

Julie: Definitely

Therapist: So, I don't believe you two have ever told me about how you both met.

Steve: Julie doesn't like to tell people about it, so. . .

Julie: No, it's okay. I'll talk about it.

Steve: If talking about it is fine with you, it's fine with me, but. . .

Therapist: It would be helpful for me to know about your past, but if you're uncomfortable-

Julie: No, it's fine. I guess I'll start. When me and Steve met I was married. My husband and I were having some problems. We had basically stopped having sex, and one of my girlfriends who was in a similar situation as me suggested that we both go on a "girls' vacation" and find some guys to have a fling with. Going into this, my intention was just to have some fun and then return back to my marriage feeling recharged. So my friend and I went on a cruise and that's where I met Steve. He was flirting with me and I really liked it because my husband had stopped saying nice things like that to me. We hooked-up several times during the cruise. It was amazing. Here was someone that I had amazing chemistry with. But my intentions were still to go back to my husband and resume married life. At the end of the cruise, I revealed to Steve that I was a married woman so this relationship wasn't going to go anywhere.

Steve: I gave her my phone number anyways in case she ever found herself in Boston and wanted to hook up again. Like she said, we had amazing chemistry together.

Julie: Six weeks after the cruise I realized I was pregnant. I knew it was Steve's baby because I hadn't had sex with my husband in months. When I told my husband he threatened to throw me out of the house, so I called Steve.

Steve: I felt really bad when I found out that I got Julie pregnant and now she was being thrown out of the house. She told me she was planning on keeping the baby and I didn't know what to do other than to buy her a plane ticket to Boston.

Julie: There was nothing for me in Indiana, so I moved in with Steve and he took care of me and the baby. And that's how we met.

Therapist: Tell me about your early years together.

Steve: They were rough.

Julie: Steve had been a bachelor for a long time and I don't think he was used to having to share his space with someone else.

Steve: I think I had a harder time transitioning to having an instant wife and child. Believe me, people told me I was crazy and my family begged me not to have her move in and marry her so soon, but what was I supposed to do? She was having my baby. I was going to have to support her and the baby even if she stayed in Indiana, so why not bring her here where I would get to see the baby?

Therapist: It sounds like it made sense at the time.

Julie: It made sense at the time, but looking back I don't think it was a good idea to suddenly move in with and marry three months later someone you only knew on a cruise ship.

Steve: We fought a lot.

Therapist: Was there ever a time in your relationship when things were really good?

Julie: I would say that the past few weeks we've been in counseling have been the best time of our relationship. We pretty much fought constantly prior to seeing you.

Therapist: It sounds like your relationship had a rough start. Do you think this has had a lasting influence on your relationship?

Julie: I think so. I don't think Steve was ready to be a dad. Sometimes Steve accuses me of getting pregnant on purpose.

Steve: I know, and I'm going to stop saying that, Julie. But it's true. Sometimes I feel like I was trapped into this marriage. I loved my bachelor days and sometimes I miss them.

Julie: Sometimes I miss those days too but you were thirty two years old, it was time to settle down.

Steve: Yes, I had passed the "age requirement" to become a husband and father, but I never expected things to happen so quickly.

Therapist: I'm sure Julie wasn't happy about things either. Do you think that sometimes you feel some resentment towards each other for the way things started?

Julie: Yes, I think so, but I'm feeling it less and less as the relationship improves.

Steve: I feel the same way. I'm not as angry anymore.

Therapist: It sounds like although the way you both met wasn't ideal, there must have been some force that kept you both together.

Julie: I think that force is our son, Aiden. Whenever I feel like giving up, I see how much he loves his daddy and how sad he would be if Steve left.

Steve: Yes, Aiden is the wonderful thing that came out of this. I would lay down my life for him, and I really mean that.

Therapist: What other good things have happened because of this relationship?

Julie: Well, before I met Steve I didn't have a career or any real aspirations, but it was Steve who really pushed me into going to nursing school. I really love my career and feel proud when I tell people I am an RN.

Steve: Although there were a lot of good things about being a bachelor, I knew I had to settle down eventually. It's nice having someone there to support you when you're going through a tough time and celebrate with you when you succeed.

Therapist: It sounds like a lot of dreams have been realized in this relationship.

Julie: Yes, I think so.

Steve: Yeah, now that I think about it, I guess there have.

Therapist: I was wondering, what are your thoughts on courtship?

Steve: It's like when you first meet someone and you are trying to get them to go out with you, right?

Julie: You try to impress each other and act very loving to try to get them to fall in love with you.

Therapist: It sounds like maybe you never had a courtship phase.

Steve: No, I guess we didn't.

Therapist: I bring it up because I feel like courtship is important for relationships.

Julie: I guess it's too late now.

Therapist: No, it's not too late. Although you can't start over in your relationship, you can still act like the young couples you see. When people are new in relationships, specifically, what kind of things do they do?

Steve: They go on lots of dates together.

Julie: The boyfriend buys little gifts for his girlfriend and she also does nice little things for him.

Therapist: Tell me more about the nice little things that people do for each other early on in relationships.

Julie: Oh you know, buy each other gifts, hold hands, give each other back rubs, make breakfast, she irons his work shirts... that sort of thing.

Therapist: So, they do little things that show each other they care?

Julie: Yeah.

Therapist: Do you guys think you could implement those caring behaviors into your relationship?

Steve: Going out on lots of dates is going to be hard since we have a kid, I think at most we could only go out once a week.

Therapist: I think having a date night once a week sounds

great. But I was actually also wondering about the small daily things you could do to show Julie that you care.

Steve: Gee, it's hard to think up stuff on the spot.

Therapist: That's okay, maybe Julie could give you some ideas.

Julie: Well, I would like it if Steve bought me flowers every once in awhile. It doesn't have to be expensive. Just a bouquet from the grocery store. I would also like it if he would take my coat off of me like you see gentlemen do. I also would like him to say "I love you" more and cook dinner occasionally.

Therapist: What else?

Julie: I'd like him to take me on one of those "date nights" and put money towards a family vacation. He knows I like it when he plays with my hair, and I would like it if he did that more often. Maybe a small present every now and then.

Therapist: Those were really great ideas, Julie. Steve, would you name some caring behaviors you would like to see from Julie?

Steve: I know it's my job to take out the trash, but I would really like it if she would take it out every now and then instead of getting mad at me for forgetting. I'd like it if she would put a little more effort into dinner and make some of my favorite meals. I'd like it if we could fool around more. I miss how she would laugh at my jokes even though I knew she didn't think they were funny. I would like it if she would express more appreciation, or if after I go to the gym she would tell me I looked sexy. That thing she said earlier about ironing work shirts sounded great too.

Therapist: That was great, Steve. Thank you. Do you feel like you both have a better idea of the little things you can do to show each other that you care?

Julie: Yes, I think so.

Steve: Sure.

Therapist: Steve, what are some things Julie didn't mention that you think you could do that would make her feel like you care?

Steve: Julie likes to get presents, so I think I could get her a small gift every now and then. I think I could also offer to stay home with our son so that she can get out and have some alone time.

Therapist: Julie, what are some caring behaviors that you think Steve would enjoy?

Julie: I can think of plenty but they're a little X-rated

Steve: ::laughs::

Therapist: X-rated is fine with me. So long as it shows Steve you care.

Julie: Oh he'll definitely know I care!

Therapist: You guys were able to think up a lot of great caring behaviors. Do you think you could start implementing them? Just a few each day? Along with trying to court each other?

Steve: I think we could do that.

Julie: I'm looking forward to it.

Therapist: Great! For homework I'd also like you to each keep a daily log of the caring behaviors you notice the other person do for you each day.

Julie: Okay.

Therapist: But you can't show each other the log until our next appointment.

Steve: Okay.

Therapist: I'll see you next week. Enjoy your weekend!

Despite not expecting the couple to tell the therapist that they had started their relationship under such dramatic circumstances, the therapist was able to help the couple see some positives about the situation and still be able to help the couple implement caring behaviors into their daily routine. Although unexpected, by preparing an alternative session plan just in case, this therapist was able to stay on track.

It may seem unlikely that you will ever encounter a couple like this, it seems more like something from a soap opera than real life.

However, in this business we are dealing with extremes. We are not in the business of dealing with so-called "normal couples." I often encounter what can only be described as "worst case scenarios" in our line of work. It is important to become comfortable with working with couples with an alternative lifestyle and be prepared to help them. Too often the people they trust have told them "It will never work out. You're crazy." Don't be another one of those people.

Sixth session outline: bringing up the past

Step 1: Ask the couple how they met

- What made them fall in love with the other person?
- Ask the couple to describe their early years together

Step 2: Specifically, how were things different then from now?

- How were things better then?
- How are things better now?

Step 3: How can romantic elements from the beginning of the relationship be incorporated into the current relationship?

- What are the things you do currently to show your partner that you care?
- What were the little things your partner did back then that made you feel loved?
- What caring behaviors can you start doing again?

Step 4: Assign homework

- Partners keep a log of daily caring behaviors

Alternate sixth session

Step 1: Ask the couple how they met

- If they met under unusual circumstances, why did they choose to remain in the relationship?
- What was their life like at the time that made these circumstances desirable?
- What was the hope they had for the relationship back then?
- Ask the couple to describe their early years together

Step 2: How has this "rough start" affected your relationship?

- Allow the couple to vent if necessary
- Positively reframe if possible

Step 3: Implement caring behaviors

- Teach the couple about the courtship phase of relationships
- Couple describes caring behaviors they would like their partner to implement

Step 4: Assign homework

- Partners keep a log of daily caring behaviors

Chapter 8

Seventh Session: Rational Emotive Behavior Therapy

You may be wondering when we are going to examine the client's childhood influences. Many psychologists have asserted the importance of exploring childhood influences in couples counseling. When I was starting out in couples counseling, I experimented with helping couples gain insight about their childhood and its effect on the current relationship. As a therapist, I love doing things like that, but I wondered, is this actually helping the client or are we just gaining insight for the sake of insight? I realized that the more sessions we had where the client did not improve, the more likely they are to drop out of therapy prematurely. So although it was interesting for me, the therapist, should a session devoted to childhood influences be part of my ten sessions?

Let me give you an example. One of my early couples counseling clients would react to her husband's behaviors in a completely overblown manner. Her angry outbursts caused significant distress in the relationship and so they came to see me to deal with the issue. I asked the client how her mother handled anger when she was angry at her father. Tears flooded out of my client's eyes as she described word for word the way that both she and her mother reacted to their husbands. She said that although she had never realized it before now, she was reenacting, almost to the T, the dysfunctional behaviors she witnessed her mother commit. What insight! I left that session feeling like a brilliant therapist, but the couple never came back for another appointment. I was left wondering what went wrong.

I realize now that although I found the session very satisfying, the couple benefited nothing from it. Some clients can look at their childhood and come to the conclusion "It is irrational for me to reenact things I witnessed when I was eight years old. I am going to act in a mature manner from now on!" but others use the insight as an excuse to continue acting the way they do; "I can't help it. I grew up in a home where people acted this way." How many times have you heard people blame their adult behavior on events that happened when they were children? And if it is true that our childhood experiences doom us to behave in certain ways as adults, how come different people can react so differently to having had similar childhoods?

It is true that some clients like this approach to therapy and do benefit from exploring their childhood experiences with the therapist, but I have found that most clients do not respond well to it in a couples counseling format. When creating my therapeutic approach to couples counseling, I only wanted to use techniques that worked for most clients most of the time. However, if you feel that exploring childhood influences is useful, you are free to experiment with that approach. Perhaps you will have more success with it than I did.

Rational Emotive Behavior Therapy (REBT)

When I provide individual counseling, REBT is my method of choice. Although many therapeutic styles focus on childhood experiences, REBT isn't one of them. I have found it very effective in individual therapy, and was wondering if I could translate REBT into a couples counseling format. Upon closer examination, I have found that many of the principles of REBT work very well for couples counseling. Since Rational Emotive Behavior Therapy is not as well known as other therapies, I thought it would be a good idea to spend some time explaining the theory of REBT before showing you how to utilize it in couples counseling.

REBT is a form of Cognitive Behavior Therapy (CBT) that was created by American Psychologist Albert Ellis in the 1950s. Although REBT is a form of CBT, it actually predates CBT as CBT did not come into existence until the 1960s. Albert Ellis started out his career as a psychoanalyst but found the process of analysis and insight to be both frustratingly slow and ineffective for most clients. He felt there must be a better way to help people change their dysfunctional thoughts and behaviors, and so developed a new therapeutic approach based upon both modern and ancient philosophies. He especially agreed with the ancient philosopher Epictetus, who said "People are disturbed not by things but by the views they take of them!" It is from this that Ellis formed his core theory of REBT that it is not events that cause us to act or feel in certain ways, but our interpretation of these events (Ellis & MacLaren, 2005).

There are countless ways of interpreting events, and how we interpret them will determine how we feel about them. My graduate Professor, Michael Murtaugh, often used this example to explain the concept that it is not events that cause us to feel certain ways but our thoughts about them: Let's use an example of four male friends at the mall. They notice a beautiful woman sitting at the food court by herself and they decide that they will each ask her out and see who she says yes to. So the first friend approaches her and asks her out on a date and she says no. He thinks to himself "I hate women! They never give me a chance! One day she'll be sorry she rejected me!" Now, if someone thinks that way, they are going to feel angry. The second friend then walks up to the her and is also rejected. He thinks to himself, "It's because I'm such a loser. I'm so unattractive. Who would ever want to go out with someone like me anyway?" How do you think that he feels? Self-talk like that will probably make a person feel very sad. The third friend asks her out and is also rejected, but he thinks "Oh, she must already have a boyfriend." A person who thinks that way probably feels neutral about the event. And actually, that is probably the most rational or realistic way of viewing the event. She probably has a boyfriend or is just attracted to a different type of man. It has nothing to do with you as a person.

When you start to look at things more rationally, suddenly feelings of anger, anxiety, and depression go away. Just to show you how much influence our interpretation of events have on our resulting feelings, can you imagine what the fourth friend would have to think in order to actually feel good about the rejection? A lot of people have a hard time with this one since most people consider rejection to be a bad thing, but there is a way of thinking about it that will make a person feel happy about rejection. The fourth friend asks the woman out and she says no. He immediately thinks to himself "It's because I'm so good looking that she's intimidated by me" and thus feels good about himself and self confident from the rejection. So as you can see, the same event caused four different reactions depending upon how each person interpreted the event.

From his theory that thoughts cause feelings, Albert Ellis created what is known as the ABCs of Rational Emotive Behavior Therapy. The A stands for Activating Event. The B stands for Beliefs, or what you thought about the event. And C stands for Consequences, or how you felt or behaved in reaction to your beliefs about the event. When the Consequences are that we react in a dysfunctional or disturbed manner, it is because of an irrational belief. Irrational beliefs can generally be identified by their absolutist nature and are characterized by "always" ("Mark always disrespects me"), "musts" ("Sarah must let me go out with my friends whenever I want or she is the not the one' for me"), "have-to's" ("We have to enjoy our company together all the time or else this isn't the right relationship"), and "never" ("You never help with the housework!")

According to Albert Ellis, irrational beliefs tend to fall into twelve categories (Ellis, 1994):

1. The idea that it is a dire necessity for adults to be loved by significant others for almost everything they do. We see this irrational belief in many clients in couples counseling. They believe that if their partner doesn't love absolutely everything about them or if they don't love absolutely everything about their partner, then the relationship should be scraped and they should start over with someone new. This belief prevents people from being happy in relationships because they believe their partner has to be perfect, but perfection simply doesn't exist.

2. The idea that certain acts are awful or wicked and that the people who perform such acts should be severely damned. In other words, if you do a bad thing you are a bad person. It is important to distinguish between being a person who sometimes does a bad thing (all of us) and being a bad person. In order to be a bad person, someone would have to do bad things all the time. However, there is good and bad in all of us. None of us does anything "all the time" or "never." When a client in couples counseling complains "My husband never helps out with the housework", I respond by saying "Never?" I then ask "what's the evidence that he does sometimes help out?" The client is always able to think of something and retract their statement. Their feelings towards their husband then go from very angry to neutral. I then teach the client to replace that original irrational belief with "My husband could help out with the housework more." This is a less distressing, more realistic, belief that can lead to changes. Beliefs like "never" and "always" don't lead to changes. Neglecting to take out the trash does not make someone a bad person.

3. The idea that it is horrible when things are not the way we like them to be. Things can not always be exactly how we want them to be, and just because we want them to be a certain way does not mean that they should be that way or must be that way. Look at the way people react to politics. People into politics look at the other side and become angry and say "why are they always wrong but never see it?!" In reality, neither side is wrong or right. They just have different proposed solutions to the same problem. Some will benefit from the solution while others will not benefit. If you are one of the ones who will not benefit, you say that the solution is wrong or horrible, when in reality it is still a solution. This belief manifests itself in couples counseling when a couple argue about who is right or who is wrong. They do not understand that there is more than one solution to a problem.

4. The idea that human misery is invariably externally caused and is forced on us by outside people and events. As discussed earlier, events don't cause us to feel certain ways, our interpretations of those events do. We hear this in couples counseling when clients say "She made me so mad!" or "He really hurt my feelings!" Upon further examination, we discover that the spouse had no intention of hurting their partner's feelings, but were simply misinterpreted. One client described an event "that made her mad" to me: "He calls me at work and says for our New Years resolution I want us to keep the house clean more often' and this made me so angry because I already clean as much as I possibly can. It's him who makes the messes!" I responded, "What he said could have been interpreted as he wants to help clean more'. What made you think he was only talking about you?" The client came to realize that she often interpreted what her boyfriend said in a negative manner and that this is what was making her so angry. It was her beliefs, not her boyfriend's actions.

5. The idea that if something is or may be so dangerous or fearsome we should be terribly upset and endlessly obsess about it. This has to do with those who ruminate and worry about things endlessly. Chronic worriers believe that they must ruminate about some feared outcome endlessly. Some have even expressed a belief that if they don't worry about something, it will happen to spite them. The truth is, if a thought is causing distress and it isn't useful, the thought should be discarded. I have worked with clients in the past who worried constantly about their partner cheating on them. There is no way to prevent a person from cheating on you, and so the thought is not useful or helpful in any way. Obsessing about your partner being unfaithful only upsets you and your partner more. In this situation, we are better off facing our fears (giving our partner trust and personal freedom) or accepting the inevitable (that if they do cheat on us that it is unavoidable and we will have to start over again with someone new).

6. The idea that it is easier to avoid than to face life's difficulties and self-responsibilities. A lot of people have the mindset that if there are difficulties in the relationship, just end the relationship and keep trying until you find someone perfect. Although this seems easier at first, in the long run it is actually harder because the search for a perfect relationship is endless. It is actually easier to try to fix the relationship you already have then to try to find a new one that doesn't require any work.

7. The idea that we absolutely need something other or stronger or greater than ourself on which to rely. The truth is, it is better to act less dependently. I think this applies to people who believe that when you are in a relationship, you must do everything with your partner and they become dependent on their partner to fulfill all their needs. Their partner inevitably fails because it is impossible to fulfill all of a person's needs. It is better for the client to learn how to fulfill their own needs in ways that are less dependent on the relationship. This is also true for people who become dependent on their therapist to solve all of their problems instead of learning how to solve problems on their own.

8. The idea that we should be thoroughly competent, intelligent, and achieving in all possible respects. Just because you are not perfectly competent at something does not mean that you are a failure at it. We can only do the best we can in all things, and that includes relationships. Even a couple that has successfully completed couples counseling will still sometimes feels annoyance towards their partner and have the occasional argument. We each have our limitations as human beings. I have heard clients express the belief to me that they're not good at being someone's significant other and shouldn't be in relationships. Upon further exploration it is revealed that they actually are adequate at being in a relationship, but because they sometimes make mistakes they decided that they are completely not good. You do not have to be perfect to be in a good relationship.

9. The idea that because something once strongly affected our life, it should indefinitely affect it. We cannot use the past as an excuse for our present behaviors. Instead of blaming the past, we can learn from it. For instance, one might say "I act dysfunctional in relationships because my parents had a dysfunctional relationship and I witnessed them fighting a lot." Another person might say "I act rationally in relationships because my parents had a dysfunctional relationship and I witnessed them fighting a lot. I knew I didn't want to have a relationship like that, so I used my parents as a model of how not to act in a relationship. I learned from their mistakes." We continuously grow and change throughout our lives. Continuing to use an event from the past as justification for dysfunctional behavior is irrational and holds us back in life.

10. The idea that we must have certain and perfect control over things. People often come into counseling because they want to control or change the other person. They either expect me, the therapist, to somehow brainwash the other person into changing, or they want me to teach them how to perform "mind control" so they can do it themselves. Therapy doesn't work that way, and life doesn't work that way in general. We can only control ourselves, but we can still enjoy being in a relationship without having to control the other person.

11. The idea that human happiness can be achieved by inertia and inaction. As people, we tend to be happiest when we are actively working on something and obtaining personal growth, but according to this belief, we shouldn't have to work hard to find happiness. You may have heard the saying that "relationships take work." Realistically, we have to work towards anything that makes us happy, and relationships are no exception. This means making sacrifices and making changes in order to achieve a relationship that will truly make you happy.

12. The idea that we have virtually no control over our emotions and that we cannot help feeling disturbed about things. I'm sort of a "no excuses" person. It bothers me when I hear clients blame their inappropriate behaviors on their emotions; "I couldn't help acting like a jerk at the party! I was feeling so sad about what happened earlier!" I don't fall for it because people have a lot more control over their emotions than they want to admit. Clients can easily be taught how to change the way they feel about things. After they've been taught coping skills and how to regulate their emotions, the excuses are over.

REBT and couples counseling

It seems that many of the principles of REBT fit well in a couples counseling format: having the therapist take a more active-directive approach, teaching the couple skills, using role play and other behavioral techniques, and having a time-sensitive approach. These are all REBT principles that work well in couples counseling. Yes, people have also used psychoanalysis in couples counseling, but the problem with taking a psychoanalytic approach is that once you discover those child influences, what's next? REBT provides a clear procedure for dealing with irrational beliefs once you have identified them. In my experience as a couples counselor, I have identified a number of irrational beliefs that get in the way of making progress in couples counseling. Although they do not exactly fit the twelve that Albert Ellis discovered, they are similar. Here are my eight irrational beliefs found in couples:

1. "If the relationship is not perfect, it is not worth keeping." Instead, couples need to recognize that no relationship is perfect or ever will be perfect. The idea of a "soul mate" or "perfect love" does not exist.

2. "My partner must agree with me on everything." We each have our own minds and our own perspectives. It is impossible to find someone that will agree with you on everything. There is also no such thing as absolute truths or being right 100%.

3. "My partner can somehow read my mind, but chooses to act differently in order to intentionally annoy me." Many people feel that their partner can somehow read their mind or should know what they want after having been together for so many years. This is a fantasy. No one can fulfill your wishes unless you ask them too. It is also unlikely that our partners would intentionally seek to annoy us.

4. "Solutions that work for me personally must also work for us as a couple." By the time we reach adulthood, most of us have figured out how to solve most of our own problems. After many years of trial and error we figure out what solutions tend to work best for us. But, just because a solution works for you doesn't mean it will work for the other person. This is a hard concept for some people to understand. It's not about finding the best solution for you, it's about finding the best solution for you as a couple.

5. "If I can not control my partner completely, I can not trust him/her." It is impossible to control someone completely.

Instead, it is better to allow them freedom and accept the inevitable.

6. "My partner must fulfill all my needs." It is not possible to fulfill all of a person's needs. Couples need to find other ways of having their needs fulfilled outside of the relationship (provided it does not violate the boundaries of the relationship).

7. "My partner must love me 100% all the time." Your partner is going to be in a bad mood sometimes and be unhappy with you from time to time. This is inevitable and true for all relationships.

8. "We must enjoy doing all of the same things. If my partner does not enjoy something I enjoy, then we are not meant to be together." Men and women rarely enjoy doing the same types of activities. That is why friends exist.

According to REBT, there are other ways couples contribute to the dysfunction in a relationship. One of the ways is by having musts and demands. It is an absolutist way of thinking where unless the demand is met, the relationship is considered awful. Let me give you an example of this. I had previously worked with a young couple in their twenties. They had dated for three years and had a very good relationship. They were young and just starting out in their careers and so were not at a point in their lives yet where they had disposable income, but were still very happy together. The girlfriend, we'll call her Liz, and Liz's boyfriend, we'll call him Brian, had decided it was about time they got married. Brian saved up his money until he was able to buy Liz a gorgeous engagement ring. He then proposed to her at a fancy restaurant. Most people would consider this to be an acceptable proposal and be excited about getting married, but Liz considered it to be absolutely awful. She refused Brian's proposal and stated she wanted to end the relationship. In a last ditch effort, Brian convinced Liz to try couples counseling.

When I began working with Brian and Liz it was revealed that the reason why Liz refused the proposal was because Brian did not propose to her in the exact and highly specific way she had fantasized about. She had never shared this fantasy with Brian, so there was no way for him to have known about it. Also, Brian lacked the income to make her fantasy a reality anyway. However, Liz insisted that he should somehow be able to read her mind and that he purposefully chose to propose to her in a less extravagant way. She simply must be proposed to in the way she demanded or the relationship should not exist. It took a lot of reality testing from me to show Liz that it is not realistic to expect someone to read your mind or that unless a proposal is exactly the way you fantasize about it that it is awful.

By the end of counseling, both Brian and Liz had developed more realistic expectations for each other. They became engaged and I imagine that they are happily married by now. So, why do we create such unrealistic expectations for each other? Just look at the type of language the wedding industry uses: "two hearts becoming one", "a perfect love", "the happiest day of your life." It's easy to see how being bombarded with messages like that can skew your perception of reality, that unless your engagement is "the happiest day of your life" then there must be something wrong with it. The remedy to musts and demands are desires and preferences. It's okay to think "I would have prefered to have been whisked away to Paris instead of proposed to in a restaurant" and perfectly natural to feel a little disappointed that your fantasy engagement did not become a reality. But it is not okay to have absolutist musts or demands in a relationship.

In addition to musts and demands, Liz also engaged in what Ellis referred to as "awfulizing." "Because I was not proposed to in this very specific way, the proposal was awful." This is irrational because saying something is awful implies that it is wholly bad. Although the proposal wasn't exactly what she wanted, it wasn't a bad proposal. One of the ways I helped Liz to overcome her awfulizing of the proposal was to have Liz come up with examples of proposals that would be worse or truly awful. Some of the examples that Liz came up with were hilarious and although we all had a good laugh, it also simultaneously pointed out the ridiculousness of awfulizing such an acceptable proposal when far worse scenarios existed. After this I asked her to rate the way Brian had proposed to her on a scale of 1 to 10 (1 being awful and 10 being perfect). Before this exercise she gave the proposal a score of 1, afterwards she changed it to a 6 or a 7. Changing her belief that the proposal was awful allowed Liz to feel better about the relationship.

Liz also engaged in what Ellis called "I-can't-stand-it-itis." Because the proposal didn't meet her demands, she decided that she "can't stand" to be in the relationship any longer. According to Ellis, when people say "I can't stand it" they usually mean that the things they don't like are so bad that they should not exist (Ellis & MacLaren, 2005). From Liz's point of view, the relationship was so awful that it should not even exist. But again, to say that the relationship is awful is to say that it is wholly bad. I asked Liz for the "evidence" that the relationship was bad ("proposal was not exactly what she wanted") and then for the evidence that it was good ("enjoy each other's company, rarely argue, great chemistry, in love, etc"). It became clear to Liz from the evidence that the relationship was not bad at all and that she could stand to remain in it.

Another error that couples make is what Ellis called "damning oneself and others." In the case of Liz and Brian, Liz damned Brian as being a bad boyfriend simply because he had not provided her "perfect" proposal. In helping Liz deal with this irrational belief, I reminded her that there is good and bad in everyone. No one is perfect, not even her. Brian then mentioned some of the ways Liz had failed to fulfill his dreams but that overall he still considered her to be a good person. Liz hadn't realized that Brian had needs and desires of his own that he had hoped Liz would fulfill. She had only been focusing on her own dreams. When she heard Brian talk about his fantasy for the "perfect" proposal, one where Liz would cry tears of joy and appreciate his efforts to pick out the perfect ring, Liz cried. No one is a wholly bad person. Instead there are only people who sometimes do bad behaviors. No one is damned.

The tools of REBT

Rational Emotive Behavior Therapy has a number of tools available to fight irrational beliefs. I am now going to teach you the ones that I have found to be the most helpful for couples counseling (Ellis & MacLaren, 2005):

Functional Disputes: Once you have identified the irrational belief, you can dispute with the client if it is functional. The therapist evaluates with the client if the belief is helping them achieve what they want in life. The therapist does this by asking questions like, "Is this belief helping you?" or "How is continuing to think this way (or behave this way, or feel this way) affecting your relationship?" If it becomes clear to the client that the belief if getting them into trouble, the client may choose to let the irrational belief go.

Now that you know more about REBT, these tactics may seem familiar. The therapist working with Mark and Sarah has already been using some REBT interventions. Remember early on in counseling how Mark had the irrational belief that he must always be right? At first the therapist attempted to point out the absolutist and irrational nature of Mark's belief. When this didn't work, the therapist disputed the functionality of the belief by asking "do you want to be right or do you want to be happy?" Since dysfunction is the very nature of irrational beliefs, functional disputes will often work where other interventions fail.

Empirical Disputes: I find empirical disputes especially helpful when couples say "always" and "never." I ask them for the evidence both for and against that something always or never happens. For instance, let's say Sarah claims that Mark never treats her with consideration. The therapist will ask Sarah what's the evidence that Mark never treats her with consideration. Sarah then describes some times that Mark treated her without consideration. The therapist then asks Sarah to give the evidence that Mark does treat her with consideration. To Sarah's surprise, she actually is able to name several examples where Mark treated her with consideration, and if Sarah can't think up any examples, Mark can certainly chime in. The therapist then asks Sarah if she still thinks that Mark never treats her with consideration. Rationally, Sarah can no longer have this belief.

Rational Coping Statements: After a belief has been successfully disputed, it helps if that belief can be replaced with something more rational. I don't want this to confused with "positive thinking." The idea is not to lie to ourselves and convince ourselves that everything is wonderful when it is not. If we go back to the example from the beginning of the chapter about the four friends who tried asking the woman out on the date, the friend who thought "it's because she thinks I'm too good for her" certainly feels very good about himself. And although it is wonderful to feel good about ourselves, that kind of thinking is too much of a stretch for someone who usually thinks "no woman would ever want to date me. I'm such a loser." Rather, we want to teach our clients to have more rational and realistic thinking like the third friend who thought "She must already have a boyfriend" or "I must not be her type."

Thinking rationally doesn't always make you feel wonderful, but it doesn't make you feel angry or depressed either. Using the earlier example "Mark never treats me with consideration" could be replaced with the more rational belief "Mark usually treats me with consideration, but he can behave in an inconsiderate way if he is in a bad mood or stressed about work." Although Sarah is still acknowledging that Mark isn't perfect, she at least no longer thinks he is horrible, which will cause a lessening in angry feelings towards him. The irrational belief that "unless the proposal is exactly as I imagined it would be, it is completely awful" can be replaced by "I would have prefered a different proposal, but I still get to marry the man I love."

Modeling: Modeling is helpful in getting a client to think outside the box. Ask the couple to describe another couple they know that has a very good relationship. In particular, how is this couple different from them? What is good about the other couple's relationship? What is bad about the other couple's relationship? Comparing their own relationship to that of a couple they respect, they can see that their relationship doesn't have to be perfect in order to still be considered good. This can help them not be so harsh about their own relationship or to pick up some pointers on things they need to change.

Referenting: This tool involves having your couple make lists of the advantages and disadvantages of changing. If you are working with a couple that is highly resistant to change, you may want to discuss with them how having spent so many years refusing to change has increasingly made things worse.

Rational Emotive Imagery: Ask your client to close their eyes and imagine themselves in a recent difficult situation with their partner. Have the client give you a signal when they have imagined the situation to the point where they are experiencing the same emotional response they felt in real life while the situation was happening (anger, anxiety, depression, rage). Now ask the client to focus on changing that emotional response to something more healthy and realistic (disappointment, neutral feeling, etc.). Have the client signal again when they have accomplished this. Ask the client to return to the room and open their eyes. You now want to ask the client what they did to make themselves feel better.

In order to accomplish this, the client must have told themselves something rational about the situation. Not all clients are necessarily verbal with their thinking. Some clients are more visual and may respond with something like "I imagined my partner as being hurt and sad and that made me feel less angry at him." Your client now has a first hand experience of how changing their thinking can change their emotional response.

Unconditional Acceptance: Humanist Carl Rogers argued that therapists should have unconditional positive regard for their clients (Rogers, 1952). That is, a therapist should completely accept their client positively regardless of any negative things the client has done. The idea is that just because you may do some bad things, this does not make you a bad person as a whole. Albert Ellis took this idea one step further by stating that everyone should display unconditional acceptance, not just therapists. Ellis argues that just because an act is bad, it does not mean that someone is a bad person. This is especially important in couples counseling. When we love someone conditionally (for example, "if you propose the exact way I want you to", "if you always agree with me") we are only loving the acts they commit, or what they can do for us. I think most people would agree that that is not true love. On the other hand, when we love someone unconditionally, we choose to love that person despite their human failings.

Positive Talk: In this exercise, each partner is asked to talk positively about the other partner or the relationship in general for a full two minutes. If the person qualifies or modifies what they say, they get a penalty of an additional thirty seconds. By not being allowed to use modifiers, the couple also practices unconditional acceptance.

Reinforcements: Behavioral reinforcements are ways of rewarding the couple for accomplishing a task. That task can be practicing their communication skills, going a length of time without fighting, or successfully disputing an irrational belief. I generally shy away from using food or doing something expensive as a reward. The last thing we want to do is replace one unhealthy habit with another. I let the couple decide what their reward should be, but try to be mindful that the reward fit the accomplishment. Minor accomplishments get minor, although reinforcing, rewards. A major accomplishment would get something more special.

Acting on Rational Beliefs: Ellis also called this "behaving the way you'd like to feel." Have your clients experiment with acting on rational beliefs. It's useful to frame this as an "experiment" since otherwise the client could interpret this exercise as you implying they can change their beliefs over night. Telling your client "as an experiment, for the next week I want you to act as though you believed the more rational belief and tell me how it made you feel" is an easier sell than "I know you don't really believe in the rational beliefs thing, but I want you to act like you do anyways."

I utilized this exercise with Liz and Brian. I asked Liz to, as an experiment for the following week, act as though she did believe that although Brian's proposal was not perfect, it was still acceptable. When Liz got home, she took her bridal magazines off the shelf and started looking through them. She even put her engagement ring back on, and was so pleased by the experience of acting on rational beliefs that she decided to leave the ring on after the week was over.

Step 1: "Tell me about the last time you got upset by something your partner did"

Now that you've learned all about REBT, let's put it into practice for today's session. When reviewing the past week with your couple, listen for any disputes between the partners. Specifically, you want to listen for one partner to say that the other partner did something that made them feel upset. If your couple says that actually they've had a great week, provide positive reinforcement for having a great week and then prepare yourself to do a little digging. The easiest way to do this is to ask one or both of them "tell me about the last time you got upset by something your partner did?" You can also ask "tell me about something that your partner did in the past two weeks that made you feel really sad or really angry." Yes, in these questions we are using the language of irrational beliefs ("someone else made you feel a certain way") so that we can better draw them out of our clients.

Ask the client clarifying questions and ask for more details until the dysfunctional belief reveals itself. Ways of doing this include asking "tell me more about that?", "if I was there with you at the time, what would I have seen?", "why did that upset you so much?" and "what was going through your mind when you became upset?" Make sure to express understanding and empathy towards the client. The purpose of identifying and replacing irrational beliefs is to help the client feel better, not to invalidate the client's experience or argue with them.

Step 2: Identify irrational beliefs

Earlier in the chapter I included a list of the eight most common irrational beliefs in couples counseling. You may want to become familiar with that list to make it easier for you to identify the irrational beliefs you will be exposed to in couples counseling. When in doubt, just listen for any absolutist beliefs, like "shoulds" or "musts." Another telltale sign of an irrational belief is if the belief causes dysfunction in the relationship. Other indications are using "always" and "never", awfulizing, I-can't-stand-it's, and someone being damned as a bad person because they made a mistake or did a bad thing.

Once I feel confident that I have identified the irrational belief, I ask the client to tell me about other times they have thought this way as well. If it is a core belief, your client has probably thought this way many different times before and in many different relationships. The more often they have relied on this type of thinking, the stronger the core belief is and the greater the dysfunction. The good news is that like all habits it can be broken, it just may take some extra persistence from the therapist.

Step 3: Educate the couple about irrational beliefs

Now that the irrational belief has been identified, you can teach the couple about what irrational beliefs are and why they are harmful to relationships. I usually start this by asking the client something like, "how else could someone have interpreted what your partner did?" This is a hard concept for people to grasp at first. We're so accustomed to the belief that we feel and act a certain way because of things that happen to us, not because of the way we think about the events. You may have to give a few examples of different ways someone could think about the event and then the resulting way they would feel about it if they thought about it in that manner.

Now that you've got your clients thinking, I like to tell the example of the four friends looking for a date to better illustrate my point of how thoughts cause feelings and subsequent behaviors. If you don't like this example, feel free to make up your own. All you need is four people who each experienced the same exact event but had different emotional reactions based on their individual interpretations of that event. Maybe you have had your own experiences in the past where you felt a certain way about an event but a friend disagreed. It is okay to turn to your own life experiences for inspiration, just make sure you are not over self-disclosing in therapy. We never want our life story to overshadow the life story of our clients in session.

After I have illustrated my point that beliefs cause feelings, I then go on to explain how irrational beliefs hurt relationships. I have found it is helpful to reword "irrational beliefs" as "unfair expectations." People seem better able to relate to "unfair expectations" because "irrational beliefs" sounds a bit like psychobabble. When was the last time you ever used "irrational beliefs" in everyday conversation? But people do know how it feels to have grown up with parents who had unfair expectations of them and to deal with a boss at work with unfair expectations. For this reason, I refer to irrational beliefs as unfair expectations when speaking with clients. Explore with the couple what expectations they hold in relationships. You can point out the unfairness by asking, are these expectations obtainable? Are they fair to the other person? Is what you're expecting even feasible?

Step 4: Challenge and replace irrational beliefs

You are now going to challenge and replace the irrational beliefs using the tools of REBT discussed earlier: functional disputes, empirical disputes, rational coping statements, modeling, referenting, rational emotive imagery, unconditional acceptance, positive talk, reinforcements, and acting on rational beliefs. You may want to use "acting on rational beliefs" as the homework for today's session. Try to become comfortable using these techniques so that they don't feel awkward to you when you are using them with a client.

There are a lot of interventions used in REBT, and I don't expect you to use all of them in this one session. Some of them may not be appropriate for particular clients. However, now that you know them, you can continue to use them in future sessions when you catch your couple making absolutist statements, expressing irrational beliefs, or stating unfair expectations. At its very basic, you are challenging any dysfunctional beliefs and replacing them with more accurate and realistic beliefs.

Seventh session vignette

Therapist: How have you guys been this past week?

Sarah: It's been great. I've really enjoyed the caring behaviors that Mark has been demonstrating.

Therapist: How about you, Mark?

Mark: I also enjoyed the increase of caring behaviors from Sarah. They were actually quite creative at times, which made me try to be more thoughtful with the caring behaviors I did for Sarah.

Therapist: Did you remember to keep a log?

Mark: Yes

Sarah: I've got mine right here.

Therapist: Would you care to read them out loud?

Sarah: Okay. On Thursday, Mark washed the dishes and gave

me a backrub. On Friday, he vacuumed the bedroom carpet. On Saturday, he picked up the house a little bit before going out with his friends. On Sunday, he went for a hike with me. Then later he took me to a diner and a movie and let me pick out the movie. Monday, he emailed me a love letter while I was at work. Tuesday, Mark made me my favorite meal. Today, he called me at work to say he loved me.

Therapist: Thank you for sharing, Sarah. It sounds like Mark put a lot of effort into the past week.

Mark: I think she missed a few things, but that's okay.

Therapist: Can you remember what they were?

Mark: I can't remember exactly what they were, but it feels like I did a lot more than just one thing per day.

Therapist: Sarah may have forgotten some things by the time she got around to writing things down, but I'm sure she appreciated everything you did at the time that they occurred. What caring behaviors did Sarah do for you this week?

Mark: Sarah also did a really good job keeping the house cleaned this week. We had some great intellectual discussions this week as well. Sarah hugged and kissed me when I came home from work and we also had sex more often this week.

Therapist: It sounds like you both had a pretty good week.

Mark: Definitely.

Therapist: I want you both to continue doing daily caring behaviors. You don't have to continue writing it in a log, although I think it would be good to acknowledge the caring behaviors in other ways, such as by expressing appreciation when you notice them being done.

Sarah: Okay.

Therapist: Although it sounds like you're both doing great, I was actually wondering if you had anything problematic to report this week?

Sarah: What do you mean?

Therapist: Could you tell me about the last time you got upset by something Mark did?

Sarah: Well... I was cleaning up the house this week and asked Mark if I could polish his desk. It hadn't been polished in a long time and was really dusty and I had the polish out so I thought "why not?" I started moving things around in order to polish and I found a piece of paper hidden under his lap top-

Mark: It wasn't "hidden."

Therapist: Please continue, Sarah.

Sarah: And just as I'm about to pick it up, Mark grabs it and gets rid of it. This sparked a huge argument.

Mark: She was screaming at me to give it back to her, but I had already shredded it. It was just a bank statement that got lost under my laptop and I had been meaning to shred it for a long time.

Therapist: Why did you become so angry?

Sarah: Because he was keeping secrets from me and after the affair he promised that there would be no more secrets.

Therapist: Do you think the paper had something to do with him having another affair?

Sarah: Possibly...

Mark: Oh come on! What could have possibly been on there that had to do with an affair?

Sarah: How would I know? You shredded it before I had a chance to look at it.

Mark: You didn't say you wanted to see it!

Sarah: Oh please!

Therapist: Sarah, right at the moment you saw the paper and Mark shredded it, what was going through your mind?

Sarah: That I felt angry.

Therapist: What did you say to yourself in your mind right before you felt angry?

Sarah: I thought "here we go again."

Therapist: As in, "he's having an affair again"?

Sarah: Yes.

Mark: What do I have to do to prove myself to you? I have done everything!

Therapist: Mark, if you could please just listen to Sarah and try to overcome the tendency to interrupt, that would be really helpful. I know it's hard when Sarah is basically accusing you of having an affair, but right now, I need you just to listen. Can you trust me on this one?

Mark: Fine.

Therapist: Sarah, can you tell me more about "here we go again"?

Sarah: It makes me feel angry, but sometimes sad and anxious too.

Therapist: Is it something you think about a lot?

Sarah: I don't know if it's something I think about "a lot."

Therapist: Do you tend to think it right before you get really mad at Mark?

Sarah: Umm maybe...

Therapist: Tell me about another time you thought "here we go again"?

Sarah: Probably when he goes out with his friends.

Therapist: And this makes you not want him to go out with his friends because it is a possible opportunity for him to cheat on you?

Sarah: Yes. My ex-boyfriend would do that. He would say he was going out with his friends but later I found out he was really cheating on me.

Therapist: Was this the first time you thought "here we go again"?

Sarah: Possibly, I know I've felt this way for years. I've had boyfriends cheat on me going all the way back to High School. I've almost come to expect it.

Therapist: And it's why you feel upset if Mark wants freedom?

Sarah: Yeah.

Therapist: Do you see the connection between "thoughts" and "feelings"?

Sarah: What do you mean?

Therapist: People generally think that events or things cause them to feel a certain way, but really it is the way we interpret or think about events that cause us to feel a certain way. You have an expectation that Mark is going to cheat on you, and because of that you get angry when he wants to go out or stay at work late. Someone without that expectation wouldn't feel that way.

Sarah: But you don't understand. Mark has cheated on me. Anyone would feel suspicious after something like that.

Therapist: It sounded to me that you had trust problems before you ever met Mark.

Sarah: Because I had been cheated on so many times.

Therapist: Which you then decided "men can't be trusted"?

Sarah: Exactly.

Therapist: Would it have been more realistic to decide "those men can't be trusted" or "those men couldn't be trusted during that period in their lives"?

Sarah: Well...

Therapist: Just because someone does something once, does that mean they can't be trusted ever again?

Sarah: Not necessarily.

Therapist: Tell me about some times that Mark has been trustworthy.

Sarah: Umm...

Therapist: ::after a pause:: Mark, could you help her out?

Mark: Whenever you ask me to do something, so long as it's reasonable, don't I always do it?

Sarah: Not always.

Mark: But most of the time?

Sarah: Well, yes.

Mark: And wasn't I there for you when you had to go to the hospital?

Sarah: Yes.

Mark: And haven't I helped out your mother a lot as well?

Sarah: That's true. You do a lot of things to help out...

Mark: And aren't I also true to my word?

Sarah: Not 100%.

Therapist: I think it's important to understand that no one is anything 100% of the time. Is it fair to expect someone to be true to their word 100% of the time?

Sarah: I suppose not.

Therapist: Thinking back over all of the years you've known Mark, what percentage of the time has he acted in a trustworthy manner towards you?

Sarah: Gee... I guess 80 or 90% of the time we've been together he has been trustworthy.

Therapist: So, for the most part, Mark has been overall trustworthy?

Sarah: Yes.

Therapist: If someone does untrustworthy things sometimes, even if most of the time they are trustworthy, does that mean that overall they are untrustworthy?

Sarah: Of course not.

Therapist: Why?

Sarah: Because saying that someone is untrustworthy would imply that they always or mostly do untrustworthy things.

Therapist: That's right. When Mark had that affair, he did a very untrustworthy thing, but that does not mean that Mark is untrustworthy as a person or that everytime he goes out with his friends he is cheating on you. When we have unfair expectations like, "Mark is an untrustworthy person" or "Mark is a cheater", it causes us to interpret the things they do in a negative manner. If instead of having the expectation of "Mark is a cheater" you had the expectation "Mark has made some mistakes in the past but overall he is a trustworthy person", how do you think you would have interpreted him shredding the paper you found under his computer?

Sarah: I probably wouldn't have thought anything of it.

Therapist: Can you think of a way you could have thought about it where it would have made you feel good about Mark's behavior?

Sarah: Hmm...I don't know.

Therapist: Would a person have felt good about it if they immediately thought something like "it must have been a receipt from a surprise gift for me he ordered online"?

Sarah: Oh I get it now.

Therapist: Do you both see how depending on how you think about an event causes you to feel a certain way about it?

Mark: Maybe.

Therapist: Let me give you guys another example just to illustrate my point that the way we think about events causes us to feel a certain way about them. Let's say that four friends are at the mall and see a beautiful woman sitting by herself at the food court. They decide that they'll each ask her out and see if she says yes to any of them. The first friend walks over to her and asks her out and she says "no." He immediately thinks "I can't stand women! She'll be sorry she ever rejected me!." Based on what he's thinking, how do you think he must have felt about the situation?

Sarah: Mad.

Mark: He sounded angry.

Therapist: That's right! He was angry. So, the second friend asks her out and she says "no" to him too. He thinks to himself "It's because I'm such a loser. If I was more attractive and had a better job women would want to date me. No one will ever love me." How do you think he felt?

Sarah: Sad.

Mark: Upset.

Therapist: He felt sad because he thought about it in a depressing way. So the third friend asks her out, gets rejected by her and actually feels good about the situation. What kind of thoughts would a person have to have in order to feel good about being rejected?

Sarah: Oh geez, I don't know.

Mark: How could someone feel good about being rejected?

Therapist: What if he thought something like "She must be intimidated by me because I'm so good looking!"

Mark: Oh okay, I can see that now.

Therapist: So finally, the fourth friend walks up to her and asks her out and is also rejected. He thinks to himself "Oh, she must already have a boyfriend." How do you think he must have felt?

Sarah: I guess neither good nor bad.

Therapist: Yeah, he probably just felt neutral about the situation. So, as you can see, there are many different ways a person can feel about an event depending on how you think about it. Of the four friends, which one do you think thought about the situation the most realistically?

Mark: The friend who just felt neutral about it.

Therapist: That's right. When we make absolutist statements like "women are horrible!" and "no one will ever love me!" that's not being realistic. Do you guys think you sometimes have absolutist beliefs or unfair expectations about each other?

Mark: Sometimes.

Therapist: Whenever you find yourself thinking something with words such as "always", "never", "have to", "should", and "must", that's an unfair expectation. When we think that way it causes us to feel unfairly angry or sad at our partner. Mark, can you give me an example of a time you felt angry at Sarah and it was because of an unfair expectation you had of her?

Mark: Sarah was asking me to do something and I thought "she's always nagging me!"

Therapist: What usually happens when you think this way?

Mark: I get angry and snap at Sarah.

Therapist: Is it useful in any way to think like this?

Mark: Not really.

Therapist: It sounds like it tends to get you in trouble with Sarah.

Mark: A lot of the time.

Therapist: What would have been a more realistic expectation to have?

Mark: That if I don't get important things done in a timely manner that Sarah is going to remind me until I do.

Therapist: I want you both to now close your eyes and think about the last time you got mad at the other person. It could be the two situations you just told me about or something different. I want you to try to mentally put yourselves in those angering situations again and try to make yourselves feel as angry as you did back then. Let me know when you feel that anger again by raising your hand and then putting it back down.

Mark and Sarah: ::raise their hands after a few minutes::

Therapist: Good. Now, with your eyes still closed and trying to picture yourselves in that actual moment where you felt angry, try to make yourself feel neutral about the event. Raise your hand when you feel neutral.

Mark and Sarah: ::raise their hands after a few minutes::

Therapist: Good. Come back to the room and open your eyes. Sarah, what did you do to make yourself feel neutral?

Sarah: I took a few deep breaths and then thought about how Mark is mostly a trustworthy person and that realistically it was probably just a bank statement or something private that has nothing to do with cheating.

Therapist: So by changing your thoughts to something more realistic, you were able to calm down. Good. How about you, Mark?

Mark: I thought about how Sarah only nags when I don't listen to her, so if I don't want her to nag, I need to make getting things done a priority over watching football.

Therapist: Good. So now you can see how changing your thoughts to something more realistic can cause you to feel less angry at your partner. I wonder what would happen if you always acted as if you had realistic expectations of each other?

Sarah: It would probably be a lot better.

Therapist: Do you think that is something you both could try? As an experiment, how about during the following week you act as if you do have realistic expectations of one another and see what happens.

Mark: Okay, I think we can do that.

Sarah: Sure.

For this session it is difficult for the therapist to give an equal amount of time to each member of the couple. One client is usually going to end up with more of the therapist's attention in this session. Due to this, the therapist chose to work more on Sarah's irrational beliefs since Sarah tends to talk less in the session and that the therapist hadn't yet addressed any lingering trust issues from the affair. You may also choose to focus more on a particular client if their irrational beliefs tend to disrupt the counseling process more. In the past, Mark's irrational beliefs (that he is always right, things must go the way he wants them to, etc) have been disruptive, but the therapist had dealt with them many times in previous sessions. It was time to work on Sarah.

The irrational belief that Sarah displayed in regards to Mark's behavior was "If I can not control my partner completely, I can not trust him", as well as damning him as a person because of a single wrong he committed years ago. The therapist may have come off as a little insensitive towards Sarah's feelings about having been cheated on, but remember that the therapist had expressed sympathy towards her in previous sessions as well as refuted Mark's statement that it was time for Sarah to move on.

Do you find yourself wondering if Mark is still cheating on Sarah? Sometimes clients can make very convincing arguments, but it's important to note that as the therapist it is not your responsibility to determine if Mark is still cheating on Sarah. If things seem suspicious to you, keep in mind that "evidence" is being filtered to you through a client's suspicious mind. Presumably, if Sarah wants someone to help her decide if Mark is still cheating on her, she can hire a private investigator. It is not the role of the couples counselor to make those determinations.

Keep in mind that if someone has an irrational belief (ie men are cheaters), their perception of the world is going to be skewed. Let's say my husband had an irrational belief that women are cheaters. As a therapist who works from home, he would have plenty of "evidence" against me. There are strange men that come to the house during the day while he's at work. They pull into the driveway in silence and leave just as mysteriously, not saying a word to anyone and avoiding eye contact with the neighbors. All of the "secret" phone calls and emails I exchange. Add some exaggerations here and there, and someone could become convinced I was cheating on my husband when really I'm just a therapist who sees clients in my home while my husband is at work. You can see how almost any situation could be twisted into "evidence" that supports a person's irrational belief. That is why it is so important not to take sides or make judgment calls in couples counseling.

Keeping in mind the common irrational beliefs seen in couples counseling, the therapist determined that Sarah had the belief "If I can not control my partner completely, I can not trust him" and quickly deduced that was why she becomes upset if Mark goes out with his friends and leaves her behind. The therapist helped Sarah see this as well. The therapist then worked with Sarah on disputing this belief and replacing it with something more realistic. So that Mark wouldn't be left out of the session entirely, the therapist included him

in a rational emotive imagery exercise. Although Mark didn't participate through most of the session, he was still able to observe and
listen to the work the therapist was doing with Sarah. Hopefully he
was able to make a connection between Sarah's irrational beliefs and
his own.

The therapist didn't come close to using all of the tools of REBT
in today's session. Depending on the couple you are working with, you
may find that you have time to use all of them in one session, or only
a couple. Either way, at the core of REBT you are simply identifying
irrational beliefs, disputing them, and then replacing them with more
rational statements. However you go about accomplishing that task is
up to you as the therapist.

Seventh session outline: REBT

Step 1: "Tell me about the last time you got upset by something your partner did?"

- Ask clarifying questions
- Express understanding and empathy

Step 2: Identify irrational beliefs

- Listen for the "shoulds" or "musts"

Step 3: Educate the couple about irrational beliefs

- Ask other ways they could think about it
- Give example of how thoughts cause feelings
- Explain how unfair expectations hurt relationships

Step 4: Challenge and replace irrational beliefs

- Functional Disputes
- Empirical disputes
- Rational coping statements
- Modeling
- Referenting
- Rational emotive Imagery
- Unconditional acceptance
- Positive Talk
- Reinforcement

Chapter 9

Eighth Session: Taking Responsibility

"Have patience with all things, but chiefly have patience with yourself. Do not lose courage in considering your own imperfections but instantly set about remedying them every day begin the task anew."

- Saint Francis de Sales

We've made it to the eighth session. After two or more months in therapy, your clients may be becoming restless and wondering what could possibly be left to work on. In the previous sessions we've focused on setting goals, learning communication skills, problem solving and compromise, bringing love and caring back into the relationship, and finally dealing with destructive irrational beliefs. Although we have planted seeds regarding taking individual responsibility, we have not yet directly confronted the couple on this matter. That is what we are going to do in today's session.

The idea of taking individual responsibility is very important. Unless we accept our own contributions, we can not make changes. A lot of people have difficulty when it comes to owning up to their own mistakes. It is simply easier to blame it on others. This phenomenon is known in psychology as the attributional bias or self-serving bias. According to the theory of attributional bias, we tend to attribute our failures to other people and our successes entirely to ourselves. In the short term this bias helps to preserve our self esteem but in the long term it can be very destructive. It keeps us from learning from our mistakes and improving (Gecas, 1982).

I love the above quote from Saint Francis de Sales. It speaks to a universal truth. It is only by accepting our faults that we can work on them. We gain nothing from putting the blame on others, but gain everything by working to correct those flaws in a productive manner. Some couples counselors try to get the couple to work on responsibility from the very first session. I have attempted this and have found that the self attribution error is simply too strong at the beginning stages of therapy to make any progress in that endeavor. Clients are feeling too hurt and too defensive to own up to their contribution right away. The therapist is better off planting seeds of responsibility and gaining trust in the therapeutic relationship by helping the couple make some progress first. After the couple has made substantial progress and become believers in couples counseling they will be ready to go through the painful inventory of owning up to their flaws and working to correct those flaws.

Step 1: "How have you contributed to the problems in the relationship?"

After you've reviewed the past week with the couple, given praise for any successes and processed any obstacles, you can get the ball rolling by asking each client "how have you contributed to the problems in the relationship?" It is unlikely that you will hear anything new during this exercise. As the therapist, after eight or more sessions of working with this couple, you probably have a very good idea of how each of them have contributed to the problems in their own way. The most common themes that come up are "I was selfish", "I was quick to anger", and "I had unreasonable expectations." It's okay to follow up with a "tell me more about that." You want to really hear specific examples of wrongdoing from the client to make sure they get it.

For example, "I was selfish" is very vague. If someone suddenly said to you "You are such a selfish person!" you would probably feel very confused. You might even dismiss what they said completely. But if someone said to you "It was selfish of you not to help your friend after all the times they have helped you", now you know what you need to do in order to not act in a selfish manner. By having the client elaborate to specific examples, not only does it help the client be more conscious about the types of behaviors that they need to avoid in the future, it also allows the listening partner to feel more that their partner "gets" how they contributed. Elaboration provides more understanding.

After you have discussed individual responsibility with one client, ask the other client for their contribution. You may notice that the other person says something very similar to what the other person says. This is not necessarily a "cop out." It is human nature to mimic the behaviors of those around us. If our partner acts in a selfish manner, we will probably act in a selfish manner as well to prevent feeling like we are being taken advantaged of. Of course, that should not be taken as an excuse. It doesn't matter who started the cycle. Trying to figure that out would be a useless and very time consuming activity. All that matters here is that each person takes responsibility for their part in the cycle.

Step 2: Each person identifies changes that need to be made to improve the relationship

Now that the couple has identified how they have contributed to the problems in the relationship, both past and present, we can work towards preventing those problems from arising again by having the couple identify necessary changes that need to be made. By the eighth session, the couple has already made a lot of changes. It is unlikely that any possible major changes still exist. But often it is the little things that bother us the most about a person and need to be changed. We are now going to address those few remaining changes.

For this exercise, I hand out pens and a notepad to each client and I ask them to make a list. I instruct the couple to make a list of three to five behavioral changes that they need to make to improve the relationship and three to five things that they feel their partner needs to change in order to improve the relationship. The reason why I have the couple make a list for both themselves and the other person is because you want to get them to both reflect on their own changes they need to make and become accustomed to asking the other person for feedback. It may seem obvious to clients the changes they need to make but then be surprised to hear that the other person came up with a completely different list for them.

Just like when you had the couple make the list describing their ideal relationship, if anything is vague, ask for clarification. You may also want to ask them why they feel a particular change is important to them. You want to get the couple comfortable with discussing changes and making specific requests for change. What we are doing now is really just practice for when the couple is outside of the session living their everyday life. Change and personal growth is a part of life, and receiving directions from a loved one makes it easier to achieve that personal growth which is so necessary to living a fulfilling life.

Couples sometimes have the irrational belief that "if he/she really loved me they would change without me having to say anything", when really it is so much easier to just tell your partner what you want from them. Couples need to understand that their partners can't read their minds and it doesn't matter how long they have been married, their partner doesn't know what they want unless they say so specifically. Encouraging couples to talk more about how to better fulfill their needs and achieve a relationship that is mutually satisfying is a very important part of couples counseling. This exercise, and the subsequent changes that occur because of it, help couples become more comfortable with asking for changes and eliciting feedback from their partner.

Step 3: Create an action plan

Ask each person if they would be willing to make the changes that both they and their partner listed. If a client objects to one of the changes mentioned, explore why they object. Sometimes a change simply isn't feasible. This then becomes an opportunity for the couple to practice problem solving or compromising. Once the couple is in final agreement of the changes they are willing to make, it is then time for the therapist to help the couple make an action plan.

As a therapist, you may have experience making action plans already. Basically, you take the goals, or changes the couple wants to make, and create a plan for how the couple is to achieve the desired changes. For example, let's say that one of the goals is to spend more time together. The first thing you will do is to help the couple identify time in their schedule for spending time together. The second step is to brainstorm some activities that they would like to do during their time together. The third step would be to schedule their first get together and activity they would like to do as a couple. Now, what if there is a problem like one works days and one works night? This will take some problem solving. Does the person have enough seniority at work to change their schedule? Would they be willing to send out applications to a new employer? Help the couple create a specific plan of action to help them achieve these goals.

Even if the couple seems to be in total agreement on making the changes, try to look for any obstacles that could get in the way of the couple achieving their goals. One way to do this is to ask "which one of these changes do you think will be the hardest to accomplish?" Then follow up with "why?" I have often found many potential obstacles with a couple by using this approach even though at first they acted as though there would be no obstacles. Sometimes it takes a little digging, but it is better to find the problems now than have them be discovered by the couple later when you are not there to help them.

Sometimes obstacles can be mental or emotional. Examples of mental obstacles include: anxiety about change, not wanting to be controlled, fear of failure, fear of investing so much of yourself into the relationship just to have it end later on anyway, stubbornness, low self esteem, and low motivation. In a lot of ways, this is the session that the couple has been fearing from the very beginning of therapy; that the problems in the relationship are partially their fault and that they need to change. Hopefully by now you have gained their trust and they have seen the power of change first hand. Still, being told you need to change by your partner can be painful. You need to be prepared for any defensiveness the client may have.

Sometimes it helps to frame change as opportunities for personal growth. Our friends often won't tell us that we need to change, and because of that, our friends rarely help us to grow as a person. Friends aren't as invested in us as our spouses or partners are. Our success as an individual isn't as important to them. By contrast, our spouses care very deeply if we win or fail, and we sometimes interpret this as control. However, I believe that this desire to see us succeed as individuals is the very act of love. They feel hurt when we feel hurt, so they try to prevent our failures. There is no better opportunity for personal growth than when we are in relationships because no other person will be more honest about what we need to change. If only we would listen.

Step 4: Implement changes

Now that the couple is in agreement about the changes they need to make and the steps they need to take to achieve them, it is time to start implementing them. But, implementation doesn't just mean "do it once and never have to change again." This is something that the couple should revisit from time to time. As the years go on and our personal circumstances change, we will have to revisit the idea of change and personal growth time and time again. The couple should understand that just as the world around us is ever changing, we need to be flexible enough to be willing to change with it accordingly.

Part of being willing to change means accepting that when our spouse complains about us, there is always at least some truth to the complaint. As painful as it is to accept that, we need to be willing to take a hard look at ourselves and ask, do I need to change some aspect about myself in order to grow as a person? Sometimes this requires having a willingness to ask your partner what changes they feel you need to make. Sometimes it means you have to be willing to ask your partner to change and help them in this task. One thing that I am certain of, is that by having a flexibility of mind and character, a willingness to accept feedback from others, means the greatest success as a human being.

Eighth session vignette

Therapist: How are you two doing?

Mark: Still good. . . I don't know if anything has really changed since last we saw you.

Sarah: We are still doing the couple's meetings and solving problems as they come along. I'd say that all the major problems have been solved by now. You were right, the communication skills have become second nature now. I don't even think about using them anymore, but I catch myself doing it all the time.

Therapist: That's wonderful, I knew you could do it! It sounds like you have made a lot of progress.

Mark: We definitely have. It kind of makes me wonder what's left to work on.

Therapist: Well, I still have two more sessions planned, but you are right, we have covered a lot over these past eight sessions. There's not a whole lot left. But one thing I thought we should work on is the idea of taking personal responsibility when things go wrong in the relationship.

Mark: Okay.

Therapist: We are always at least 30% responsible for any problems in our relationship and it is important to always look for your contribution because that is the one thing you can change. You can't change what the other person is doing, but you can change yourself.

Sarah: Hmm, that's true.

Therapist: I was wondering. . . looking back on the history of this relationship, how do you feel you have each contributed to the problems in this relationship?

Sarah: Should I go first?

Therapist: Sure.

Sarah: To be honest, I think my anxiety and my tendency to become overwhelmed has contributed negatively to me and

Mark's relationship. I know I have at times driven him away by becoming angry and irrational. My mother had anxiety issues so I know it can be hard to be around a person like that, and Mark has done the best he can to deal with that side of me. I know my job as a real estate agent has been tough for the relationship as well. Sometimes I have to leave last minute to do a showing for a client and Mark has been very understanding of that despite me acting like a chicken with it's head cut off when the phone rings. The money can be very good, but it's not always stable. Sometimes I take my frustrations out on him, and for that I am deeply sorry.

Therapist: Thank you, Sarah. I know it is not easy to own up to one's mistakes. Mark, how do you feel that you have contributed to the problems in the relationship?

Mark: I think I can get defensive and be very touchy. I know that I hurt Sarah a lot when I had the affair and continued to hurt her for years afterwards by being so quick to anger when she brought it up. I think that I could have helped out with the housework a lot more considering her busy schedule. I also think I can act condescending and that has a lot to do with needing to feel superior to other people, but I'm going to try to limit my condescending remarks from now on.

Therapist: Mark, that was wonderful. Thank you. How does it feel to hear the other person take responsibility instead of playing the blame game?

Sarah: It feels good actually. What Mark said touched me so deeply that I'm fighting back tears.

Mark: It was long overdue.

Therapist: I want you to try to make this a habit. Try to recognize your own contribution and if you make a mistake, admit to it readily.

Mark & Sarah ::nods::

Therapist: ::hands out pens and notepads:: I want you guys to do a little writing now, if that's okay?

Sarah: Okay

Mark: Writing's fine.

Therapist: I want you to each write down three to five changes that you need to make in order to improve the relationship and three to five changes that your partner needs to make.

Sarah: I think we can do that.

Therapist: ::Waits about 15 minutes until the couple seems to be done writing:: Everyone all set?

Mark: Done.

Sarah: I just finished.

Therapist: Sarah, maybe you would like to start by reading the things you wrote down that you need to change?

Sarah: Okay. I wrote down that one of the things I need to change is my anxiety.

Therapist: How do you think you could reduce your anxiety?

Sarah: I was thinking that I could start seeing a therapist after I finish couples counseling. Do you see people individually or do you just do couples?

Therapist: No, I see a lot of people individually as well.

Sarah: Would it be okay if I saw you as an individual therapist after we finished couples counseling?

Therapist: I would be honored.

Sarah: Great! Okay, umm.. next I wrote that I needed to nag less and show more empathy for Mark's point of view. I also wrote that I need to work on not making Mark feel guilty when he goes out with his friends.

Therapist: Thank you, Sarah. Mark, what are some things you wrote that you thought Sarah needed to work on changing?

Mark: I wrote that I would like Sarah to express more appreciation for what I do–

Therapist: Can you tell me more about that?

Mark: Well, sometimes I wonder if the extra things I do for her goes unnoticed because she doesn't say anything about it. For example, washing dishes is Sarah's chore but one day this week I saw that the dishes were really piling up so I washed all of them. Sarah didn't say anything about it.

Sarah: I saw that you washed all the dishes and that's why I gave you a kiss on the cheek. I guess I need to be clearer. But I did appreciate you doing all of the dishes.

Therapist: So it sounds like Mark is asking for verbal praise.

Mark: I guess so. The kiss sounds good now, but at the time I thought you were doing that "just because." I didn't put the two together.

Sarah: I will kiss you and tell you why from now on.

Mark: The other things I put on my list were for Sarah to go out with friends more so I can go out and not feel guilty about it, for Sarah to put her make-up away in the morning instead of leaving it out on the sink, and to cook healthier meals because I'm trying to watch my weight.

Therapist: How do those sound Sarah?

Sarah: I think I could do them.

Therapist: Which one do you think would be the hardest to follow through on?

Sarah: I think cooking healthier meals would be harder. I like the taste of my cooking and I don't need to lose any weight.

Therapist: Is there any way to compromise on this?

Mark: You can still cook your favorite meals once in awhile.

Sarah: What if I just modified my regular recipes to make them lower in calories, like use less oil?

Mark: We could try that. But I think that if in three months from now that's not working we should consider trying my idea.

Sarah: Okay.

Therapist: Sounds like a deal. Mark, what are some changes you need to make in order to improve the relationship?

Mark: I wrote that I need to use less condescending humor, I should put more effort into our dates, and buy Sarah more presents.

Therapist: Sarah, what did you write that Mark needs to change?

Sarah: I wrote that Mark needed to try to be more respectful when we are having an intellectual discussion-

Therapist: Tell me more about that.

Sarah: Sometimes it feels like he's talking down to me and it can be really insulting.

Mark: I'm sorry, Sarah. I'm going to try to work on that.

Sarah: Okay, but it really hurts my feelings when you act intellectually superior to me.

Mark: You're a very intelligent woman, Sarah. I mean, just look at all the houses you've been selling lately. You obviously have a lot of talent.

Sarah: ::smiles::

Therapist: Is there anything else on your list?

Sarah: I wrote that I would also like it if Mark did a better job cleaning up after himself. Like, if I'm gone and he decides to cook something, he will just leave the mess for me when I get home. I know it's my job to clean up after dinner, but I don't think it should count if I'm away.

Therapist: What do you think about that, Mark?

Mark: She's probably right. I was being selfish. I shouldn't leave messes for her.

Sarah: I also wrote for Mark to try to act more enthusiastic about dates. Sometimes he acts like it's a chore almost.

Mark: It's hard for me to do dates on weeknights. I feel tired from work.

Sarah: You'll go out with your friends on weeknights and not act tired.

Mark: That's true. I don't know what to say about that. You might have a point there.

Sarah: Another change I would like to see from Mark is for him to compliment me more and not ignore me when his friends are around.

Therapist: What do you think about the changes Sarah has suggested?

Mark: I think I could do them.

Therapist: Which ones do you think will be the hardest to do?

Mark: The hardest ones probably are the ones having to do with changing my personality. I don't think personality is something that can be changed.

Therapist: I disagree. I want you to look back at your life starting from when you were a child through to present day. Your personality has changed a lot over the years.

Mark: I never thought about it like that. But I do think that there are "core" parts of ourselves that cannot be changed.

Therapist: Is being condescending a core part of you?

Mark: Well...

Therapist: It seems more likely that it is a behavior that was learned. That good news is that behaviors can be unlearned or replaced by other more adaptive behaviors. This is how we grow as people. By taking a careful inventory of ourselves and changing the parts of us that we don't like. You are a dynamic human being. People change every day.

Mark: Hmm...

Therapist: I believe that both of you have the ability to change. This is one of the values of relationships. No other person encourages us to grow and change as people more than our partners. There is a lot of good that can come from listening to feedback from our partners, and personal growth is one of them.

Sarah: That's true.

Therapist: I think it helps to create a plan when we are trying to implement changes. You guys already created a plan for cooking healthier and seeing a therapist. Can you create a plan to achieve the other goals?

Mark: I'm not sure if a plan could be made for the other ones on the list. I think they have more to do with having a conscious awareness of what you do and how it affects other people.

Therapist: ::nods::

Mark: Sometimes it's almost like I'm on "automatic." I just do things without thinking or out of habit. I'm going to try to slow it down and do things more deliberately until they become a new habit, like the communications skills.

Sarah: I'm going to do that too.

Therapist: It's important to realize that we are always going to have to grow and change. I want you to continually strive to improve and ask yourself "how can I be a little bit better today?" If you continue to do this and ask each other for feedback, I have no doubt that you can achieve something really special.

Mark & Sarah: Okay.

The couple wasn't enthusiastic about the idea of making personal changes, but they seemed willing to try, which is really the most you can ask for. In this session, the therapist was very confrontational towards Mark, especially his belief that we have "core" parts of our personality that we can't change. It may indeed be true that we have core parts of our personality, which seems to be more of a philosophical debate that the therapist was not going to engage in with Mark. Rather than challenge the idea of core personality traits, the therapist challenged the idea that condescending humor was one of them. The therapist also brought up the point that it was unlikely that Mark had always used condescending humor, even as a child, which is what a "core personality trait" would suggest.

In general, I don't advocate arguing with your clients. If Mark had continued to disagree with the therapist, the therapist would have dropped it, being happy to just plant a few seeds in the process. Unlike arguing, confrontation can be helpful in the later stages of therapy. We've used confrontation before. Remember "do you want to be right or do you want to be happy?" The goal of using confrontation in therapy is not to assert your will over the client, but to help the client recognize the dysfunctional nature of the beliefs they have been asserting in counseling. The therapist then asks a thought provoking question (for example, "do you want to be right or do you want to be happy?" "Is condescending humor a core personality trait?") that reveals the dysfunction of the belief to the client.

Yes, confrontation is a powerful technique that can get clients unstuck in therapy when nothing else can, but keep a few things in mind before deciding to use it. Confrontation is uncomfortable for clients (and uncomfortable for the therapist too!). It should only be used when the client is demonstrating a self defeating behavior or belief that is limiting progress in therapy, not when you think the client is "wrong" and you are "right." Confrontation should also not be used until you have established a therapeutic alliance or trust with your clients. Using confrontation too soon in counseling can cause you to appear to be condescending. Remember, in general we want to use as many positive statements in counseling as possible, and reserve confrontation for when we really need it.

Another comment-worthy event in this session was that Sarah asked the therapist if she could continue individually with the therapist to work on her anxiety issues. I think I should comment on this because I do not recommend that therapists see clients individually and as a couple at the same time. What Sarah requested was okay because the individual counseling is to begin after the couples counseling ends, which is in two more weeks. I have heard of a lot of therapists who will see a family for family therapy, then also see the parents for couples counseling, and then see each individual family member for individual therapy. Although this is a great way to fill up a caseload, it is not a good way to conduct therapy. It is also considered unethical behavior.

In order to be a good couples counselor, you have to be objective. This is why talking to a counselor is more effective than talking to a friend. The friend has an emotional involvement which clouds their judgment. Because the therapist doesn't have the bias that the friend does, the therapist is able to see crucial things that the friend misses. When we start seeing a couple individually as well, we begin to form a bias. It doesn't matter how good of a therapist you are, you will no longer be objective if you see a couple in individual counseling too.

Some therapists will argue "but the couple asked if I would also see them individually. What if I refer them to another therapist and they don't like the other therapist and never get the help they need because I refused to see them?" There are many capable therapists out there who can help your couple. But if you are truly doing it for the client's benefit and not for the financial benefit of increasing your caseload, consider this: if you see the couple individually, the odds of you helping them with their relationship issues decreases. You become a less effective couples counselor, and having a bad therapy experience is something clients hold on to for a long time. It hurts the whole profession, not just your business. So, for the sake of your clients, have only one therapeutic relationship at a time.

I don't find anything wrong with seeing a client individually once couples counseling has ended. I do find something wrong with seeing both partners in individual counseling (again, due to a loss in objectivity), so one should be referred out to a trusted colleague if both are requesting individual counseling. You will find that if a couple is pleased with you, they will often ask to remain working with you for other issues as well. I consider it to be one of the benefits of couples counseling, but do not abuse your client's trust by allowing multiple therapeutic relationships to exist at the same time.

Eighth session outline: taking responsibility

Step 1: "How have you contributed to the problems in the relationship?"

- Ask each client how they have contributed
- Get specific examples of wrongdoing from each client

Step 2: Each person identifies changes that need to be made to improve the relationship

- Couple writes down 3-5 changes they need to make and 3-5 changes their partner needs to make
- Couple takes turns reading their list out loud in session

Step 3: Create an action plan

- Therapist helps couple to break down the specific steps they need to take to make these changes possible
- Therapist identifies obstacles and helps find solutions

Step 4: Implement changes

- Continually grow and change as a couple and as an individual

Chapter 10

Ninth Session: Forgiveness

We've nearly reached the end of our couples counseling sessions. How do you feel about the couple you have been working with? Have they made a lot of progress? Do you feel confident that they can continue to make progress on their own? Today's session is both about preparing for the future and letting go of the past. You will be preparing the couple for life without a couples counselor to guide them through their relationship troubles. You've taught them all the skills necessary to have a wonderful relationship and so long as they continue to use them and grow and change as a couple, you should feel confident that your couple will continue to prosper without your presence. However, there is one thing that I have found can sabotage all the progress your couple has made and eventually cause them to revert back to dysfunctional behaviors, and that is emotional baggage from the past.

Past hurts will be an issue for all of the couples you work with. Because we are so fallible as human beings, inevitably we have done something in the relationship to hurt our partner. For some of the couples we work with, the past hurts will be huge, such as multiple affairs over the course of a relationship. Others may have lingering bitterness resulting from more "minor" hurts like having to give up on a career opportunity because it interfered with your partner's plans. The very nature of being in a relationship means there must be sacrifices. Some dreams will be realized through the relationship while others will have to go unfulfilled. An inability to forgive your partner for dreams left unrealized can erode the progress in a relationship overtime.

Many clients have misconceptions about what forgiveness is and isn't. Forgiveness doesn't mean you just take past offenses and brush them under the rug. It also doesn't mean forgetting about past hurts. Forgiveness also doesn't mean condoning bad behavior. Some clients will say "but he doesn't deserve forgiveness!" That is where they are wrong. Forgiveness isn't something you do for the other person, it is something you do for yourself. What a lot of people don't realize is that refusing to forgive hurts them a lot more than it does the other person. The other person has probably moved on with their life and doesn't think about the transgression nearly as often. However, the person without forgiveness seethes in anger and continues to suffer much longer than the person who "deserves it." Forgiveness is ultimately something you do for yourself.

Forgiveness comes easier when people are in a good place in the relationship, which is why we have waited until nearly the last session to address this very important topic. If we had attempted to do this session earlier in counseling, the session would have probably resulted in an unproductive argument, resulting in deepening hurt and increasing the odds that your couple would have dropped out of counseling completely.

In a lot of ways we have "brushed it under the rug" up until now. Clients usually come prepared to talk about past hurts starting at the very first session and they are often surprised when the therapist informs them that they won't be discussing the past today. It is very easy for clients to fall into a competition of who hurt who more in the beginning stages of counseling. That is why those topics are best delayed until the couple learns to speak to each other in a controlled respectful manner, using empathy and validation to help their partner feel understood. Some therapists view talking about the past as taking a step back, stating that the past doesn't matter. I always say that you can't get rid of baggage until you've unpacked it, going through each item piece by piece, deciding what to keep and what to get rid of. You will be helping your couple go through that process today.

Step 1: Unpack the baggage

It is entirely possible that your couple has never had the opportunity to discuss past hurts without their partner becoming defensive or having it turn into an argument. This is your couple's opportunity to express their past hurts in a controlled respectful manner, something they may have never done before. Expressing their pain with control and respect is key in order for this to work. If the client cries while doing this, that's okay and is in fact encouraged. If you can see your client fighting back tears, say something like "It's okay to cry. Let it out." It is also okay for your client to express anger. For some clients, emotional expression is part of the process. But keep in mind that it is not okay for clients to engage in personal attacks or condemning the other person. The exchange must be respectful at all times.

In order to really unpack that baggage, you might have to help the client do a little digging by asking follow up questions like "how has this affected the relationship?", "how has it affected your life in general?", or "really make him/her understand the hurt they have caused you. Get it all out." The other person is not allowed to interrupt or "correct" what their partner is saying during this time. Rather than respond in their usual manner by becoming defensive, the other person is to have a couple's dialogue or apologize, and that's it. The act of "unpacking baggage" sounds very simple but it is actually a very powerful technique. Clients often report feeling "lighter" afterwards and more at peace.

Step 2: Therapist asks the couple what their thoughts are on forgiveness

After each person has had their chance to unpack their baggage, the therapist then asks them what their thoughts are on forgiveness. People often don't know what to make of the idea of forgiveness. I often hear a lot of misconceptions about forgiveness from clients when I ask them this question. Typical responses are "It means forgetting", "it means condoning the other person", and "accepting the other person's apology." This is your opportunity as a therapist to clear up any of these misconceptions. Especially the one that forgiveness is a one-time thing. Forgiveness is a process that may take years to complete. One answer that a client gave that I did like was that "forgiveness is accepting that you can't change the past."

You may want to ask some follow up questions like "tell me about a time that you forgave someone and you felt bad about it?" Many people will describe memories from childhood when a sibling would wrong them and their parents would demand that they forgive the sibling after the sibling's phony apology, just to have the sibling wrong them again moments later. Experiences like these leave a bitter taste in people's mouths because it implies that forgiveness is agreeing with the wrongful behavior. You can use this as an opportunity to explain to the couple how forgiveness should never be forced, but given of your own free will when you feel ready. Now ask the couple to talk about a time that they gave forgiveness and felt good about the situation. If the couple is unable to think of a situation where they felt good about forgiveness, educate them how the purpose of forgiveness is to heal and let go of hurt from the past. When forgiveness is done correctly, they will find they feel good about it.

I know what it's like to have a hard time forgiving someone first hand. One of my most difficult experiences with forgiveness was after my car accident. I was driving to work and another driver ran a red light and struck the rear of my car. I was always a careful driver and hadn't gotten into a major accident like this before. Naively I believed that so long as it's clearly the other person's fault, you had nothing to worry about, and clearly it was the other driver's fault. He sped through a red light and then hit the back of my car, what could be clearer than that? When we pulled over to exchange insurance information, the other driver casually denied running the light and actually insisted that I was the one who did! I couldn't believe that someone would lie so boldly! He then proceeded to lie about his registration and insurance information and drove away without a care in the world. Although there were plenty of witnesses, no one had stopped. I was able to track down his real registration and discovered that he had a long history of doing these sorts of things. However, my insurance didn't want to pursue the matter. Because there were no witnesses, I had no proof. I had to pay the full deductible even though I had done nothing wrong. Getting my car repaired was also a nightmare which only added to my anger.

I spent a long time feeling angry about this situation until I realized how unfair that was. The driver who ran the light probably never thinks about it, but here I am ruminating in anger about it much of the time. What good was it doing to hang on to that anger? I learned it was better for me to forgive. The best "revenge" was to live a good and happy life while he continued to live an irresponsible life that would eventually catch up with him. I decided that it was a valuable learning experience. I bought a dashboard-cam (like what the police use) so that if such a situation ever happened again I would have all the proof I needed.

Try to think of your own experiences with forgiveness. You don't have to share this experience with your clients, but it helps to better understand where they are coming from. As a therapist, what are your own thoughts on forgiveness? Do you tend to hold a grudge? Why is it so hard to let go of anger? Try to get in touch with your own feelings on forgiveness so that you can better understand what your clients may be going through.

Step 3: Ask the couple how not forgiving their partner has negatively impacted their lives

As I mentioned earlier, holding on to bitterness hurts the victim more than it hurts the transgressor. Ask each client how not forgiving their partner has negatively impacted various aspects of their life. On the surface, it seems they are only negatively impacting the person they haven't forgiven, but we now know that the transgressor is actually little affected either way. Ask the client to describe how it's affected their own personal happiness, their relationship with their partner, their relationships with others, and life in general. People are often surprised how far reaching an effect it has had on their life.

Often after hearing their partner describe how negatively their life has been affected, the transgressor will apologize without prompting from the therapist or the other person. This then often causes the other person to forgive them. This is a beautiful thing when it happens. Throughout this couple's counseling process we, the therapists, have been very active and direct with our clients. However, now is the moment for the therapist to be more passive. If the transgressor doesn't want to apologize and the victim doesn't want to forgive them, don't try to lead or manipulate them into doing so. They may just be waiting until they are in private to do it. If and when the couple decides to apologize or forgive, it should be of their own volition. If your couple chooses not to do so at this moment, just have faith that they will on their own when the time is right.

Step 4: Prepare for termination

Although at the first session you and your couple agreed upon ten sessions and you are at the ninth one now, you can't expect them to have been keeping track of sessions. I have found that most clients have no idea how many sessions it has been and are often shocked to discover it has been nine already. This is why you have to take some time out of today's session to prepare them for termination.

I usually get the ball rolling by saying something like "So, how do you feel that couples counseling has been progressing? Have we worked on all of the things you wanted to have worked on when you first agreed to do this?" After I have given the couple a chance to discuss their feelings about how things have either progressed or haven't progressed, I'll say "We had originally agreed upon ten sessions and today is our ninth session. How would you feel about next week being our last session?" Clients typically react in one of two ways; they are either overjoyed to have finally finished couples counseling or go into panic mode at the thought of not being able to rely upon you anymore. Some couples will want to continue working with you for a few more sessions.

It's not unusual for a couple to want to continue seeing you for a while longer. After having struggled with conflict for years, ending counseling after just three months can seem premature. When a couple asks if they can continue to see me past the ten or twelve sessions, I'll first discuss with them that the goal of counseling is always to terminate. I then ask them why they wish to continue. If the reason is because they still have some ongoing issues, I will ask them why they feel they cannot continue to work on those issues on their own. If the couple still insists that they want to continue working with me, I will agree to continue but make sure that they understand that the responsibility to make progress lies with them. I let them know that for each additional session we have, it is their responsibility to come up with an agenda to work on in counseling.

Remember Steve and Julie from Chapter 7? They have just finished discussing forgiveness and gained some valuable insights. The therapist has done a lot of great work with this couple and is just about to let them know that next week could be their last session. However, Steve and Julie don't feel ready to leave counseling just yet. Let's see how the therapist handles this situation:

Therapist: So, how do you feel that couples counseling has been progressing?

Julie: I think that it's been progressing slowly but surely.

Steve: I feel satisfied with the way things are going. In the beginning I used to dread coming here, but now I actually look forward to it. It has definitely made a difference in my life.

Therapist: Do you feel that we've worked on all of the things you had wanted to work on when you signed up for couples counseling?

Steve: Going into it, I just wanted us to stop fighting. Now that that problem has been solved, other problems have been brought to the surface. I see the value of counseling and I want to use it to improve other parts of my life as well. I think me and Julie could really benefit from receiving parent coaching from you.

Julie: Yeah, I think it would be great if you could help us with our parenting next.

Therapist: Going into this we had agreed upon ten sessions and today is our ninth session.

Julie: I thought this was only the sixth session!

Steve: Oh geez...

Therapist: How would you feel about next week being our last session?

Julie: I think it would be too soon!

Steve: Is there anyway we could keep seeing you?

Therapist: I only want to keep seeing you guys if it will continue to benefit you. The whole idea of counseling is to help you to become your own counselors so that you will no longer need me anymore. Is there any reason why you feel you cannot continue to make progress on your own after next week?

Steve: I think it has really helped just to have an objective third party person. You have helped us to see things in a way we wouldn't have otherwise.

Julie: Yeah. I think it also helps to have someone else holding us accountable to actually make these changes.

Therapist: If we do continue, you will have to take a more active role in counseling. I will want you to make an agenda and goals for each session to make sure we are still actively making progress in each session.

Julie: Absolutely! Next session we could work on parenting stuff.

Therapist: Okay. Next week come prepared with an agenda to work on and we will continue to evaluate if counseling is still needed on an ongoing basis. I look forward to discussing parenting techniques with you.

In this case, the therapist has experience with parent coaching, so it is appropriate for them to continue counseling. You may encounter couples that want you to continue working with them but it is to treat an issue you are not qualified for. In that case, it is appropriate to refer to a provider who has experience working with those issues. The idea of encouraging clients to be independent from the therapist may seem counterproductive. After all, we've all heard of the therapist who will continue to see the same clients for many years. You can find yourself in an ethical conflict. On the one hand, it's good for clients to be independent but on the other hand we therapists need to make a living and our pay is tied to our ability to keep clients in therapy. In a lot of ways, counseling is a poor business model. We are in the business of putting ourselves out of business.

I believe in helping clients get better as quickly as possible. At first this seemed like a strategy that would ultimately put me out of business, but I have instead found a steadily growing list of clientele. When you provide good services, people tell their friends about you, you gain a good reputation in the community, and often one or both partners will want to continue on with you in the form of individual counseling. When you refer out to more qualified providers, people appreciate your efforts and you start to build a referral network with another therapist. The odds are good that that therapist will return the favor for you one day. Providing excellent customer care and doing the right thing is ultimately good for business. I'll discuss more about client referrals in the next chapter.

The majority of your clients will be happy to be finishing couples counseling. Do not take this as an insult. It means that you have done your job well as a couples counselor. Keep in mind that many people aren't proud of having to see a couples counselor and will view the conclusion of couples counseling as having overcome a major hurdle in their lives. For those that feel ready to have next week be their last session, ask them to think of any remaining issues they would like to have addressed in their last session and tell you about them next time.

Ninth session vignette

Therapist: How have you been this past week?

Sarah: Pretty good.

Mark: We're still doing well.

Therapist: Last week we talked about making some changes, how did that go?

Sarah: I've been using less oil and less salt and experimenting with other ways of making my recipes healthier and I've found that it really doesn't affect the taste that much, so it's good. I want Mark to be healthy so that we can live together for many more years.

Mark: It's too soon to say if I've gotten healthier as a result of her modifications to her cooking, but I appreciate the effort. Sarah has also been nagging less and when I went out with my friends last week she didn't make me feel guilty at all. It was great.

Sarah: Mark has been making changes too. He's been acting a lot nicer and a lot less condescending.

Mark: It's going to take time, but I'm trying.

Therapist: Good! It sounds like you both have put a lot of effort into changing.

Sarah: We definitely have.

Therapist: I thought that for today's session we would work on something a little different. So far we had been focusing mainly on the future and what skills we can learn and changes we can implement to make things better. In order to do this, some issues have been brushed aside. I would like to work on those issues now.

Mark: What issues are you referring to?

Therapist: Before you had made progress in counseling, you had each hurt one another. Although I think we have moved past that stage of hurting one another and being hurt, I think that it is still important that we discuss those hurts and take some steps towards healing them. It's important that while we take turns discussing the way we had been hurt in the past that the other person not interrupt or correct what the other person is saying. I want you to just listen. It's important that you each have an opportunity to say your piece. If you keep those hurts bottled up inside of you, they will continue to fester and could undo the progress you have made so far. It's also important that when you express your hurts that you do so in a controlled respectful manner, with consideration for the other person's feelings. Can we do that?

Sarah: Okay.

Mark: Alright.

Therapist: Sarah, you've never really had a chance to talk about Mark's affair. Would you like to talk about that now?

Sarah: Okay...Mark, it really hurt me when you cheated on me. It killed my self confidence and I still think about it sometimes. I feel like there are things I can't talk to you about anymore. It has also changed my views on men in general.

Therapist: What kinds of fears have you been dealing with?

Sarah: ::cries:: That he will cheat again and I will have no one. I lost so many friends after I took him back. Even my own family threatened that they wouldn't take me in if I went back to Mark. If Mark cheats on me again, he'll be fine but I will be completely destitute.

Therapist: Really make him understand the hurt he has caused you. Get it all out.

Sarah: I trusted you so much in the beginning, and now I feel like I will never be the same way again. I feel that a piece of my heart has died. It has changed who I am as a person.

Therapist: Is there anything else, Sarah?

Sarah: No, I think that's it. God, I had been holding onto that for so long.

Therapist: Mark, being careful not to invalidate or disagree, what are your thoughts on what Sarah has just said?

Mark: I think her feelings are legitimate. I let her down. There were better ways I could have handled the situation but I chose to be selfish. I don't know what else to say.

Therapist: Maybe you could take a moment to talk about your own hurt?

Mark: There have been a lot of hurts in the past, sure. Sarah hasn't done any one big thing like what I did to her, but there are a lot of little things too. Before we started coming here, I would have to deal with this daily negativity from her. I would actually dread coming home from work because it was so stressful. All I wanted to do was go home and relax and the second I came through the door she would start with me. I would actually find reasons to work late! It was better than going home.

Therapist: Is that something you still think about and feel angry about sometimes?

Mark: Things have been going a lot better for a while now, but I still find myself feeling moments of dread when it's almost time to leave work. I still feel apprehensive about spending time with Sarah because of the memory of it.

Therapist: Sarah, what do you think about what Mark just said?

Sarah: It makes me feel sad. I didn't know he felt that way about me.

Therapist: I want to know what each of your thoughts are on "forgiveness."

Sarah: Forgetting about past wrongs and moving on.

Mark: To wipe the slate clean and stop being angry about the past.

Therapist: Forgiveness isn't about forgetting and it doesn't mean you condone the other person's behavior. Forgiveness is also a process and not a one time thing. Tell me about a time that you forgave someone and then felt bad about it afterward.

Mark: I used to get picked on by my brother a lot. I would complain to my mother about it and she would make him give some phony apology and then force me to forgive him and "play nice", but as soon as she turned her back on us he would go right back to picking on me. I felt angry about that for a long time.

Sarah: I forgave my ex after the first time he cheated on me. He told me I needed to forgive him in order for us to stay together, and that it was the right thing to do, so I did. Later I found out that he continued to cheat on me with three more girls. I felt like such a fool.

Therapist: So, forgiveness that is forced or coerced by another person feels bad, especially when their apology is insincere and they go on to wrong us again. Tell me about a time that you forgave someone and it helped you to feel better.

Mark: I spent a long time feeling mad at my brother. Once I moved out of the house, that was it, I didn't talk to him for years. I couldn't get over the stuff from when we were kids. Then a few years back he actually reached out to me. He called me up on the phone and apologized for bullying me when we were kids. We caught up and it was clear that he had changed a lot since then. We have a good relationship now and I am glad that I forgave him. I feel a lot better letting go of all that anger.

Therapist: What about you, Sarah?

Sarah: I had a similar experience to Mark's. I grew up feeling really mad at my parents and feeling like I had an unfair childhood. My parents worked a lot and I grew up feeling like they didn't really care about me because we didn't spend a lot of quality time together. But then I realized that they were doing the best they could for us. Unlike most of the people I know, I didn't have any student loans from college. My parents completely paid for my education and my three siblings' college education. Once I took a step back and realized where they were coming from, I was able to forgive them and not feel so angry or neglected anymore.

Therapist: After having listened to both of you, it becomes clear that forgiveness is really something you do for yourself, not the other person. The fact of the matter is that it hurts you a lot more than the other person to hold on to all of that anger. How do you think not forgiving Mark has negatively impacted your life?

Sarah: It's like you said, I'm left holding on to all this anger. It's like I can never have any peace if he is away from the house because I'm imagining that he's cheating on me. It's prevented me from making friends because I'm worried there's going to be another friendship fall-out when Mark cheats on me again. It has definitely had an impact. I don't want to live this way anymore.

Mark: I'm sorry for how I have hurt you. I promise you that I will never cheat on you again. I know now that I should have had us go to couples counseling instead of selfishly having my needs met outside of the relationship. I feel truly sorry for what happened and how it has continued to affect you since.

Sarah: I want to forgive you. I want to move towards forgiveness. I want to let go of all of the anger.

Therapist: I think it will be a process, but that by continuing to grow and change as a couple you will eventually achieve forgiveness. You will be able to accept that you can't change the past. Mark, how has not forgiving Sarah negatively impacted your life?

Mark: It's made me feel uneasy in my own home. It's made me feel hesitant to work towards my own personal growth because I think changing means somehow condoning her behavior. But I do need to change and I do need to become a better person, and that means forgiving Sarah.

Sarah: I feel terrible that I made you not want to come home. I feel really awful about it. I'm sorry, Mark

Mark: I forgive you, Sarah. I want us to move forward and really create a relationship that is something special.

Therapist: How does it feel to forgive Sarah?

Mark: It feels good. It really does. And I hope that Sarah can come to forgive me as well, when she's ready.

Therapist: It sounds like you both gained some valuable insights about forgiveness today. How do you feel that couples counseling has progressed overall?

Sarah: I think it has been good.

Mark: We've made a lot of progress so far.

Therapist: Have we worked on the things that you wanted to work on when you agreed to try couples counseling?

Sarah: Definitely. We've worked on so much!

Mark: It's hard to think of anything that's left. I've felt very satisfied with the work we've been doing here.

Therapist: We had originally agreed upon ten sessions and today is actually our ninth session.

Sarah: Wow, I can't believe it's been nine already!

Therapist: How would you feel about next week being our last session?

Mark: I think I would feel pretty good about it.

Therapist: I would feel good about it too. At this point I feel confident that you can continue to make progress on your own without me.

Sarah: I suppose you're right, I mean, what else is there left to work on?

Therapist: I want you to spend some time this week really thinking about if there are any final issues you want me to work on with you next time. Also let me know if you change your mind about ending couples counseling. In the meantime I will be prepared for next week to be our last session.

It is interesting how when first starting couples counseling the couple is eager to air their grievances, but now they seem almost hesitant when the opportunity finally arises. Mark and Sarah did a good job of not invalidating the other person's pain and offering genuine remorse for their transgressions. The support they were able to offer one another was helpful towards the healing process. Although reluctant at first, couples often later express gratitude at the opportunity to express their pain and be understood by their partner. Forgiveness is a powerful force in people's lives.

Mark and Sarah sounded ready to terminate as well. In fact, they probably high-fived each other when they left the office. For most clients, ending couples counseling is seen as a good thing and they welcome the opportunity to be independent once more. However, the process of termination should not be taken lightly, which is why we are giving our couple some warning ahead of time despite the short-term nature of couples counseling.

Ninth session outline: forgiveness

Step 1: Unpack baggage

- Have couple express in a controlled respectful manner how past betrayals and hurts within the relationship have continued to affect them both in the relationship and in life in general

Step 2: Therapist asks the couple what their thoughts are on forgiveness

- Clear up any misconceptions about forgiveness
- As the couple to describe both good and bad experiences with forgiveness

Step 3: Ask the couple how not forgiving their partner has negatively impacted their lives

Step 4: Prepare for termination

Chapter 11

Tenth Session: Termination

Congratulations! You've made it to the finish line! We're down to the final stretch but the work's not done yet. We still need to terminate with the couple. "Termination" is a fancy word that basically means "ending therapy." Although the word has a negative feel to it, it is really a positive experience for both therapist and client and not something that should be dreaded. In order to terminate successfully with your couple we will need to accomplish a few goals in this final session: tie up loose ends, review progress, remind the client that they can always come back should problems arise again, and let the couple know that you would appreciate their personal referrals.

A colleague once told me that we should prepare for termination starting from the very first session. I believe that we accomplished that by discussing with the client at the first session the fact that our time together was limited and generally only lasted ten to twelve sessions. We then reminded the client again when we were at the "halfway point" in couples counseling, around the fifth session. And finally, towards the end of the ninth session we asked the couple how they felt about terminating at their next session. Termination should never come as a "surprise" for the client.

Saying "goodbye" is hard for a lot of people. Some clients may have visions of tears and sappy goodbyes. I try to make my terminations as upbeat as possible. I don't cry in the session or say "Oh my God, I'm going to miss you guys so much!" no matter how much I might want to. I try to channel the same kind of vibe I got from my father when

I graduated college. My father didn't act sad that I was graduating even though it meant I was an independent adult and didn't "need" him anymore. He was proud! I try to show that same kind of pride towards my clients and add emphasis to the accomplishment of having repaired their relationship/marriage. Finishing counseling is no small achievement. I do my best to help my clients feel good about that.

Some clients will want to thank you by giving you a gift at this final session. In my office policies it states explicitly that I do not accept gifts. My reward is in seeing the clients get better and attaining personal growth. However, some clients will still give me a gift anyways. When I receive a gift from a client of course I am very grateful, but it is in no way expected. You may want to put some thought into your gift policy. Some therapists will refuse any gifts or donate them to charity. I feel that if despite my no-gift policy, a client still wants to give me something, then that must be part of their own personal process and I had better just accept it as graciously as I can. If gifts make you feel awkward, put some thought into your own gift giving policy and take the time to explain it to your client.

Step 1: Tie up loose ends

At the end of the last session you asked the couple to put some thought into any final issues they would like you to address. Some couples will come prepared with some final issues they would want to work on, but you will find that most report they couldn't think of anything to work on. This makes sense since part of termination is when the client feels they no longer have anything to work on in therapy. If you have been following these sessions step by step, most likely the couple is prepared to deal with their own issues moving forward.

If the couple comes to the session without any last topics to discuss, you might want to just do a quick review of some of the most important topics we've discussed thus far. Maybe there was a particular communication skill that the couple didn't seem to ever grasp. It is fine to review that now. Have some last minute inspiration you would like to share with the couple? That is fine too. Spend a few minutes to tie up those loose ends.

If the couple doesn't have anything they want to work on with me, I like to spend a few moments reviewing all the major points from each session: that we should continuously set goals in our relationships and strive to accomplish them, that we should communicate in a clear and considerate manner, that we should strive for solutions and compromises where everybody wins, that sometimes it's better to be wrong than to be right if it means being happy in our relationship, that we should continue to put as much effort into the relationship as we did when we first met our partners, that we need to challenge irrational beliefs that sabotage our relationships, that we need to own up to our own contributions to problems in the relationship, and forgive our partner for hurts that have happened along the way.

224 CHAPTER 11. 10TH SESSION: TERMINATION

Step 2: Review progress with clients

Take a trip down memory lane with your clients and remind them how much progress they've made. Maybe when you first met them they were so angry they couldn't even talk to one another but now they waltz into your office smiling and holding hands. Discuss the strides you've seen the couple make and invite them to discuss this as well. Ask the couple what positive changes they've noticed. It may also be helpful to ask what they found to be the most helpful topics worked on in therapy. Most clients will talk about the early sessions in therapy being the most helpful, which I always find interesting considering that clients seem the most miserable and resistant in the beginning stages.

In addition to discussing all the good parts of counseling, you should also be willing to ask for the bad parts. No one likes negative feedback, and although it's too late to correct a client's negative experience, it's not too late to change things for the next client. Negative feedback helps you to ultimately become a more skilled therapist. In my opinion, this is my client's real parting gift, the opportunity to become a better counselor. Some of the criticisms that clients give you may be things outside of your control. For instance, a client once suggested that he would have felt "safer" in counseling if the office door had been left open. Unfortunately I can't accommodate that request due to confidentiality issues, but I have always done my best to implement changes according to client feedback.

In addition to discussing the progress that has been made in counseling, you also want to ask your clients what progress has been yet unrealized. Remember, just because you didn't fix their problems 100% doesn't mean that therapy cannot be terminated. The question is whether or not they can continue to make progress on their own. Talk to the couple about how they can go about addressing these remaining problems. I recommend my clients continue to have once a week couples meetings to work on issues. I remind them that I've taught them all the communication and problem solving skills they need, and feel that they can continue on without me. Most clients will agree.

Step 3: Thank them for having been excellent clients

Don't take all the credit for your couple's success! Even if you felt that you worked really hard and struggled a lot with this particular couple, give them most of the credit. Without our clients we wouldn't be in business no matter how brilliant we are. By taking credit for your client's progress, you rob them of their achievement. I always thank my couples profusely for the honor of having worked with them and tell them that they were all excellent and above-average clients. This leaves the client feeling good about their efforts and will hopefully encourage them to continue making efforts even though counseling is now over.

Sometimes we deal with clients that just make things miserable for us and we are happy to see them go. It's one of the dirty little secrets of therapy, but it happens to the best of us. Sometimes we work with a couple that we just don't mesh with and when that last session finally arrives it can't come soon enough. Hopefully you are skilled enough as a therapist that your clients can't tell when you genuinely don't like them. Even if you are happy to see them go, try to be as gracious towards them as you would with a couple that you truly liked. Mention some qualities about them that you did like and thank them for having been excellent clients. This can actually do a lot for the relationship if they ever plan to come back someday. I have found a lot of problem-clients are better the second time around.

It's important to remind your clients that they may come back to counseling at anytime in the future should problems arise again. Sometimes clients do need to come back to therapy for a boost. This does not mean that couples counseling was a failure the first time. Circumstances change over time and sometimes clients can find themselves feeling overwhelmed again. Sometimes a client may want to come back for counseling but for issues unrelated to their relationship. It is not uncommon for a previous couples counseling client to return to therapy but to work on individual counseling instead. Previous clients who have seen first hand the power of your work can easily become repeat customers.

Step 4: Ask for referrals

A lot of therapists hate asking clients for referrals, and I can understand why, because I was one of those therapists. The thought of asking clients for referrals made me feel very uncomfortable. It seemed cheap and conjured images of pushy salesmen. There were also ethical considerations. By asking for referrals was I taking advantage of a vulnerable client? At the same time, word-of-mouth marketing has been proven to be one of the most effective forms of marketing (Diana,

2010). By neglecting client referrals, was I missing out on a powerful marketing tool? I had to put a lot of thought into this.

I decided that it was not an ethics conflict because I was waiting until the end of the very last session to bring it up. Clients wouldn't feel obligated to do special favors for me since in a few minutes they would most likely never see me again anyway. I would also not be pushy by limiting my efforts to just one sentence. At the end of the session I simply say "If you have been happy with my work, I always appreciate referrals if you know any other couples that could benefit from my services." I put a lot of time into crafting that statement, making it as pressure free as possible, yet I have also found it to be effective in generating referrals.

My assumption was always that if the couple was happy with me, naturally they would tell their friends about me. I have rarely found that to be the case. When people have positive counseling experiences they'll tell people "I tried counseling and it worked great for me. You should try seeing a therapist too." Statements like that are great for the industry as a whole but do nothing for you personally. I think just adding in a quick statement about appreciating referrals is enough to make people say "I tried counseling and it worked great for me. You should try seeing Marina. She's really good. Here's her phone number." I have found that personal recommendations is where the majority of my clients come from. Do not underestimate the power of word-of-mouth marketing.

Tenth session vignette

Therapist: How has the past week been?

Mark: Good.

Sarah: About the same.

Therapist: Did you put any thought into any remaining questions you might have for me?

Sarah: We talked about it during the week but couldn't really come up with anything. The only question I have is what if we start experiencing problems again?

Therapist: I want you to know that you can always come back if problems were to arise again. Do you still have the magnet

I gave you on the first session with all my contact information on it?

Sarah: Yep, it's on the fridge.

Therapist: Just hang on to that magnet and call me anytime you want to come back.

Sarah: Okay.

Therapist: Are you worried that things will get bad again once you stop counseling?

Mark: No, I think we feel pretty confident that we can handle our own problems from here on out, but just in case. You never know what could happen.

Therapist: Oh, I see. I think those are valid concerns.

Sarah: We just wanted to be prepared.

Therapist: I think you two have really made a lot of progress. Do you remember in the beginning how much you used to argue?

Sarah: We were in pretty bad shape.

Therapist: But now look at you! I've really seen a lot of growth and change from both of you over the past ten weeks. It has truly been a pleasure to work with you.

Mark: Thank you. It's been a pleasure to work with you as well. I don't think we could have done it without you.

Therapist: Oh, I don't know about that. I think you both were ready to change. You did all the work. I just did maybe 10%.

Sarah: No, really, you've been wonderful. I see the way Mark and I have changed and I'm amazed.

Therapist: Tell me about the progress you've seen.

Sarah: Well, for one, we used to fight every day. Every day! I don't think I realized how bad it was until I was out of the situation, but looking back, it was a living hell. I'm glad we finally agreed to do couples counseling instead of breaking up or just continuing to suffer in a bad relationship. Sometimes I think, "God, why did I live like that?"

Therapist: I don't think the relationship was necessarily bad, you just didn't know the skills yet to make it good. A couple is going to have poor communication if they don't know good communication skills.

Mark: I think it's also a willingness to take a hard look at yourself and realize you need to change for the good of the relationship.

Therapist: That's so true, Mark. What progress have you noticed?

Mark: I've made a lot of changes. It's funny, going into this I made a promise to myself that I wasn't going to let anyone convince me to change. I figured that if a relationship required me to change then it wasn't a relationship worth being in. Now I know that is foolish. We grow and change every day. Why not make some changes for the better?

Therapist: What changes have you made?

Mark: I've changed the way I talk, not just to Sarah, but to everyone. I've found the communication skills helpful with friends, family, and even coworkers. I've also tried to be more sympathetic and sensitive about the way I treat others.

Therapist: I've noticed that too. You've definitely made a lot of hard changes. I'm so proud of you both.

Mark: Thank you. I've put a lot of effort into this.

Therapist: I can tell. I'm wondering... what was the most helpful part of therapy for you?

Mark: Probably the communication skills. Up until then, excuse my language, I thought this was all bullshit. But then when I started practicing the communication skills and saw that they actually worked, that was a turning point for me. I started to think there really might be something to this couples counseling thing. I also found the session on problem solving to be really helpful.

Therapist: What about you, Sarah?

Sarah: I liked the beginning when we defined our goals and made lists of how we wanted our relationship to look like. I think it set up a foundation of things to work on. I also liked bringing back the caring behaviors from when we first met.

Therapist: Were there things you didn't like or didn't find helpful?

Sarah: Oh... I don't know...

Therapist: I find negative feedback helpful so I know what to improve and can grow as a healer and a professional.

Mark: At times you were difficult to get a hold of.

Therapist: Thank you for sharing that, Mark. I'm going to make it a goal of mine to make sure I get back to all my clients in the same day from now on. I am sorry if I was sometimes hard to get ahold of.

Sarah: I guess something I didn't like was the lack of magazines in the waiting room. There was nothing to do but stare at the wall.

Therapist: Are there any magazines you would suggest?

Sarah: Vogue, Glamour, Redbook... magazines like that.

Therapist: Thank you for the suggestion, Sarah. I'm definitely going to look into that. As far as progress made in therapy goes, do you think there is still some progress left to made?

Mark: Well, I think there's always room for more progress. I'm sure there's always going to be more things me and Sarah can work on.

Therapist: Such as?

Mark: I think the major issues have been covered here. It's really just some little things. Just a few tweaks here and there that could make things even better.

Therapist: Do you have any thoughts on progress, Sarah?

Sarah: I agree with Mark that a few things still remain, but we've covered all the major stuff. I think we could still be nicer to each other at times and try to include each other more with friends, but overall I think we've solved the difficult issues in counseling.

Therapist: Have you put any thought into how you want to continue to make progress now that couples counseling has ended?

Sarah: I guess just by continuing to do what we've been doing here.

Mark: By continuing to apply the skills we've learned in this room, I suppose.

Therapist: It may help if you continue to use this allotted time as a time to work on couples issues, applying the techniques you've used here to solve ongoing problems.

Sarah: Sounds good.

Mark: We could do that.

Therapist: Well, I wanted to let you guys know that you have been excellent clients. In the ten weeks we have been working together you have always been on time and have never missed an appointment. You always did the homework assignments and made lots of progress. Honestly, I wish I had more clients like you.

Sarah: You've been wonderful as well. I wish there were more therapists like you.

Therapist: Thank you, Sarah. And remember, you can always come back should problems arise again. And if you've been happy with my work, I always appreciate referrals if you know any other couples that could benefit from my services.

Sarah: Actually, there is a couple that we've been meaning to recommend to you.

Mark: Do you mean Emily and Joe?

Sarah: Yeah.

Mark: Yes, they could sure use some couples counseling. We know lots of couples, actually, that could use a good couples counselor.

Therapist: Thank you. I always appreciate referrals. And it's been wonderful working with you.

Mark and Sarah came into today's session not needing any more suggestions or relationship skills. Indeed, they seemed quite ready to terminate counseling. This session would be considered a successful termination because the couple received warning about the termination beforehand, felt ready to leave counseling, had made measurable improvements, and had the option of coming back at any time should they feel the need to again. The couple was given the opportunity to say "goodbye" and expressed feeling good about their experience in couples counseling. As you probably noticed, the mood was very positive in this session. Just because it was the last session doesn't mean that people have to cry and be sad about leaving.

I try to end things as positively as possible. As therapists, we always want people to leave counseling while feeling good about it. This is not only good for us, but good for the profession as a whole. People who feel good about their counseling experience will not only be more likely to return to counseling should they experience other problems in their lives, but they are also likely to recommend it to others who are experiencing difficulties. There's enough negativity in the counseling profession, let's add something positive!

Tenth session outline: termination

Step 1: Tie up loose ends

- Answer any final questions the clients may have for you

Step 2: Review progress with clients

- What changes have the couple made?
- What was the most helpful part of therapy?
- What was the least helpful?
- What progress still needs to be made?

Step 3: Thank them for having been excellent clients

- Remind clients that they may come back to counseling at anytime in the future should problems arise again.

Step 4: Ask for referrals

- Let them know that if they have been happy with your work, you always appreciate referrals if they know any other couples that could benefit from your services.

Conclusion

I hope that you have found this book helpful. Couples counseling has been called the most difficult form of counseling to administer, and many therapists either refuse to participate or do so badly. When I was starting out in couples counseling, I found professionals quick to criticize the practice but offer little in the way of improving things for struggling therapists. It was my goal to write a straightforward, easy to understand book that would help more failing therapists succeed at this sorely needed therapy. My hope is that this book has helped you to feel more prepared to treat couples in need. I have found that my methods work better when therapists feel free to modify them to better fit their "therapeutic style." I want to encourage you to do the same.

You may want to reread this book again before attempting these techniques on a real couple. Remember, confidence is key in delivering effective couples counseling, so you should feel free to reread this book until you are confident in executing its methods. Ideally, you want to know the concepts and techniques so well that they just roll off your tongue in a real session. That may mean having to read this book a couple of times and reading a certain session chapter again right before meeting with your couple. Eventually you will get to the point where you only need to glance at the session outlines as a quick reminder. That is why I have put all the session outlines together for quick access for those of you who have gotten to the point where you only need a reference for during a session or after the session when you go to write your therapy notes.

Most importantly, I want to thank you, the reader, for devoting your time and energy to reading this book. It was a pleasure for me to write it and I hope it serves you well professionally. I do plan to write many more books and I hope that you find them equally helpful to your development as an expert healer!

First session: intake

Step 1: Build Rapport

Step 2: Gather Information

- Occupations
- Who they live with
- Medications and medical conditions
- Psychiatric history
- Trauma history
- Presenting problems or concerns
- Frequency of problem behaviors

Step 3: Educate clients about the process of couples counseling

- Get a firm commitment for 10 sessions

Step 4: Express confidence that the relationship can be saved

- Normalize their experience
- Let them know that you can help
- Highlight the good points of the relationship

Second session: reveal potential

Step 1: Review Progress

Step 2: Explain the writing assignment

- Ask couple to each make a list (at least 10 items) of changes they would like to see in the relationship

Step 3: Process the list

- Have partners take turns reading the list aloud and put check marks next to the items on their list that are the same or similar.
- Therapist intervenes to clarify items that are vague and to help client define them in behavioral terms.

Step 4: Assign homework

- Therapist assigns couple homework assignment of creating a new list together and bring it with them to next session.

Crisis intervention outline

Step 1: Let the couple tell the story of the crisis

Step 2: Reflect, validate, empathize, and work towards a solution

- Practice active listening and unconditional positive regard

Step 3: Problem Solve

- Ask partners how they would like to solve the problem
- Brainstorm possible solutions
- Suggest a compromise if necessary

Step 4: Moving Forward

- Get a commitment from partners to move forward

Third session: communication skills

Step 1: Review homework

- Couple reads aloud their shared list
- Therapist critiques or offers insight about list if necessary

Step 2: Have the couple argue

- Therapist observes couple have an argument and then provides positive reinforcement for what they do well while arguing

Step 3: Educate the couple on "the four horsemen"

- Criticism
- Contempt
- Defensiveness
- Stonewalling

Step 4: Teach basic communication skills

- Avoid harsh start-ups
- Use repair attempts
- Be clear and be considerate

- Avoid blame
- Have couple's meetings

Step 5: Assign homework

- Therapist assigns couple to practice communication skills during daily couple's meetings

Fourth session: couple's dialogue

Step 1: Review homework

Step 2: Teach the couple how to have a couple's dialogue

- Write on an index card the four steps
- Reflecting, Validation, Empathy, Problem Solving

Step 3: Practice, Practice, Practice

- Therapist uses role-play and role-rehearsal with each partner
- Couple then practices with each other

Step 4: "Do you want to be right or do you want to be happy?"

Fifth session: problem solving & compromise

Step 1: "What problems are you currently experiencing that haven't been addressed yet in couples counseling?"

Step 2: Help the couple to find the core "themes" in their arguments

- Trust vs Mistrust
- Appreciation, or Reality vs Expectations (example: division of labour)
- Respect vs Disrespect
- Unity vs Discord (example: meddling in-laws, kids, parenting disagreements)
- Closeness vs Distance

- Finances, or Short-term vs Long-term Security
- Sex, or My Needs vs Your Needs

Step 3: Teach the couple how to problem solve

1. Define the problem
2. Finding common ground; what do you both agree with?
3. Each person proposes several different solutions (3 is a good number)
4. Weigh the pros and cons of each solution
5. Decide to try one or two solutions as an "experiment"
6. Review the effectiveness of the solution

Step 4: Teach the couple how to compromise

Step 5: Assign Homework

- Continue to solve problems and compromise during couple's meetings

Sixth session: bringing up the past

Step 1: Ask the couple how they met

- What made them fall in love with the other person?
- Ask the couple to describe their early years together

Step 2: Specifically, how were things different then from now?

- How were things better then?
- How are things better now?

Step 3: How can romantic elements from the beginning of the relationship be incorporated into the current relationship?

- What are the things you do currently to show your partner that you care?
- What were the little things your partner did back then that made you feel loved?
- What caring behaviors can you start doing again?

Step 4: Assign homework

- Partners keep a log of daily caring behaviors

Alternate sixth session

Step 1: Ask the couple how they met

- If they met under unusual circumstances, why did they choose to remain in the relationship?
- What was their life like at the time that made these circumstances desirable?
- What was the hope they had for the relationship back then?
- Ask the couple to describe their early years together

Step 2: How has this "rough start" affected your relationship?

- Allow the couple to vent if necessary
- Positively reframe if possible

Step 3: Implement caring behaviors

- Teach the couple about the courtship phase of relationships
- Couple describes caring behaviors they would like their partner to implement

Step 4: Assign homework

- Partners keep a log of daily caring behaviors

Seventh session: REBT

Step 1: "Tell me about the last time you got upset by something your partner did?"

- Ask clarifying questions
- Express understanding and empathy

Step 2: Identify irrational beliefs

- Listen for the "shoulds" or "musts"

Step 3: Educate the couple about irrational beliefs

- Ask other ways they could think about it
- Give example of how thoughts cause feelings
- Explain how unfair expectations hurt relationships

Step 4: Challenge and replace irrational beliefs

- Functional Disputes

- Empirical disputes

- Rational coping statements

- Modeling

- Referenting

- Rational emotive Imagery

- Unconditional acceptance

- Positive Talk

- Reinforcement

Eighth session: taking responsibility

Step 1: "How have you contributed to the problems in the relationship?"

- Ask each client how they have contributed

- Get specific examples of wrongdoing from each client

Step 2: Each person identifies changes that need to be made to improve the relationship

- Couple writes down 3-5 changes they need to make and 3-5 changes their partner needs to make

- Couple takes turns reading their list out loud in session

Step 3: Create an action plan

- Therapist helps couple to break down the specific steps they need to take to make these changes possible

- Therapist identifies obstacles and helps find solutions

Step 4: Implement changes

- Continually grow and change as a couple and as an individual

Ninth session: forgiveness

Step 1: Unpack baggage

- Have couple express in a controlled respectful manner how past betrayals and hurts within the relationship have continued to affect them both in the relationship and in life in general

Step 2: Therapist asks the couple what their thoughts are on forgiveness

- Clear up any misconceptions about forgiveness
- As the couple to describe both good and bad experiences with forgiveness

Step 3: Ask the couple how not forgiving their partner has negatively impacted their lives

Step 4: Prepare for termination

Tenth session: termination

Step 1: Tie up loose ends

- Answer any final questions the clients may have for you

Step 2: Review progress with clients

- What changes have the couple made?
- What was the most helpful part of therapy?
- What was the least helpful?
- What progress still needs to be made?

Step 3: Thank them for having been excellent clients

- Remind clients that they may come back to counseling at anytime in the future should problems arise again.

Step 4: Ask for referrals

- Let them know that if they have been happy with your work, you always appreciate referrals if they know any other couples that could benefit from your services.

Suggested Reading

I've included a list of suggested reading to further help develop your skills as a couples counselor. There are a lot of books on relationships and sadly I've found a lot of them to not be very helpful. I've only included on this list those that I personally have found to be insightful. You will notice that some of these books are "self help." I like self help books because they avoid a lot of the psychobabble that our average client isn't going to understand. I have found that reading self help books is good for learning how to phrase things in a way that is relatable to the layperson. Enjoy.

Carnegie, D. (2009). How to win friends and influence people. Simon & Schuster.

Dryden, W., & Neenan, M. (2006). Rational emotive behavior therapy: 100 key points and techniques. Routledge.

Ellis, A., & MacLaren, C. (2005). Rational emotive behavior therapy: A therapist's guide (2nd ed.). Impact Publishers.

Gottman, J. M. (2002). The relationship cure: A 5 step guide to strengthening your marriage, family, and friendships. Three Rivers Press.

Gottman, J. M., & Silver, N. (2000). The seven principles for making marriage work: A practical guide from the country's foremost relationship expert. Three Rivers Press.

Johnson, S. M. (2004). The practice of emotionally focused couples therapy: Creating connection. Routledge.

Hendrix, H. (2007). Getting the love you want: A guide for couples, 20th anniversary edition. Henry Holt & Co.

Kirshenbaum, M. (2012). I love you but I don't trust you: The complete guide to restoring trust in your relationship. Berkley Trade.

MacDonald, L. J. (2010). How to help your spouse heal from your affair: A compact manual for the unfaithful. Gig Harbor, WA., Healing Counsel Press.

Runkel, H. E., & Runkel, J. (2011). Screamfree marriage: Calming down, growing up, and getting closer. Crown Archetype.

About the Author

Marina Williams, MA, LMHC is a Licensed Mental Health Counsellor who specializes in treating relationship issues, depression, and anxiety disorders. She graduated with a Masters Degree in Clinical Psychology from Bridgewater State University. She currently works in private practice, offering both individual and couples counselling in the Hyde Park neighbourhood of Boston, Massachusetts.

In addition to providing counselling, Marina Williams works as an independent author. She has written and published the books "Couples Counselling: A Step by Step guide for Therapists", "Tricks of the Trade: How to be a Top Notch Mental Health Counsellor in an Age of Competition", "Results Directed Therapy: An Integrative and Dynamic Approach to Psychotherapy", and "Ending the Power Struggle: A Step by Step Guide for Couples Counsellors".

Marina Williams also has a number of resources available for therapists who are looking for support or further training. She is the founder and creator of TherapistCE.com, an affordable continuing education provider for therapists. She also has a blog intended for other therapists that can be found on her website MarinaWilliamsLMHC.com. The website for her private practice is CounselingWithMarina.com.

Would you like to earn continuing education units while improving as a therapist?

You know that one of the keys to becoming a great therapist is professional development and continued training. Unfortunately, many continuing education opportunities cost $40 per CE or more. You want quality continuing education but you also dont think you should have to spend so much of your hard earned money just to get training. Thats why I created TherapistCE.com.

On TherapistCE.com you can watch continuing education videos for just $5 per video. Best of all, you can watch them anywhere and anytime, which means you wont have to miss any of your appointments. TherapistCE.com is an approved continuing education provider with the BBS, NASW, and NBCC. This means that TherapistCE.com is an approved CE provider for therapists in nearly every State!

References

Amato, P. R. (2000). The consequences of divorce for adults and children. Journal of Marriage and Family, 62(4), 1269-1287.

Beck, J. S. (2011). Cognitive behavior therapy: Basics and beyond. (2 ed.). New York, NY: The Guilford Press.

Bringle, R. G., & Byers, D. (1997). Intentions to seek marriage counseling. Family Relations, 46(3), 299-304.

Carnegie, D. (2009). How to win friends and influence people. Simon & Schuster.

Curtis, J. T., & Wang, Z. (2003). The neurochemistry of pair bonding. Current Directions in Psychological Science, 12(2), 49-53.

Diamond, L. M. (2004). Emerging perspectives on distinctions between romantic love and sexual desire. Current Directions in Psychological Science, 13(3), 116-119

Diana, D. P. (2010). Marketing for the mental health professional: An innovative guide for practitioners. Hoboken, NJ: John Wiley & Sons, Inc.

Doheny, K. (2011, September 05). 10 surprising health benefits of sex. Retrieved from http://bit.ly/M0Zb3w

Donnelly, D., Burgess, E., Anderson, S., Davis, R., & Dillard, J. (2001). Involuntary celibacy: A life course analysis. The Journal of Sex Research, 38(2), 159-169.

Drigotas, S. M., & Barta, W. (2001). The cheating heart: Scientific explorations of infidelity. Current Directions in Psychological Science, 177-180.

Elliot, S. S., & Saunders, B. E. (1982). The systems marriage enrichment program: An alternative model based on systems theory. Family Relations, 31(1), 53-60.

Elliot, D. B., & Simmons, T. U.S. Census Bureau, American Community Survey Reports. (2011). Marital events of americans: 2009. Retrieved from U.S. Census Bureau website: `http://1.usa.gov/KoiLZc`

Ellis, A. (1994). The essence of rational emotive behavior therapy. New York, NY. The Albert Ellis Institute.

Ellis, A., & MacLaren, C. (2005). Rational emotive behavior therapy: A therapist's guide (2nd ed.). Impact Publishers.

Farouky, J. (2008, December 04). Mother-in-law problems: They're worse for women. Time World. Retrieved from `http://ti.me/MOqp6h`

Franck, D. (2000). Single adults-a population group too large to ignore. Enrichment Journal, Summer 2000, Retrieved from: `http://bit.ly/K2jBLm`

Gecas, V. (1982). The self-concept. Annual Review of Sociology, 8, 1-33.

Gottman, J. M., Coan, J., Carrere, S., & Swanson, C. (1998). Predicting marital happiness and stability from newlywed interactions. Journal of Marriage and Family, 60(1), 5-22.

Gottman, J. M., & Levenson, R. W. (2000). The timing of divorce: Predicting when a couple will divorce over a 14-year period. Journal of Marriage and Family, 62(3), 737-745.

Gottman, J. M., & Silver, N. (2000). The seven principles for making marriage work: A practical guide from the country's foremost relationship expert. Three Rivers Press.

Kemeny, M. E. (2003). The psychobiology of stress. Current Directions in Psychological Science, 12(4), 124-129.

Halford, W. K. (2001). Brief therapy for couples: Helping partners help themselves. New York, NY: The Guilford Press.

Hendrix, H. (2007). Getting the love you want: A guide for couples, 20th anniversary edition. Henry Holt & Co.

246

Johnson, S. M. (2004). The practice of emotionally focused couples therapy: Creating connection. Routledge.

LeCroy, C. W. (1989). An experimental evaluation of the caring days technique for marital enrichment. Family Relations, 31(1), 15-18.

Olson, D. H. & Defrain, J. (1994). Marriage and the Family, Diversity and Strengths. Mountain View, California: Mayfield Publishing Company.

Pew Research Center. (2010, November 18). The decline of marriage and the rise of new families. Retrieved from: http://bit.ly/KtBBNW

Rogers, C. R. (1952). A personal formulation of client-centered therapy. Marriage and Family Living, 14(4), 341-361.

Schultz , S. (2007). 5 stages of committed relationships. Retrieved from: http://bit.ly/LcA4Gj

Stuart, R. B. (1980). Helping couples change. New York, NY: The Guilford Press.

Tjaden, P, & Thoennes, N. National Institute of Justice and the Centers of Disease Control and Prevention, (2000). Extent, nature and consequences of intimate partner violence: Findings from the national violence against women survey. Washington, DC: U.S. Government Printing.

Treas, J., & Giesen, D. (2000). Sexual infidelity among married and cohabiting americans. Journal of Marriage and Family, 62(1), 48-60

Twenge, J. M., Campbell, W. K., & Foster, C. A. (2003). Parenthood and marital satisfaction: A meta-analytic review. Journal of Marriage and Family, 65(3), 574-583.

University Of California - Irvine (2002, September 26). Still Mulling Over Last Night's Argument? It Could Affect Your Heart. ScienceDaily. Retrieved from: http://bit.ly/M1O9Nd

U.S. Department of Justice, Bureau of Justice Statistics. (2006). Criminal victimization, 2005. Washington, DC: U.S. Government Printing.

Willis, M. (2007). Connection, action, and hope: An invitation to reclaim the "spiritual" in health care. Journal of Religion and Health, 46(3), 423-436.

Made in the USA
Middletown, DE
09 May 2024

54083686R10146